WILD

—AT—

HEART

WILD

— AT —

HEART

AMERICA'S TURBULENT
RELATIONSHIP *with* NATURE, *from*
EXPLOITATION *to* REDEMPTION

ALICE OUTWATER

St. Martin's Press ☰ New York

www.stmartins.com

Photograph credits: Introduction: Sandra Selle-Rodriguez, The Old Juniper Tree. Figure 2: Erik Lam, Greater Swiss Mountain Dog. Chapter 1: Frank Fiske, Mrs. Jack Treetop, State Historical Society of North Dakota, 1952-0110. Chapter 2: George Inness, The Lackawanna Valley, National Gallery of Art, Washington, DC, circa 1855. Chapter 3: Thomas Annan, Scotland, 1868, printed 1900. Close No. 101 High Street (-8) LACMA M.2008.40.98.8.jpg. Chapter 4: Ole Worm's Cabinet of Curiosities, Museum Wormianum, 1655, Smithsonian Institution Libraries. Chapter 5: Smithsonian Institute Archives, Image #MNH-43843. Chapter 7: Frederic Edwin Church, Niagara Falls, from the American Side, 1867, National Galleries of Scotland, Edinburgh, Scotland. Presented by John S. Kennedy 1887. Chapter 8: Anonymous photograph taken in New York City, circa 1905. Chapter 9: Tule Lake Relocation Center, Newell, California, Francis Stewart, War Relocation Authority photographer, National Archives and Records Administration, NARA record: 8464475. Chapter 10: LeRoy Woodson, photographer for the EPA, July 1972 (NARA record: 2368875) National Archives Archeological Site. Chapter 11: Stuart Franklin, Julia Butterfly Hill in Luna

Designed by Meryl Sussman Levavi

Library of Congress Cataloging-in-Publication Data

Names: Outwater, Alice B., author.
Title: Wild at heart : America's turbulent relationship with nature, from exploitation to redemption / Alice Outwater.
Description: First edition. | New York : St. Martin's Press, [2019] | Includes bibliographical references and index.
Identifiers: LCCN 2018041157| ISBN 9781250085788 (hardcover) | ISBN 9781250085795 (ebook)
Subjects: LCSH: Nature—Effect of human beings on—United States—History. | Human ecology—United States—History. | Environmentalism—United States—History. | Conservation of natural resources—United States—History.
Classification: LCC GF75 .O87 2019 | DDC 304.2/80973—dc23
LC record available at https://lccn.loc.gov/2018041157

First Edition: April 2019

10 9 8 7 6 5 4 3 2 1

This book is for the butterflies and bees, the deer herd, the bear and her cub, and the jackrabbits, coyotes, and ravens who live beside me.

We need the tonic of wildness—to wade sometimes in marshes where the bittern and the meadow-hen lurk, and hearing the booming of the snipe; to smell the whispering sedge where only some wilder and more solitary fowl builds her nest, and the mink crawls with its belly close to the ground.

—HENRY DAVID THOREAU, *WALDEN*

Contents

WILD
— AT —
HEART

Introduction

Our land is wild, a spread of high desert covered with sagebrush and old junipers cut by a swale that carries water during storms or snowmelt. The neighbor's irrigated fields and cattle lie half a mile away down a gentle slope, with two irrigation ditches and a barbed-wire fence between us. There's a den of coyotes that lives in the stand of ancient juniper trees on the slope above the ditches.

In the dry, high desert, a juniper can occupy its place on Earth for as long as 800 to 1,000 years, and each one is a singular presence. In pagan days, every tree, stream, and hill was believed to have a soul, along with some animals, plants, rocks, mountains, and rivers. Even ephemera like thunder, wind, and shadows could have their own spirit. British ethnologist Robert Ranulph Marett wrote that trees were generally regarded as maternal deities or forest spirits, and when a tree's life was taken for human use, woodcutters would beg forgiveness before they felled it. The souls of trees didn't disappear in antiquity; in Thai forests today, Buddhist monks tie pieces of cloth around trees in the jungle to remind rogue woodcutters that the trees' spirits are under the monks' protection. Wilderness has long been seen as a community of beings.

Judeo-Christianity, in contrast to pagan and Asian religions, established a dualism between humans and nature where humans have souls and the rest of the world does not. God created nature but was not part of it, and created humans in his image. The Old and New Testaments put people at the pinnacle of creation with dominion over nature, which was made for human use. Before biblical times, the spirits in natural objects had protected nature from humans. According to the Bible, humans held an effective monopoly on souls. Old inhibitions against profiteering from nature collapsed.

In the New World, natives lived in the wilderness and settlers lived apart from it. An English settler in the early 1600s described wilderness as "a dark and dismal place where all manner of wild beasts dash about uncooked." Wilderness was a Godless place full of things that could be eaten or sold. By that definition, my land's uncut trees and unmolested deer herd make it wilderness enough.

Being remote, I wanted a dog for company and safety. Dogs live on the boundary between humans and wildness; they are a bridge between nature and human culture. As the only large domesticated predator, dogs maintain a keen interest in other animals (a particularly useful trait in bear country) and are happy to lend you their ears and eyes, pointing out creatures you may have missed. But a dog's ability to slip into nature and back can be deadly with a coyote den nearby.

Coyotes are notoriously tough on dogs. Small dogs are like hors d'oeuvres, while dining on larger dogs takes some planning: a single member of the pack will lure a big dog back to their den, where they eat him as a group project. Coyotes are the most vocal local mammal, and they howl on a moonlit night in layers of sound that build and then recede. When pups whelp in the juniper grove every spring, their high-pitched baby voices join the lower voices of their parents in a nightly chorus, called group yip-howls, of *ar-ar-ar-aroooooo*. Coyotes have an imposing profile, but are less than fifty pounds of canid dressed up in a long-haired coat. I chose a dog the size of a small pony with the hope that God's dogs would leave it alone.

Titus arrived as a fifteen-pound puppy, and weighed 125 pounds by his first birthday. There is nothing natural about a Greater Swiss Mountain dog: the breed was created by humans to pull loads and manage cattle. Titus was a farm dog scaled large and muscular who grew so fast that he'd flip ass over teakettle at a dead run because he wasn't entirely certain where his feet were. Titus collected antlers that he used as chew toys, and chased rabbits through the sagebrush; he'd occasionally catch and eat one. A coyote is part of nature while Titus, with his handsome tricolored coat and enormous appetite, embodied human mastery over nature.

One day on our morning walk, the young bulls next door were grazing right next to the barbed-wire fence. I thought Titus would enjoy meeting them. The dog had known deer since he was a puppy—one of his jobs was to move deer off the landscaped area—but deer move so fast that there's not much interaction. As soon as Titus ducked under the fence to join the young bulls in their pasture, he understood that he was a drover dog. Herding dogs gather cattle together and hold them still, so it is easier to catch a rogue dog. Drover dogs drive cattle in front of them, and Titus had no end point. He drove the young bulls for forty-five minutes, with great joy. He did it well, too: he never touched them, and never stopped. He had mad skills. But they weren't our bulls, so his behavior was completely unacceptable.

Around here, dogs who chase livestock are shot because it is a law of nature that dogs are made to protect cattle, not harass them. This cultural definition of a natural law is as implacable as the law of gravity in rural Colorado, where everyone has a gun and the jury already ruled. There is literally no room in these wide-open spaces for dogs who run stock.

As soon as Titus saw the bulls, my husband, Bob, jogged back to the house to get the car. I climbed the fence and chased the dog as he moved the cattle into the corner, moved them into the cattails by the ditch, moved them back and forth across the field. The rancher whose house overlooks the field arrived with a leash. Bob arrived with the car. The owner of the cattle and his friend came out with their dogs, so in the end there were five people and two dogs trying to divert Titus from the yearling bulls. When I finally caught him, he had so much adrenaline that he leaped at the end of the leash like a 125-pound fish.

My dog had found his nature, his essence, and his central fact of existence.

A neighbor, who uses dogs to manage her sheep, heard that Titus had misbehaved, and called me that evening. She gently explained to me that my dog's training regime was insufficient, and she would be willing to supervise his education. She delivered three boxes of books, CDs, games, tools, harnesses, leashes, and training aids the next day, and Titus's schooling began in earnest.

Titus had been pulling a seventy-five-pound cart for months (full-grown males can pull more than a ton) and had mastered the normal range of commands, but this was like doggy college. I started wearing a treat bag stuffed with liverwurst, cheddar, and salami for three lessons a day: we worked on command fluency so he'd respond in all situations and locations; molding behavior, where I'd lure him to do things and then connect a word with it; long line, where we'd practice walking a mile with his eyes on me (instead of the bunnies); and cavaletti, using low bars to teach him how to jump like a horse, to refine his body placement. I was guided through the latest dog-training techniques. Three weeks into our new regime, we were out on a walk when Titus looked down the hill and realized that the fields where he had chased cattle were adjacent to our land. He was off in a beeline, at top speed. He looked like a small horse on a critical, lifesaving mission.

It took fifteen minutes to catch him that Thursday afternoon, with Bob and a neighbor helping. Friday morning, we were coming back from a walk when he saw that cattle were grazing right down the hill from our house. He leaped over the two irrigation ditches like a steeplechase champ and ducked under the barbed-wire fence to drive them. Two hours later, he was down there again.

And that was the end of Titus.

Once he became aware of his true nature, he had to be leashed. Instead of free run of a hundred acres, he was stuck within ten feet of me. He gazed through the windows at cattle grazing half a mile away and plotted his escape. You could see it in his muscled flanks and big brown eyes: he was going to be shot before the week was out.

Titus left Colorado three days after he discovered freelance herding. He started a new life as a stud dog in Oklahoma, and is training for the show ring. He'll be caged or leashed for the rest of his life. Titus grew up with a lot of exercise, and was very handsome. There aren't many dogs in the United States that get to have sex, and Titus has taken to it with gusto. The breeder says that he's yodeling with happiness. I missed my dog, and was sorry he'd lost his freedom until a friend pointed out that he'd probably consider his new job a promotion.

∘ ∘ ∘

Our dominion over nature was taken as the natural order until the 1859 publication of Charles Darwin's *On the Origin of Species*, which presented the uneasy reality that people could not hold themselves to be separate from nature. It took more than a century for people to fully embrace the concept that we are not a lot *like* animals; we actually *are* animals.

Wilderness was considered a dark and forbidding place full of wild tribes, the opposite of Eden, until the 1700s, when urban populations increased and people's perceptions of nature changed. Jean-Jacques Rousseau believed that humans in nature are uncorrupted, and that civilization brings vice. Instead of Satan's home, wilderness was seen as an uninhabited temple of nature where God could be encountered directly. Nature and the ecstatic sublime were primary subjects of painters J. M. W. Turner and Thomas Cole, authors Ralph Waldo Emerson and Henry David Thoreau, and poet William Wordsworth. Valuing nature became part of western culture.

Environmental historian William Cronon noted that the final Indian Wars were fought as the government started setting aside national parks and wilderness. Native Americans were removed from their land and confined to reservations, creating the uninhabited wilderness that the government then protected. And wilderness has been defined as uninhabited from that time to this. Humans are not unnatural and North America was inhabited long before Europeans arrived, but wilderness was codified in the Wilderness Act of 1964 as "an area where the earth and its community of life are untrammeled by man, where man himself is a visitor who does not remain." For land to be wilderness, humans must be separate from it.

Our concept of nature has evolved over thousands of years. Wilderness as we know it today—empty, wild land that is protected from human intervention—is a cultural construct from the 1800s that includes the national myth of the frontier and its cowboys, and of the sublime, where wilderness is Nature's cathedral.

Wildness is something else entirely: it is the part of nature that is beyond human control. It is undomesticated and uncultivated. It is autonomous. Ecologically speaking, wildness is defined by how individuals are affected by natural selection. Modern civilization insulates us from disease, hunger, weather, and predation, and we live in cities—built environments—that further mitigate risk. We are not wild, and neither was Titus.

Titus couldn't stay (unless we acquired a herd) because he knew that he was a drover dog. His mental picture of the world was clear, and personal. He was autonomous. You can't get less wild than a creature whose genetic makeup originated in a Swiss canton, bred under human control for centuries. But he was a wild soul who refused to have his world defined by my parameters. As poet Gary Snyder said, "A person with a clear heart and open mind can experience the wilderness anywhere on earth. It is a quality of one's own consciousness. The planet is a wild place and always will be."

Our relationship with nature has run the gamut from hellish to heavenly, from outside us to within us. Our relationship with nature is influenced by economic systems and spiritual beliefs; there are no universal standards, and actions that are unthinkable in one culture or era are unremarkable in another. But the deeper truth known to Darwin, dogs, and philosophers alike is that all living beings are inextricably part of nature. And nature is beyond our control.

That also means that human nature is beyond our control. We are wild at heart.

There is wildness everywhere, and within us all.

∘ ∘ ∘

Nature and wildness exist separately from humans, and we can't control it. But we now have the ability to destroy everything alive. We can kill the wildlife, manage the waterways, reshape the land, and pollute the air, land, and water in ways that are incompatible with life. This means that our relationship with nature matters; our individual choices and collective actions will determine the survival of nature and all her glories. The sad truth is that if the past is prologue, nature is doomed. The world is changing fast, and time is running out. We have the ability to learn from the past. History can help us understand how we arrived at the present, so we can create a future that we'd want to live in.

Let me tell you a story about nature that begins at the beginning.

1

Nature and Native America

*The long memory is the most radical idea
in America.*

—U. Utah Phillips

Mrs. Jack Treetop, a member of the Húŋkpapȟa Lakȟóta (Hunkpapa Sioux), was photographed in 1908 wearing a Mona Lisa smile, a lovely stole of cylindrical bone beads, and a fortune in dentalium shells. Her shells are the basis of a strange story: they had been harvested nearly 1,500 miles away under sixty feet of water off the west coast of Vancouver Island; some of them may have been gathered centuries earlier. Dentalium was used throughout the Great Plains, Great Basin, Central Canada, Northern Plateau, and Alaska for as long as 3,500 years for every kind of jewelry and clothing decoration. It was used as currency for at least a thousand years, and perhaps much longer. What looks like decorative beads is actually money.

Nature and money have always been intertwined. Until recently, nature was the source of everything people used, and this bounty was distributed in different ways. From time immemorial, natural resources have been bartered, gifted, and sold for money.

Dentalium, like most money, is durable, portable, uniform, and scarce. These shells rarely wash up on shore. Ethnographers claim that they were harvested exclusively by the Nuu-chah-nulth people (formerly called Nootkas) of the Pacific Northwest, who collected the shells a few at a time from sandbars about sixty feet below the surface of the ocean.

The shells were deeply valuable. For some California tribes, twelve fine shells bought a redwood dugout canoe. The highest-quality shells were about two and one-fourth inches long, and some native traders had measurements tattooed on their arms to verify the length of their dentalium (Anglos called them Indian bankers).

More than 600 tribal nations lived on the land that became North America, and these people had a wide range of economic and social systems. There was great diversity of language and architecture, but two systems were widely shared. Hundreds of tribes participated in a complex, far-flung trade network that stretched from Central America to Alaska, and used dentalium to buy food, hides and furs, fabrics, ceramics, baskets and canoes, turquoise, macaw feathers, and even slaves. And almost without exception, tribal peoples believed that spirits resided in many living and nonliving beings. Nature was full of lives that were much like human lives.

To provide a range of native attitudes towards nature, I chose three tribes with different histories from distinct areas and environments. The temperate rain forests of the Pacific Northwest (near the dentalium beds) supported some of the densest populations of native people in North America, and the area was undisturbed by Europeans until the 1700s. The Chinook people were the best traders in the region, and many of the earliest explorers and traders wrote of Chinook life. I have a Hopi friend from the southwest desert of New Mexico, where his ancestors have lived for thousands of years. And I have a soft spot for the Western Abenaki, who once lived on the land I grew up on in Vermont. These tribes all saw nature differently.

∘ ∘ ∘

In the Pacific Northwest, people relied on salmon and other fish for food, and the runs never failed. It was a fat life, and the region supported dense populations of well-fed people for thousands of years. But the plentiful food, long residence, and wet, temperate climate did not create an egalitarian and unified society. Instead, it was an area with exceptional linguistic diversity and a highly stratified social system. When tribes that live in a small area speak unrelated languages, it means they aren't talking with each other. The six major language families in the Pacific Northwest were so different that native traders used a pidgin called chinuk wawa, made up of words from all the local languages.

People bought and sold things with dentalium, and these tribes also participated in a gift economy centered around potlatch, a ceremony in which food and goods are given away or destroyed for status and political gain. "Potlatch" may be anglicized from the Nuu-chah-nulth word *patshatl,* or "giving," and these celebrations of birth, adulthood, marriage, or death featured competitive feasting, speechmaking, and gift giving. A potlatch isn't just a party: it's a political struggle among people jockeying for economic and ceremonial privileges within the social hierarchy. Pre-contact gifts included storable food, canoes, copper sheets hammered from chunks of raw ore, dentalium, and slaves.

The essence of potlatch is reciprocation. Presents were given and returned as a measure of respect. Potlatch gifts reinforced a web of obligations, and were used to settle the hierarchy within clans, and between tribes, confederations, and nations. People passed their winters in a cheerful round of gatherings that redistributed the wealth throughout a community, though guests of higher status received more things.

Ownership and property are not simple, stand-alone concepts; they are socially defined relationships between people and things and nature. Can you own land? Wildlife? Trees or water? Native Americans had different relationships with property and wildlife than Europeans, and many tribes relied on a gift economy. As early as 1765, Thomas Hutchinson wrote in *The History of the Colony of Massachusett's Bay* that "an Indian gift is a proverbial expression, signifying a present for which an equivalent return is expected." In Vermont two centuries later, a friend who gave a gift and wanted it back was called an Indian giver.

Property and ownership are complex legal constructs and, regardless of the economic system, gifts often come with strings attached. A gifting culture relies on reciprocity, so an individual retains some rights to a gift. Even today, when you buy something, some fraction of a purchase often remains the property of someone else. When you buy a book, for example, the arrangement of words belongs to the author even though the book itself is sold and owned. You have the right to read my book, but I retain the rights to that particular set of words. Curiously, modern scientists follow the rules of a gift economy: those who give the best papers and contribute the most to their field are gifted with grants. Information often gains value through sharing, and it's possible that the exchange economy was dominant during the Industrial Age, and a gift economy is returning as we enter the Information Age.

The Chinook tribe was based around the mouth of the Columbia River, a major travel route for indigenous peoples. Nearly every dentalium shell that was harvested by the Nuu-chah-nulth people (who also made canoes) was traded by the Chinook. If you follow the money, you end up at the Chinook, who also traded ninety-pound packs of dried, pulverized salmon encased in cord-laced fish skins and rush baskets, edible for up to two years, as a standard trade item. Their other major trade items were canoes (often made by other tribes) and slaves.

The Chinook, master traders, had close contact with early European traders, and repeated smallpox epidemics nearly wiped out these intrepid middlemen by the mid-1800s. The surviving tribal members burned their ancestral villages to get rid of the bad spirits that made them ill, and stayed with other tribes. Their language was nearly replaced by the pidgin trading language chinuk wawa. Traditional Chinook life was so altered by European exposure that the diaries of early traders and explorers offer some of the clearest glimpses of pre-contact Chinook life.

To understand how the Chinook saw nature, I wanted to experience their world. What did a Chinook see from day to day? The Friends of the Ridgefield National Wildlife Refuge in Washington just built a Chinook plank house, so it's now possible to sit in a traditional Chinook home. I'm all in.

The plank house is twenty miles north of Portland in a grassy coastal area where wetlands fed by slow tributaries to the Columbia River are interspersed with a coastal forest of Douglas fir and some gigantic Oregon white oak trees. People have lived here for at least 2,300 years, and the plank house is well adapted to the rainy climate. It's spacious, nearly eighty feet long and half as wide with a ridgepole over twenty feet high, and two large rectangular hearths down the center of the building provide heat during the winter. A platform runs down one side of the plank house, with woven cattail mats perpendicular to the walls dividing the long house into cozy, private nooks. Traditionally, each family slept together in their own section with private storage rooms underneath the floor for extra possessions and food, providing psychic reassurance that there will be plenty for tomorrow. The reconstructed plank house isn't an exact replica—there are risers on one side to seat people for presentations and no cellars—but even so it feels warm and safe.

In 1806, on a drizzly January day, Meriwether Lewis wrote a long journal entry that detailed the domestic clutter of Chinookan daily life. People smoked fish in frames that stood close to the fire in the sunken hearth running down the center of the house, and smoked meat in the rafters. The family with the highest status lived farthest from the entrance, while the slaves and lower-status people lived near the door. The plank-house door was an oval opening, often carved or painted to look like a human or animal mouth, and Chinook backed into the single door buttocks first, a deeply non-threatening position.

The Chinook had more slaves per capita than the surrounding tribes because they were such good traders. Female slaves carried water, hewed wood, and made baskets and mats while male slaves built and repaired the houses, fished and hunted for meat, cured and preserved foods, and paddled their master's canoe. In 1810, a male slave in Chinook country could be bartered for ten to a dozen blankets; farther north, male slaves cost seventy-five to a hundred dentalium, while females cost fifty to seventy shells.

When you share a large house with slaves, it's important to look different from them. The Chinook people wore very little, and did not use clothing to indicate their status. Instead, tattoos and jewelry were used as social signifiers, and they molded their babies' heads to make an elegant, angular profile that was easily distinguished from the rounded foreheads of their slaves. A flattened head was a badge of aristocracy and a sign of freedom. (Chinook wore European hats sideways, since their heads were wider ear to ear.)

Two centuries later, it is surprisingly easy to piece together what the Chinook thought about nature. One of the most important rituals of Chinook life was the First Salmon feast, honoring the salmon with elaborate ceremonies to thank them for returning. People did not take salmon from the river, they accepted a gift and its obligations. The first salmon of the season was ritually prepared to ensure a successful fishing season, and after the fish was cooked, people feasted, danced, and gave thanks. The bones and skin of the fish were returned to the river so the rest of the salmon could see that the first salmon—a gift from the sea—had been respected, so they would continue to swim up the river in great numbers.

Chinook believed that nature was made up of spirits, including wind, water, plants, animals, mountains, and many others. People had guardian spirits, often animals, who taught them skills. In addition, objects had spirits, from the house to the dish and spoon. All spirits had supernatural powers and human characteristics, both good and evil. Some spirits were good and helped people who pleased them, while others were bad and harmed individuals or the tribe.

The Chinook lived in a world where nature was alive, and they were part of nature. Sharp trading was second nature, and a dentalium-based exchange economy allowed people to sell things to strangers with no strings attached. Then the Europeans came, and one of their first gifts was venereal disease. As the best traders, Chinook had the most contact with the Europeans, and natives as far away as Alaska were soon calling sexually transmitted diseases "Chinook."

The tribes of the Pacific Northwest had avoided contact with the global economy until 1741, when a Danish sea captain named Vitus Bering was hired by Czar Peter the Great to explore the Siberian Pacific. His brig was shipwrecked on an uninhabited northern island that was home to a wide variety of sea life. Georg Steller, Captain Bering's naturalist, discovered Steller's sea cow, a relative of the dugong and manatee that grew to up to thirty feet long with sweet blubber and meat; it became extinct in twenty-seven years (if that's not a record, it should be). The sea otter, the heaviest member of the weasel family and one of the smallest sea mammals, was another of his discoveries, and it has the misfortune of bearing a sumptuous coat.

The sea otter trade changed the Chinook's relationship with nature. Captain Bering's crew returned to Russia with 900 sea otter pelts that they had bought from local tribes, and most of these skins were sold in Chinese markets. Sea otter fur became a favorite of the Mandarins, who used it to trim their silk robes. It is the densest fur in the world, more valuable than sable, and each pelt was about a year's salary for a worker. Enterprising traders soon sailed from China, Great Britain, and Spain. Captain James Cook, Juan Pérez, and other foreigners exchanged dentalium, copper, and iron for sea otter skins and sex, and by the 1760s, the Pacific coast fur rush was on.

The tribal people of the Pacific Northwest believed that all animals had spirits, but the sea otter was particularly valued. Some natives knew the sea otter as "the brother"; among some tribes, only chiefs and experts were allowed to hunt sea otters or wear their fur. Luxuriant, dense, and soft, sea otter fur was worn as chiefs' regalia and was given in potlatches to mark coming-of-age ceremonies, weddings, and funerals. For people to kill and sell thousands of sea otter skins, their relationship with nature must have changed. Instead of being respectful of their sea otter brothers, they killed these animals for manufactured goods and dentalium, and for a time they prospered.

Global trade changed the Pacific Northwest. More than a hundred American ships traded for furs on the northwest coast between 1788 and 1803, using Hawaii as a resupply point to deliver furs to China. In 1794, the *Resolution*'s bill of lading listed a typical cargo of trade goods, including 378 iron swords, 52 copper sheets, 11 muskets, 7 pistols, 8 copper-mounted cutlasses, and 150 fathoms of dentalium. The captain purchased furs with dentalium, and bartered for furs with metal and weapons. A single ship could bring thousands of skins to market. Captain Charles Carey, for example, assembled a cargo in 1820 that included over 23,000 skins for the hold of his ship, the *Levant*, and sailed to China where he bartered the furs for tea to sell in Europe.

The enormous cultural and linguistic divide between the Europeans and the tribes made the fur trade a dangerous business. Hundreds of fully armed natives would paddle out in large canoes to inspect the trade items laid out on the deck. A few ships were commandeered by natives over the years, and surely many locals were killed by guns. But the greatest threat was germs.

Venereal diseases came first, and smallpox followed shortly thereafter. Historian Elizabeth Fenn explains in *Pox Americana* that smallpox likely first struck the Chinook as part of a continental pandemic that started near Boston in 1774 and eventually spread from Mexico to Alaska. When the first British expedition surveyed Puget Sound in 1792, navigator George Vancouver noted that the area was a necropolis, with skeletons "promifcuoufly fcattered about the beach, in great numbers." Their naturalist, Archibald Menzies, noted of the natives that "several of them were pock markd . . . [and] a number of them had lost an eye."

The natives were immunologically unprepared for European diseases, and single epidemics would kill as many as three-quarters of the people in a village. After an epidemic, the survivors would torch their lodges and possessions to appease the bad spirits. But the foreign illnesses kept coming. Academic estimates of the pre-contact Chinook population range from 5,000 to 22,000. In 1825, the Hudson's Bay Company counted a total of 550 Chinook, with 170 slaves; thirty years later, a total of 56 Chinook managed 23 slaves.

Chinook did not bury their dead. The corpses of high-ranking individuals were placed in canoes that were raised on poles onshore, along with goods for the next life. But when epidemics overwhelmed a village, many of the dead were slipped into the grassy tidal rivers where they bumped along the banks of their tributary to the Columbia River and then out to sea. The prevailing current at the mouth of the Columbia is north to south. After an epidemic moved through the villages, a steady stream of bloated corpses piled up along the beaches south of the Columbia, fattening carrion eaters and famished dogs. For years, jumbled drifts of human bones lay bleaching on the gray and windswept shores.

The Chinook, who surely must have seen themselves as part of nature, lost their language, livelihood, and land. They lost 98 percent of their tribal members, and their villages were either burned or taken over by other tribes. The land hasn't changed much since then, but the Chinook's concept of nature has all but disappeared. The spirits that once inhabited their world are gone.

○ ○ ○

In the Pacific Northwest, the Chinook saw nature as being made up of the spirits of all things. The Hopi concept of nature is fundamentally different: in Hopiland, nature was controlled by spirits. The Hopi, through their *kachinas* (embodied spirits), helped rain clouds come visit their high desert fields and coaxed the snow to fall.

The Hopi live in the high desert of the southwestern United States where they still speak their language and practice their religion on land they never left. According to the Hopi Tribal Government, their reservation in northeastern Arizona encompasses more than 1.5 million acres, with twelve villages on three mesas that have never moved. The Hopi have lived on their row of mesas in the desert Southwest since prehistoric times, the oldest continuously occupied settlement in North America. They built large, defensible apartment house complexes, or pueblos, of local stone, and in spite of long periods of outside aggression, the tribe has endured. According to the 2010 census, more than 18,000 Hopi live in the United States.

Their religion is still alive. Many Hopi have maintained a sacred covenant with Màasaw, the ancient caretaker of the Earth. In 1955, David Monongye, a Hopi leader from the Fire Clan, explained, "This land at first glance appears to be of no value, mostly rock and sand, hardly any trees, hardly any water, but we came to this person (Màasaw) who will take care of us if we follow this life plan, and all will be provided for us."

Hopi Indians were known as careful micro-agriculturalists of corn, beans, and squash who cultivated reverence and respect for all things. According to the *Hopi Dictionary*, *Hopi* translates as "behaving one, one who is mannered, civilized, peaceable, polite, who adheres to the Hopi way." The Hopi ideal is to live as peaceful and humble farmers with men working on the women's land. "The family, the dwelling house and the fields are inseparable, because the woman is the heart of these, and they rest with her. . . . The man builds the house but the woman is the owner, hence all of its possessions are hers; the man cultivates the fields, but he renders its harvests to the woman's keeping, because upon her it rests to prepare the food, and the surplus of stores for barter depends upon her thrift."

Their land is mostly too dry for trees and rainfall is erratic. To grow corn in these marginal fields, the Hopi need the help of spirits who control nature.

My husband, Bob, became friends with Terry Gasdia, a

Hopi from the Fourth Mesa, about ten years ago. We met at an annual Christmas market held at the local high school where Native American artists sold their jewelry, pottery, and paintings. He was in his midforties then, midsize but very strong with long hair that he wore in a ponytail. We brought home a big watercolor of a kachina in blue and red, which has hung in my office since then. For years, Terry would drop by every now and then, and Bob would stop by his place.

The Hopi have refined their own strains of corn for millennia. Bob and I have lived on a farm for decades, and always have room for an interesting handful of seeds. One year, Bob grew a big patch of Hopi corn from a mixed batch of seeds Terry brought him. Some of the corn plants grew eight feet tall, while others were barely four feet. There was red corn, blue corn, yellow and white corn; long ears, medium ears, and round ears; varieties of corn I'd never seen or tasted. It was too tough to eat on the cob, but the cornbread we made from dried kernels ground in a coffee grinder was as sustaining as meat.

Terry had a house in town for a while, and he usually had a niece or nephew around who he was watching out for. He was often making art, and we'd often buy it. Terry worked in a variety of mediums, from paper to stone, mostly making kachinas.

Hopi kachinas are supernatural beings—life forces of the cosmos—that embody the spirits of living things and affect various aspects of the natural world. There are kachinas for rain, corn, butterflies, dragonflies, and coyotes; stars, sun, and water; the clown, the ogre, and even death. Most of Terry's kachinas are cottonwood effigies—little statues or dolls—that Hopi artists have sold as art objects since the late 1800s. The dolls are identified by their colors, tools, and accessories, by the clothes and feathers they wear, all of which are symbols laden with meaning. Each kachina has a backstory that explains every detail of their dress.

According to the Hopi, kachinas can change nature, and often come to the mesas in the form of rain clouds. Each of these kachinas, regardless of their appearance, is like a person in the spirit world. They are messengers who accept gifts and prayers for health, fertility, and rain and carry them back to the gods. They are friends who are loved, cared for, and ceremonially fed. (The dolls like a little ground corn, a few strands of tobacco, and some salt crystals placed before them, as surely as Santa likes a sandwich and a bottle of beer.) Kachinas are a connection between the human world and nature, and a properly treated kachina can make the rain come, the snow fall deep, or crops grow tall and strong. Their role in the water cycle is particularly important to the Hopi, whose harvests on the high, arid desert of northeastern Arizona have always been precarious.

Kachinas have lives that are separate from humans. One night, Terry had a dream of a kachina that he didn't recognize, who asked him to hike up Junction Creek to meet him face to face. Terry hiked up the creek and saw the new kachina there. He carved it from cottonwood root, painted it the way it had presented itself by the creek, and brought it down to Hopiland for the kachina season. He then danced dressed as his new friend.

The old folks saw him and said, "I haven't seen that kachina since I was a kid! I thought he was gone. Where did you find him?" And when Terry told the story of their meeting up Junction Creek, they all agreed that it was a fine thing to have that spirit back in the village after such a long absence.

Many cultures have kachinas. European kachinas include elves, tomtes, the tooth fairy, vampires, werewolves, and Santa

Claus, who embodies generosity. Like all kachinas, Santa has a complete backstory including Mrs. Claus, a sleigh and a team of reindeer, and a workshop staffed with elves at the North Pole, where he spends most of his year. Santa enters the human world for one long night, while Hopi kachinas spend half the year in the village, and then most of them go to the top of the San Francisco Mountains on their off-season. During the winter solstice, kachinas take on their physical form and enter the Hopi villages to launch the complex ceremonial calendar that lasts until the summer solstice, when they go back to their mountains.

The kachinas help the Hopi survive. Hopi kachinas have three forms: kachina spirits often appear as a rain cloud; kachina dolls are roughly six inches high, carved from cottonwood roots; and kachina dancers are masked and costumed Hopi men. Kachina dancers personify these spirits, and assume their powers and prestige. With a mask, costume, and paint, the dancer becomes infused with the spirit of a particular kachina, and for a time the kachina and the dancer become one. During the time that dancing men become kachinas, they can cure sickness, grow corn, bring clouds and rain, and reinforce order in the Hopi world.

One summer, I saw deer kachinas dance at Chimney Rock, a sandstone spire near Durango where the moon lingers during its cycle. About a thousand years ago, there was a 200-room settlement on top of Chimney Rock. The stone floor where the kachinas danced was finished for the first time in 1084 and rebuilt in 1972.

It's mostly sagebrush on the land below, but there is more moisture on the high flat areas where snow collects in the winter: dusty blue-green juniper trees and some craggy Gambel oaks with moss-green leaves grow near the ceremonial platform, along with sparse tufts of grass. The small audience included natives, some people from nearby towns, and a few tourists; we all brought our own folding chairs.

The deer kachinas dance to bring game and deep winter snow for a good harvest the following year. They danced the night of the full moon in early summer, and all the details were prescribed by tradition. The dancers wore antlers, with juniper branches over their faces so you couldn't see their eyes. They wore turquoise-colored armbands and held three-foot sticks in their front hands, leaning on them to make their stance into that of a deer. A deer kachina is not a deer; it's a spirit with skills, sidekicks, and a role in the water cycle to bring deep snow the next winter. During the dance, there was some alchemy where the dancers actually became the spirit they had summoned, and the little boys dancing as small deer were also transformed. Shape-shifting is not part of my daily round, but it was clear that those pueblo men dancing atop that stone spire in the full moon (as their ancestors had) were speaking an ancient language of motion, rhythm, and symbols that had summoned spirits from a different plane. I don't remember if the winter snow was deep that year, but the Hopi believe that dances like these are necessary to maintain harmony and balance in the world and bring water.

∘ ∘ ∘

In the forested Northeast, the Abenaki used shamans who traveled between nature and human society in a trance state to manage the weather or help with healing or hunting. Shamanistic traditions are based on the premise that nature's invisible forces or spirits affect our lives and can be managed. Shamans have existed around the world since prehistoric times, and they get into a trance state by singing, dancing, taking drugs, meditating, and drumming. Often plants, including ayahuasca, peyote, or psilocybin, are used as entheogens ("generating the divine within") to bring on a spiritual experience.

During a shaman's trance, his spirit leaves his body and enters the supernatural world. Once in the spirit world, the shaman communes with spirits and with animals that act as messengers and spirit guides. Mircea Eliade, a Romanian historian of religion, believed that shamanism underlays all other spiritual traditions, and that shamanism's most distinctive feature—but not the only one—was the journey to other worlds in an altered state of consciousness.

According to oral tradition, many Abenaki could leave their bodies and enter nature as an animal. All shamans could transform themselves into at least one animal form and the last great shaman of the Abenaki, Old John Neptune, or Bungawarrawit, was credited with having seven animal forms. (Henry David Thoreau described visiting him in 1853 in *The Maine Woods*.) "The Wabanakis saw a spirit in every tree and waterfall, and a malignant or benevolent influence in many animals; and, in order to propitiate these beings, the class of sorcerers became, of course, a positive necessity," said the 1908 *Encyclopedia of Religion and Ethics*. "The conjuror could transform himself into an animal at will." Strange occurrences involving wildlife were regularly attributed to shamans at play.

Shamans work with nature to control the weather, see the future, interpret dreams, and travel to other worlds. "Shamanism is not a belief system," explained anthropologist Michael Harner. "It's based on personal experiments conducted to heal, to get information, or do other things. In fact, if shamans don't get results, they will no longer be used by people in their tribe. People ask me, 'How do you know if somebody's a shaman?'

I say, 'It's simple. Do they journey to other worlds? And do they perform miracles?'"

Village leadership normally resided with a dominant local family, and a chief or sagamore (from the Eastern Abenaki sȧkǝmɑ) usually held a leadership position for life. Some leaders were shamans and some were not, and political power in this patrilineal society depended on personal charisma.

Christianity came with the fur trade in the 1500s, changing Abenaki attitudes toward nature. The colonists were so brutal—and their diseases so devastating—that most of the Western Abenaki self-deported to Canada around 1670, and Jesuit missionaries moved to their new villages to convert them. Jacques-René de Brisay de Denonville wrote in 1690, "Of all the Indian nations, the Abenaqui is the most inclined to Christianity," and many of the letters written by Jesuit missionary Sébastien Râle in the late 1600s reported that the Abenaki in Quebec were admirably sober and Christian. Nowhere in his letters did I find a description of how the Abenaki felt about nature.

By oral tradition, Abenaki mythology is divided into three time periods. The first was the Ancient Age, when animal and human life was undifferentiated. Next came the Golden Age when animals were still human, but quantitatively different. The last period is the Present Age, in which animals and humans are completely different. According to their mythology, the Abenaki people were once one with nature and are now separate from it.

Apart from their mythology, we have just a bare sketch of Abenaki life in the 1500s. When the Europeans arrived, the Abenaki hunted, gathered, and farmed corn, beans, and squash. The northern woods are not very productive, and the Abenaki hunted on a fraction of their family hunting territory each year to give the animal population time to recover. They maintained a balance between human and animal needs. There was no money and no inheritance, with hunting territories and houses owned by the family as a whole; gifts were used to distribute hunting surpluses and items made by specialists.

At the time of first contact, the Europeans were shorter than the Abenaki, lived fewer years, had less leisure time, and were more likely to die from violence. By objective measures, European culture did not look like a better system. But the arrival of Europeans marked the beginning of rapid and drastic changes to the Abenaki way of life, and the near disappearance of the tribe. French and English trading posts were established throughout Abenaki territory, and there was brisk trading of beaver pelts for European manufactured goods. The Abenaki participated in the transatlantic economic system, and within decades copper pots replaced native bark containers and earthenware, guns replaced bows, and glass beads replaced porcupine quills. Suddenly an exchange economy based on beaver skins superseded the gift economy.

Of course, germs came, too. An unidentified epidemic swept down the St. Lawrence River in 1535, bringing pestilence down the East Coast. Another epidemic struck between 1564 and 1570, and typhus killed thousands in 1586. According to the *Handbook of North American Indians*, there were perhaps 12,000 Western Abenaki in New Hampshire and Vermont in 1600. Father Pierre Biard, a French Jesuit missionary, noted in 1616 that the Abenaki "are astonished and often complain that since the French mingle and carry on trade with them they are dying fast, and the population is thinning out." That same year, British trader Captain Richard Vines wintered on the coast of Maine and wrote that the natives "were sore afflicted with the Plague, for that the Country was in a manner left void of inhabitants." This catastrophic epidemic spread down the coast between 1616 and 1619, making room for the Pilgrims in 1620.

As new generations succumbed to disease, traditional culture fractured. After each biological disaster, the survivors of neighboring villages and tribes merged together, and their identities became blurry even in oral history. There had been dozens of distinct tribes in the Northeast before European diseases arrived, but after contact, tribal history was about attrition and regrouping. There were major epidemics at least every decade: smallpox, flu, diphtheria, and measles depopulated entire regions.

The Western Abenaki population dropped from perhaps 12,000 to 250, losing 98 percent of their people. Their language nearly disappeared, and their sagamores no longer took on animal shapes. The long human alliance with other species disappeared, and the Vermont mountains lost their animal friends as well: the wolves and wildcats, deer, beaver, turkey, and moose soon vanished from the state.

∘ ∘ ∘

Balance. Respect. Gratitude. The Chinook of the Pacific Northwest believed in the power of gifts, and gave thanks for nature's bounty. The Hopi of the arid Southwest relied on kachinas to interact with nature and bring rain. And the Abenaki believed that people could become animals and return to human form. These tribes saw Nature as alive, full of beings with lives as complex and rich as their own. They trusted in the power of gifts, and measured wealth by what you gave away. Animals were message bearers and representations of spirit guides, and hunters maintained a balance between human and animal needs.

The riverside grasslands and forests that sheltered the Chinook are uninhabited now, and the wind that rustles through the tall grasses is unheard and unseen. The Canada geese that winter near Cathlapotle have no fear of Chinook arrows, and the salmon that swim up the rivers are no longer a gift from the underwater king. The Hopi no longer live on corn grown by the grace of rain-bearing kachinas, but they continue to welcome these spirits every winter and dance their ceremonial dances to ensure that the world keeps spinning and the sun still rises. On the East Coast, the sagamore no longer sits upon the mountaintop. A bond between the human and animal worlds was broken, and cannot be remade. What has been lost shall never be returned, but the reverberations of these cultures continue to resonate within us. The thankfulness of the Chinook, the reverence of the Hopi, and the restraint of the Abenaki reflect a relationship with nature that models the sustainable balance we are trying to create today.

2

Nature as Sublime

England was the first country where human labor was replaced by machines on a grand scale, and the changes trig-
gered by the invention of new spinning and weaving machines
actually altered the landscape. The new machinery increased
demand for high-quality iron. The development of canals and
railways allowed the ingredients to make iron—iron ore, coal,
and limestone—and other heavy goods to be transported at a
reasonable cost. There were improvements in the banking,
transportation, and communication systems and increased

iron production, fuel use, and trade. All of these factors contributed to the Industrial Revolution, and paradoxically a new-found appreciation for nature.

In the old order, peasants had provided their lord with food, crafts, and services in exchange for military protection. This social arrangement was upended by the Industrial Revolution. When workers shifted from rural agriculture to urban industry, nature was transformed from the 1611 King James Bible's "waste howling wilderness" to a Romantic expression of the sublime. After factories replaced agricultural society and cottage industries, nature became a way for people to connect with God.

To a peasant farmer, wilderness is unimproved land lacking in food and water, apt to harbor bandits and to be avoided when possible. In 1620, William Bradford wrote of the New World's "hideous and desolate wilderness, full of wild beasts and wild men." Thomas Hobbes, no fan of nature, wrote in 1651 that the life of man in nature is "solitary, poore, nasty, brutish, and short." Hobbes argued that people should enter into a contract with a powerful leader and exchange some freedom for security. Nature was not a healthy state to be in.

An agrarian society is characterized by wealth inequality and a lack of social mobility: like unfettered capitalism, it's a winner-take-all society. When land is the major source of wealth, the social hierarchy is based on landownership rather than labor, and a handful of people usually end up owning everything. The country of El Salvador, for example, was owned by fourteen families (*Las Catorce*). In Europe, an underclass of vassals were bound to cultivate their lord's land, often for generations, and the upper class kept landownership to a small fraction of the population. Britain enjoyed centuries of primogeniture, where estates were deeded to the eldest son, and the second Domesday list of 1873 showed that all the land in England was owned by less than 5 percent of the population.

British landowners adopted a series of agricultural reforms that created a landless and hungry workforce long before the Industrial Revolution. Although British laborers didn't own land, they had traditionally augmented their diet in the common forests by fishing and hunting small animals. Villagers could scavenge their firewood there, taking any dead limb that could be broken off with an iron hook or a shepherd's crook (by hook or by crook), and people could graze a few animals or grow a small garden on common fields. Gleaning, where people gathered up the useful remnants of a crop after harvest, was allowed on the commons and provided up to a quarter of the year's grain for the poor.

The 1723 Waltham Black Act claimed deer, rabbits, hares, and fish as private property and barred British laborers from harvesting them. Poaching became a hanging crime, and the enclosure movement followed, literally fencing off land from the peasantry with hedges or stone fences. Private owners took over about one-sixth of England between 1760 and 1870, enclosing vast acreages of common pasture and forestland. In many parts of England, villagers lost access to land where they could fish, hunt, pen a pig, and graze a goat or gather wood or peat for fuel, willows for basketry, or reeds for thatching. Gleaning was outlawed, and the living standard of commoners took a nosedive.

There was no doubt that large enclosed farms were more productive than scattered peasant plots: fewer hands worked the same acreage and yields increased. Unfortunately this left landless peasants with no way to grow or gather food. Instead, they needed cash to buy it. Home textile production and soon factory jobs provided work for the whole family. By the nine-teenth century, England had become an industrial society where people were paid to make things, and bought most of their food with money.

This societal shift worried Swiss philosopher Jean-Jacques Rousseau, who believed that, in nature, humans were funda-mentally good and lacked the passions that generate vices. He held that vices start to develop as soon as people organize themselves into societies. He deplored the "fatal" concept of property, and described the dystopia that results from individ-uals owning the Earth. Civil society, as Rousseau describes it, provides order and ensures the right to property, which is good for the rich. Rousseau saw inequality as a feature of the long process by which people become estranged from nature.

The shift to industrial production may have made Rous-seau wish for the days of the noble savage. For workers, the new industrial social order brought crushing poverty and a lack of social mobility. Before collective bargaining, industrial soci-ety exploited a population whose access to common land had disappeared with enclosure, and whose cottage industries had been eradicated by new inventions. Factory owners used the military to quell protests.

Humans have been weaving for at least 9,000 years, and fine fabric has been traded abroad for millennia. The Indus-trial Revolution was based on new weaving and spinning machines as well as laissez-faire capitalism, the end of rural life, and globalization. It's fair to say that textile manufacturing is a reflection of our complex relationship with nature.

Cloth is a useful, complicated product that requires a lot of specialized labor and knowledge and wildly diverse raw mate-rials. Silk fiber is made by the spinneret on a caterpillar's lip that loops a cocoon around its body before it pupates; the cocoon has to be carefully unwound before the fiber is spun into thread. Wool fiber, sheared from sheep, has a natural crimp that allows it to be spun (unlike hair or fur), but you need to feed a whole flock year-round. Plant fibers from flax and hemp stalks need to be cultivated and harvested before being fermented for a week or two to make the fiber usable, while cotton fibers are plucked directly from the boll that protects the seeds.

Collecting and harvesting the fibers was just the first step. By the 1700s, fabric making required the skills of many guild-regulated artisans. After farmers grew and harvested the raw fiber, retters soaked the flax or hemp while sorters washed and graded the fleeces. Then rovers and carders cleaned, separated, and combed the fibers parallel; spinners made these processed fibers into thread; dyers colored the thread; weavers made it into cloth; and fullers or walkers finished the fabric after it was woven. As a sector of the economy, fabric making was ripe for incremental improvements in many areas.

In England, cottage fabric production had been based on artisans working at home for a master who provided the raw materials. In 1760, the production for English fustian, a strong cotton-and-linen twill, was described as follows: The master gave out linen warp and raw cotton to the weaver and received woven cloth back, paying the weaver for both spinning and weaving. In two weeks, a family would spin almost seventy-five miles of thread to weave a twelve-pound piece of linen-cotton fabric.

According to a 1780 description of Lancashire, home weaving was a good life. The weavers kept their

> dwellings and small gardens clean and neat,—all the family well clad,—the men with each a watch in his pocket, and the women dressed to their own fancy,—the church crowded to excess every Sunday,—every house well furnished with a

clock in elegant mahogany or fancy case,—handsome tea services in Staffordshire ware.

The workshop of the weaver was a rural cottage, from which . . .
he could sally forth into his little garden, and with the spade
or the hoe tend its culinary productions. The cotton wool
which was to form his weft was picked clean by the fingers of
his younger children and was carded and spun by the older
girls assisted by his wife, and the yarn was woven by himself
assisted by his two sons.

Industrialization transformed cottage weavers into factory workers, but it didn't happen all at once. Each step in the
cloth-making process had to be improved, invention by invention. We think of industrialization as a matter of machines
replacing handwork, but it is a cumulative process that includes
transportation systems, social and economic systems, as well
as machinery.

The first major improvement to cloth making came in 1733,
when John Kay patented the flying shuttle at the age of twenty-
nine. The basics of weaving on a loom are: A loom holds the
long warp threads under tension and heddles raise or lower the
warp threads to create a shed. The shuttle holding the horizon-
tal weft thread is slipped through from one side to the other.
Pulling the beater towards you pushes the weft into place, and
foot or hand pedals reverse the up-and-down threads of the
warp. Throw the shuttle through to your left hand, pull the
beater towards you to smash the thread into place, and use pedals to reverse the warp threads again, all day long. Weaving was
traditionally men's work because it takes significant upper-body
strength to beat the threads together on a wide piece of cloth.
Since the shuttle had to be passed from hand to hand,

cloth could only be as wide as the weaver's arm span, no more than sixty inches. For wider cloth, the weaver hired two people—often a child and an adult—to throw the shuttle back and forth while he operated the foot pedals and the beater. The flying shuttle was a tricky invention that allowed weavers to make cloth without throwing the shuttle hand to hand, from one side of the loom to the other. A weaver with a flying shuttle could make twice as much cloth in a day as a weaver using a hand shuttle.

Working people were not happy about it. According to Charles Dickens, the natural balance between spinning and weaving was so much disturbed that John Kay was "mobbed and nearly killed for his pain. He escaped, wrapped in a sheet of cotton wool, and was thus carried bodily through the mob." Historian Paul Mantoux wrote that the flying shuttle took decades to appear in some districts, and violence against the "engine weavers" continued for thirty years. Kay moved to France and died in poverty in 1779.

The new flying shuttles created a thread shortage, because weavers could work twice as fast. Wages rose for spinning, carding, and roving, and a number of new machines followed. The spinning jenny, invented by James Hargreaves in 1764, was a spinning wheel with eight spindles, and later sixteen or more. Hargreaves built his machines in secret and used them for his own workshop. When neighboring spinners heard about his invention, they broke into his workshop and smashed the machines. Too late, though: by the time Hargreaves filed patent no. 962, many Lancashire spinners had already built bootleg copies.

People used spinning jennies at home, but the next spinning improvement was placed squarely in factories. Richard Arkwright's 1769 water frames were powered by falling water and soon coal-powered steam engines. Four rollers drew out strands of cotton and a spindle twisted them into thread, allowing for continuous spinning. Arkwright built the first spinning mill three years later. His five-story building needed 200 people to tend the machines and ran twenty-four hours a day, in two twelve-hour shifts. Most of the workers were women and children, with the youngest just seven years old. Cromford Mill—now a UNESCO heritage site—was so successful that Arkwright soon built more mills, and eventually employed a thousand people. He built housing for the workers along with a market and company store, and was knighted in 1786. When he died in 1792, Sir Arkwright was the wealthiest self-made man in England.

Ten years after the water frame was invented, Samuel Crompton (who died a pauper) combined it with the jenny to make a spinning mule. The spinning mule had two long, parallel carriages on wheels, with bobbins of roving (aligned and lightly twisted fibers) on one side, and spindles for the spun thread on the other. Two hundred spindles was the norm in 1790, and eventually a single spinning mule turned more than a thousand spindles.

The spinning mule was operated by brute force. According to testimony made to the British Parliament, a carriage carrying 336 spindles weighed 1,568 pounds. The spinner used his hands and knees to return the carriage to the closed position. This action was described as requiring "the same mechanical exertion which would raise 160 lbs. the distance of six feet in the same time," done 5,000 times a day. With a spinning mule, one brawny operator did the work of a thousand spinsters at their wheels.

In the new economy, traditional roles were reversed. Home spinning had been done by women and the elderly, but the strength needed to operate a spinning mule made it a man's work. Handloom weaving had traditionally been a man's occupation, but by 1788, two-thirds of the workers hired by cotton mills in England and Scotland were children.

Gender roles in fabric manufacturing were upended, and so were the professional societies that controlled the various artisans required to make cloth. Guilds had managed fabric manufacturing for centuries, but they had no power in the new economy. The entrepreneurs who built factories were industrialists, not artisans. A guild policed its members' professional practices, investigated complaints of poor workmanship and unfair competition, fined masters who violated the guild's rules and standards, and supported widows and orphans. The industrialists were not guild members: their products were not controlled by guild rules, and they emphatically did not provide support for widows and orphans.

Home spinning had been a commonly shared year-round task for many millennia, but by the dawn of the nineteenth century this job had disappeared entirely. Thanks to British spinning mules, no place on Earth made cheaper thread. In eighteenth-century India, spinners took 50,000 hours to spin a hundred pounds of raw cotton into fine thread. In 1795 Britain, they needed just 300 hours with the water frame to spin that same hundred pounds of raw cotton. Labor costs in England were suddenly much lower than in India.

Inexpensive, machine-made thread spurred artisan weavers, and thousands of villagers spent endless hours on their looms. But then the power loom was invented, and cottage weaving was gone in a generation. After the weaving mills were built, a home weaver couldn't make enough cloth to feed his family.

Meanwhile, the pretty little weaving village of Lancashire

had been transformed into a bleak collection of mills. An 1814 description of the area wrote of

> hundreds of factories in Lancashire that are five and six stories high. At the side of each factory there is a great chimney which belches forth black smoke and indicates the presence of the powerful steam engines. The smoke from the chimneys forms a great cloud which can be seen for miles around the town. The houses have become black on account of the smoke. The river on which the Manchester stands is so tainted with colouring matter that the water resembles the contents of a dye vat.

The factories ruined the local environment, and they were filled with an entirely new class of laborers that had no access to nature—no land to pen a cow, no right to forage for rabbits and quail—and no way to earn a living by spinning or weaving at home. The new machines were clearly destroying a centuries-old economic system of home-based fabric production, and there was widespread regret at the disappearance of village life.

You'd expect people to be glad that the worst jobs disappeared. The carders and rovers, for example, who combed and prepared fibers for spinning, were so often afflicted with anthrax that it was called wool-sorter's disease. But even the carders wanted to keep their jobs. In 1786, after 170 carding machines were installed in Leeds, four men wrote a petition on behalf of the carders and rovers:

> A full four thousand men are left to shift for a living how they can, and must of course fall to the Parish, if not timely relieved. . . . How are those men, thus thrown out of employ

to provide for their families; and what are they to put their children apprentice to, that the rising generation may have something to keep them at work, in order that they may not be like vagabonds strolling about in idleness? ...

Signed, in behalf of THOUSANDS, by Joseph Hepworth, Thomas Lobley, Robert Wood, Thos. Blackburn.

Anthrax be damned; these men wanted their jobs.

Every newly invented machine made a whole class of jobs obsolete. After thousands of years of spinning, there were no more spinners. After carding since the dawn of civilization, the profession disappeared. Rovers? Fullers? Walkers? The surnames still exist, but these ancient trades disappeared with the new machinery of the Industrial Revolution.

Many weaving and framework knitting communities were on the verge of starvation. Their products could not compete against factory-made goods, and they sent petitions to Parliament, begging for help. These petitions were ignored. The government had embraced the new laissez-faire economic doctrine, and was relying on the market to solve the problems of industrialization.

Laissez-faire (which translates as "allow to do") was a product of Enlightenment. Freedom of thought, free trade, and free competition were all related to the higher principle that the natural world is a self-regulating system, and that natural regulation is the best type of regulation. Laissez-faire was "conceived as the way to unleash human potential through the restoration of a natural system, a system unhindered by the restrictions of government," wrote Lebanese economist Toufic Gaspard in 2004. Laissez-faire claims that individuals following their selfish interests ultimately contribute to the general good (provided you ignore air and water pollution). Adam

Smith, author of *An Inquiry into the Nature and Causes of the Wealth of Nations*, saw laissez-faire as a moral issue: the market is the way that men ensure the rights of natural law. According to Smith's invisible hand, an individual's pursuit of his own interest benefits society more than if his actions were intended to benefit society. It's straight from Voltaire's overly optimistic Pangloss in *Candide*: we live in the best of all possible worlds and it couldn't possibly be any better.

In a laissez-faire economy, the government's role is to protect private property, administer justice, and not interfere with business. Tuscany, Spain, and Sweden adopted laissez-faire economic principles, and British industrialists quickly realized how well this new economic system aligned with their own interests. After 1776, laissez-faire economics also became popular in the United States.

The global market had been unleashed, and the government protected the manufacturers, with soldiers when necessary. Machines had displaced labor, and the new industrial regime tore up the eighteenth-century social contract. This aggressive new class of manufacturers was not managed by the state.

People protested against the machines with petitions, marches, and machine-wrecking that historian E. J. Hobsbawm called "collective bargaining by riot." Workers had broken machines in disputes with factory owners for decades, but the Luddites were systematic about it.

Luddites were textile workers in Nottinghamshire, Yorkshire, and Lancashire whose jobs had been replaced by machines. They had no money and no food, and by rioting they risked hanging or deportation to Australia. These people were desperate. The first Luddite riot was on March 11, 1811, in Arnold, a village in Nottinghamshire. Stocking makers broke into shops, smashed the wide knitting frames, and used the name "Ludd" for the first time.

Ned Ludd was said to be an apprentice weaver who (the apocryphal story goes) had smashed a loom decades earlier in a rage after his master beat him. Whenever frames were sabotaged, people would say with a wink, "Ned Ludd did it." Frame breakers were known as Luddites, with King, Captain, or General Ludd as their mythical leader. Letters and proclamations were signed "Ned Ludd."

According to the *Nottingham Journal*, there were nearly nightly attacks on wide knitting frames in March and April 1811, with no arrests. Luddites warned knitting masters to remove the new frames from their shops, and if the masters left them in place the Luddites used massive sledgehammers to smash the machines. A letter to the Home Office dated November 13, 1811, requested that the government send the militia because "2,000 men, many of them armed, were riotously traversing the County of Nottingham." These were artisans protecting their craft and their livelihood. They had nothing left to lose. Doggerel recorded in 1812 reads:

> Chant no more your old rhymes about bold Robin Hood,
> His feats I but little admire,
> I will sing the Achievements of General Ludd
> Now the Hero of Nottinghamshire.

Lord Byron, poet and Nottinghamshire landowner, spoke in the House of Lords before they passed the 1812 Frame-Breaking Act that ruled frame breakers should hang. "These men were willing to dig," said Byron, "but the spade was in other hands; they were not ashamed to beg, but there was none to relieve them. Their own means of subsistence were cut off;

all other employments pre-occupied; and their excesses, however to be deplored and condemned, can hardly be the subject of surprise." The other lords had less compassion, and 12,000 troops were sent to put down the protesters.

Luddites frequently joined people who were rioting for food and political reform, and their sabotage brought attention to the sad straits of people whose skills had become obsolete at the start of the Industrial Revolution. They enjoyed widespread support from their communities, but the movement was defeated by government troops. After a few dozen agitators were hanged, the attacks ended.

The destruction of the Luddites by the military established a principle that has been followed ever since: industrialists have the right to impose new technology without negotiating with society at large. Neither the public nor the operators have a say in whether or not the technology is adopted. Genetically modified foods, nuclear power, oil pipelines, and many chemicals, including pesticides, herbicides, and toxic household cleaners, have been introduced to society with the same principle.

In an agrarian society, large landowners often co-opted legal, religious, and military institutions to justify and enforce their ownership. As it turned out, industrial society is no better: industrialists co-opt civic institutions in order to make the rules, shape the landscape, and sell whatever they like.

Industrial society needed people to operate the machines, but factory jobs did not create strong and healthy workers. A tragic side effect of industrialization was that removing people from nature took away their vitality, health, and joy. Farm laborers had been hale, but people who worked in factories were sickly and weak. After the Luddites were crushed, generations of working-class men, women, and children worked twelve hours per day for very low wages, their lives metered out to the rhythm of the machines.

> Any man who has stood at twelve o'clock at the single nar-
> row door-way, which serves as the place of exit for the hands
> employed in the great cotton-mills, must acknowledge, that
> an uglier set of men and women, of boys and girls . . . would
> be impossible to congregate in a smaller compass. Their
> complexion is sallow and pallid. . . . Their stature low—the
> average height of four hundred men, measured at different
> times, and different places, being five feet six inches. Their
> limbs slender, and playing badly and ungracefully. A very
> general bowing of the legs. Great numbers of girls and
> women walking lamely or awkwardly, with raised chests and
> spinal flexures.

The workers did not thrive, but the mills did. By the 1830s, nearly all the cotton in the world was woven in South Lancashire, and the charming village of home weavers had become an industrial wasteland.

About sixty miles away, William Wordsworth and his poetry helped codify the romantic experience of Nature, where humans communicated directly with the divine.

The Enlightenment's scientific concerns and rational thought was a natural companion to industrialization. Enlightened thinkers had demoted nature from an active creative agent to the inert product of creation. Instead of being seen as a divine generative power, nature was viewed as merely an aggregate of rocks, twigs, and clouds.

Romantic philosophy, on the other hand, embraced heightened emotion as a way to experience the mysterious and infinite. Individual communion with nature could provide experiences that utterly consume us, overwhelm rationality, and allow us to be humbled by the wonder of creation.

Wordsworth was born in 1770 and was sent to boarding school in Lancashire when he was eight, after his mother died. Lancashire was the epicenter of cotton manufacturing, and Wordsworth grew up as mills were constructed and nature disappeared. His father died when Wordsworth was thirteen, leaving him an orphan in care of his uncles. Wordsworth went to Cambridge University where he started the daily discipline of writing poetry, and took a walking tour of the Alps and their sublime scenery when he was twenty.

Wordsworth arrived in Paris on the anniversary of the storming of the Bastille, and was swept up in revolutionary fervor. He returned to Cambridge University for his degree and was back in France by November 1791, where he fell in love. Annette Vallon was pregnant in less than three months. In Paris that year, Wordsworth met John "Walking" Stewart, an English philosopher who had spent the last thirty years walking from India to Europe. Wordsworth was deeply impressed by Stewart and his philosophies on nature. He left France, penniless, just weeks before his daughter Anne-Caroline was born.

For the rest of his life, Wordsworth spent much of his day walking. He composed poetry during his daily ten-mile perambulation, and is believed to have walked about 175,000 miles in his lifetime. In 1795, he met the poet Samuel Taylor Coleridge, and they quickly developed a close friendship. They were both walkers, but Wordsworth preferred gravel paths while his friend Coleridge bushwhacked through the fields. Wordsworth and his sister Dorothy moved just a few miles away from

Coleridge in 1797, and the next year Wordsworth and Coleridge produced *Lyrical Ballads*, a collection that started the Romantic movement.

The poems were written in everyday language and presented Wordsworth's philosophy of nature.

> For I have learned
> To look on nature, not as in the hour
> Of thoughtless youth; but hearing oftentimes
> The still, sad music of humanity.

According to Wordsworth, nature brought joy and healed sorrow. Nature was an elevating influence, and there is a "mystic intercourse" between humans and nature, a spiritual communion. In his eyes, "Nature is a teacher whose wisdom we can learn, and without which any human life is vain and incomplete." As he explains in the "Immortality Ode,"

> To me the meanest flower that blows can give
> Thoughts that do often lie too deep for tears.

Rather than the biblical concept of a soulless wilderness, Wordsworth believed that nature was infused with a divine spirit, a kind of mystical pantheism. Like Rousseau, Wordsworth considered people who are raised in close contact with nature as purer and less corrupt than people raised in the city. Humans were essentially good, though humans in cities were suspect.

Wordsworth received his inheritance at thirty-two, and provided a lump sum for his daughter's support in Paris before he married a childhood friend. They had five children in rapid succession, and Wordsworth kept walking and writing poetry. His poetry was panned by critics for decades, but Wordsworth had become nature's foremost spokesperson by the time he died at eighty.

○ ○ ○

There was a perverse correlation between industry and the romanticization of nature. As Great Britain became an industrial nation and the lower classes were reduced to landless factory workers, western intellectuals embraced farming. According to Thomas Jefferson, a yeoman farmer who owned a modest farm and worked it with family labor was the ideal American. This concept of an honest, virtuous, hardworking, and independent citizen was an early force in American politics. The Republicans, led by Thomas Jefferson, promoted local government and an agrarian economy based on small independent farmers. (Since Jefferson and forty other signers of the Declaration of Independence owned slaves, they embraced the ideal of a yeoman farmer in theory but not in practice.)

Like yeoman farmers, artisans saw themselves as central figures in a republican order where competence in their craft provided an independent living, hard work brought success, and these virtues made them good citizens. Artisans made up half the urban population in the United States, from weavers and printers to silversmiths, including Paul Revere.

The Industrial Revolution spread to the United States shortly after it took root in England, and the first New World spinning mill was built in Pawtucket, Rhode Island, in 1790. Francis Cabot Lowell opened his first mill in 1823, when he claimed in a bout of grandiosity to have invented the factory system "where people and machines were all under one roof." Lowell wanted complete control of the fabric-manufacturing process, and his Boston Manufacturing Company built a complex of mills and factories along the Merrimack River. Two decades later, Lowell bought raw cotton and shipped out finished cloth from a series of buildings that were all staffed by Lowell employees.

As the number of factory jobs in northeastern cities grew, so did the focus on the natural world and nature. Ralph Waldo Emerson made his living lecturing about nature and Romanticism. His 1836 essay "Nature" laid the foundation of Transcendentalism, an idealistic philosophical and social movement that taught that divinity pervades all of nature and humanity (its members also held progressive views on feminism and communal living). Ralph Waldo Emerson, Henry David Thoreau, and Amos Bronson Alcott were neighbors and central figures in the Concord-based intellectual circle that defined Transcendentalism. God is in nature, they said, and God can be understood by studying nature.

In spite of Emerson's fame, his writings don't wear well. "The universe is composed of Nature and the Soul," he wrote, which may have been insightful in the 1800s but seems oddly restrictive today. Many of his statements reflect the boundaries of New England village life: "Every spirit builds itself a house; and beyond its house a world; and beyond its world, a heaven. Know then, that the world exists for you." A rhinoceros would disagree. In Emerson's world, humans were made in God's image, the Earth was created for our use, and nature was an inchoate spiritual force. "Nature is not fixed but fluid; to a pure spirit, Nature is everything."

Nonetheless, Emerson and the Transcendentalists promoted an American perspective that nature held intrinsic value. Wilderness was not just home to wild beasts and men; it could act as an antidote to the corrupting influence of industrialization. Transcendentalism launched camping as a recreational activity, where people could escape the degradations of city life. Visiting the wilderness for a few nights cultivated manly qualities and provided young men with the opportunity to discover their true nature.

Henry David Thoreau, who loved nature with abandon, tutored Emerson's children. Often called the father of American nature writing, Thoreau was thirty-four when he wrote "in Wildness is the preservation of the World" in his 1851 essay "Walking." He lived for two years in a cabin on Walden Pond, and this experiment in simple living led to his Transcendental classic *Walden; or, Life in the Woods*, published in 1854. Simplicity, self-reliance, and the belief that humans were part of nature are the themes that infuse this book.

A century and a half later, *Walden*'s phrases have slipped into the vernacular: "Lives of quiet desperation"; "marching to a different drummer"; and his opening paragraph, "I went to the woods because I wished to live deliberately, to front only the essential facts of life, and see if I could not learn what it had to teach and not, when I came to die, discover that I have not lived." Thoreau speaks right to my heart.

Philosophers and poets embraced nature as a spiritual force after the Industrial Revolution, as did artists. Thomas Cole was born in 1801 and moved from England to Philadelphia in 1819 to become a painter. Cole made three oil paintings on a steamboat trip up the Hudson River, and exhibited the paintings in a frame shop in New York City. They were seen by the president of the American Academy of the Fine Arts, who promoted Cole's work and launched the Hudson River School of landscape painting.

According to Romantic philosophy, Nature was heavenly, and humans were an insignificant presence. Sublime experiences in nature and in art inspire awe and reverence, and an emotional understanding that transcends rational thought, words, or language. Thomas Cole's paintings of the Hudson Valley and Niagara Falls present wilderness as tabernacle. These painting have a religious element to them: either God is in Nature, or Nature is God.

Niagara Falls became an American symbol of nature. It was possibly the most painted site in North America, appearing in advertisements as early as 1830 to hawk shredded wheat and baldness cures. Images of Niagara Falls were sold to the public through art and advertisements, literature and magazines, newspapers, dioramas, panoramas, and ceramics. Napoleon's younger brother honeymooned at Niagara Falls in 1804, and soon a honeymoon tour with a stop at the falls was a defining American experience. Waterfalls, with their roaring waters, treacherous currents, and deadly whirlpools, could easily represent the dangers and delights of love. The falls were a visual spectacle, an auditory overload, newlyweds felt the pounding water reverberate through them, and were covered with spray. Niagara Falls, like marriage, was approached with a mixture of awe and dread. Women were allowed to be swept away by nature, presumably without loosening their corsets.

"I wept with a strange mixture of pleasure and pain," wrote Mrs. Frances Trollope in 1832, "and certainly was, for some time, too violently affected in the physique to be capable of much pleasure; but when this emotion of the senses subsided . . . my enjoyment was very great indeed."

3

Nature and Health

While the Romantics were emoting over their connection to Nature, the working class was suffering from their separation from nature. Physically suffering, that is, because health and nature are deeply intertwined. Nature provides clean air and water, food, fuel, and other necessities for human health. In addition, nature makes people healthier by reducing stress.

Before urbanization, most families lived in rural villages surrounded by nature. After moving to urban housing near the mills, the same families that had produced strong farmhands for centuries became feeble and infirm in a single generation. The working class enjoyed cheaper material goods and rising wages after industrialization, and it was long assumed that more clothes and more money meant they had a better life. Instead, those economic benefits did not balance the miseries of urban housing and high food costs. Wages rose, sure, but everything else cost more except clothing. Between diseases and bad living conditions, harsh child-rearing practices, and simply too little food, the urban working class failed to thrive.

During the first half of the 1800s, the height of an average worker in the United States and Britain declined, along with the average lifespan. In general, healthier people live longer. The average height of a population is a subtle indicator of public health, reflecting the nutritional deficiencies that each individual encounters throughout their development. A child whose diet is low in calories or protein will become a shorter adult. A child with light clothing and bedding in a cold climate will use more calories to keep warm, and have fewer calories to grow on. Repeated bouts of childhood disease can reduce adult height, as can physically strenuous work. Too much pollution or too little oxygen during childhood will result in shorter adults.

Before the days of picture IDs, height records were common. Many institutions, including armies, schools, factories, jails, plantations, and poorhouses, routinely measured their members. In the United States, for example, soldiers have been measured since before independence. The reduction of average height that accompanied industrialization was first noticed during the national mass measurement of the Civil War, when it was postulated that perhaps Americans didn't reach their full height until the age of thirty. Urban life was hard on people's health, and it took more than a century for industrial workers to regain the height and longevity that their rural ancestors enjoyed.

Height records yield some uncomfortable insights into human nature. In the United States, we think of markets as a good thing that would improve a farmer's standard of living. Instead, height records show that farmers who sold their goods at weekly markets were typically shorter than farmers with no market access: they had more cash, but their children had fewer calories to grow on. Farmers who can sell their crops routinely trade away nutritional benefits by growing non-food cash crops like flax, hops, or cotton, or by selling the most nutritionally dense farm products. When a dairy farmer sells butter and cheese, for example, his children (and there might be a dozen) drink skim milk. In the early 1800s, Irish men were taller than English men in spite of their poverty, and US southerners were taller than northerners. After industrialization, people who lived closer to nature were both taller and poorer than people who lived in cities.

People worked hard in the 1800s, and they needed more food than we do today. Working-class women expended between 2,750 and 3,500 calories a day, working-class men between 3,000 to 4,500 calories a day, and men who built roads and railways needed more than 5,000 calories a day. Total calorie requirements were even higher during the winter months, when homes and workplaces were barely heated.

Rapid urbanization made food and fuel more expensive. Industrialized areas produced less food per capita, and there was higher demand for food that reached urban markets. Height is closely related to protein consumption, and in the

1800s, the human population grew faster than the number of cows, sheep, and pigs in the countryside. There was a shortfall of protein in Britain and New England, although villagers had more access to protein and dairy products than city dwellers. The amount of food per person decreased in the first half of the nineteenth century as the countryside emptied out and urban housing costs increased.

As the price of food and housing rose, factory workers could not afford to feed the whole family. A nationwide survey of British eating habits in 1863 showed how laboring families divided the family calories: working men in Gloucester ate bread, cheese, vegetables, dumplings, and tea, while their wives and children ate bread and water. Working-class children usually went without milk, and many were hungry most days but Christmas.

Finally, the nature of employment changed after industrialization. There is always work in an agrarian society, although there are busy and slow times. In an industrial society, people either work or are unemployed, so their income is more volatile. All of these factors whittled away at a worker's biological standard of living.

The reduction in average height during the 1800s was found across regions and occupational groups, but it was not evenly distributed. The upper classes prospered during industrialization, and wealthy cohorts like passport holders and Harvard students maintained their height or grew taller, decade after decade. By 1883, fourteen-year-old boys from fee-paying public schools in England were more than seven inches taller and twenty-five pounds heavier than boys from industrial schools. Urban workers lived truncated lives, shortchanged in height, weight, and years.

In the 1800s, the tallest people lived farthest from the industrial economy. The Cheyenne Indians—a buffalo-eating Plains tribe—were the tallest measured people in the world. According to the biological record, industrialization was bad for human health.

∘ ∘ ∘

The Industrial Revolution and the rise of global trade allowed many diseases to spread around the world. Faster ships, more trains and rails, and better roads and carriages meant that sick people carried disease farther. Epidemics that had been confined to a single country or continent could finally expand into global pandemics.

Some of the diseases of the 1800s were recently imported, and some were old favorites that appreciated the new urban concentrations of warm bodies. Dense urban populations allowed diseases to spread more rapidly, and people who worked together indoors were more likely to infect each other. Measles, diphtheria, whooping cough, tuberculosis, cholera, and typhoid were a constant threat to every nineteenth-century household, and smallpox killed more than 400,000 Europeans a year.

One of the new diseases was yellow fever, which sailed from Africa to the Caribbean in the 1600s. This mosquito-borne virus spread to the coastal cities of the New World, where epidemics caused terror and economic disruption, and filled 100,000 to 150,000 graves. Scarlet fever was one of history's worst child killers, spread by sneezing and responsible for up to a quarter of all deaths in some regions. Typhus, caused by *Rickettsia* bacteria carried by body lice that live in the seams of wool clothing, was so common that it had three names: putrid fever, ship fever, and gaol fever. Found among prisoners, soldiers, sailors, and the unwashed poor, typhus killed more than 100,000 wool-clad Irish during the 1830s.

Diseases that spread through feces were big winners in the 1800s. Typhoid fever, caused by a strain of salmonella, took a steady toll in many cities and is believed to have killed 2 percent of the Union Army in the Civil War. Cholera, a diarrheal disease that killed by dehydration, was confined to India until traders carried the infection west to southern Russia in 1817, and British soldiers carried it east to China, Japan, and Indonesia. Cholera is caused by the bacterium *Vibrio cholerae*, and killed more people more quickly than any other epidemic disease of the 1800s. No place was safe from these diseases: country villages were as likely to be affected as big cities.

Finally, tuberculosis was a major killer in the cold, damp, crowded cities, responsible for about one-third of all deaths in England and over half the deaths in many Massachusetts towns. Known since antiquity, people believed that tuberculosis was caused by foul or sooty air, and common remedies included red cabbage, rose jelly, frogs, mercury, hydrocyanic acid, and the use of a swing. And not just any swing; the therapeutic swing invented by Charles Darwin's grandfather, Erasmus Darwin, spawned a variety of knockoffs, including one that promised that by "increasing its velocity, the motion be suddenly reversed every six or eight minutes . . . the effects are, an instant discharge of the contents of the stomach, bowels, and bladder, in quick succession." And if that didn't help you feel better, you could wash up and take another ride.

Doctors had no idea how to help. In the 1800s, the cure for most communicable diseases was bleeding, blistering, vomiting, or a bout of diarrhea, based on their understanding that disease came from an imbalance of the four humors: red blood, yellow bile, black bile, and translucent phlegm. (Gentler remedies included hot or cold baths, dietary changes, and many herbs, including opium, chamomile, lavender, and yarrow.)

Doctors could not cure disease, but they had an idea about where disease came from. For thousands of years, people in Europe and Asia believed that disease was caused by nature. Miasma, the putrid smell emitted by decaying plants or animals, made people sick. "All smell is, if it be intense, immediate acute disease," wrote a sanitary reformer in 1846, "and eventually we may say that, by depressing the system and rendering it susceptible to the action of other causes, all smell is disease." According to miasmatics, disease did not spread from person to person; instead, the stink of rotting organic matter contaminated the air, and anyone who inhaled it could get sick. Cities would literally empty out when a fever came to town, with as much as nine-tenths of the population decamping in the face of an epidemic.

For centuries, miasma was understood to be an amoral stench created by nature that struck the rich and poor alike, with saintly folk as likely to fall ill as sinners. By the 1800s, it was understood that the people most likely to die from a miasma were morally weak, physically intemperate, or from inferior cultures (i.e., recent immigrants). The cold, hungry poor in densely populated urban slums died younger than the warm, well-fed rich in their mansions, proving the point.

Whatever the disease, patients were usually nursed at home. The bedroom was transformed into a sickroom, and the wife, mother, sister, or servant tended the patient. Sickrooms were kept closed to prevent the miasma that caused the disease from traveling through a window and reinfecting the patient, and patients were given extra bedding to keep warm.

The bad air that gave you disease and bad morals that made you susceptible to it were blamed for bacterial and viral diseases spread by water, mosquitoes, flies, lice, airborne droplets, and direct contact. Curiously, it was the focus on sin, particularly sloth, that inspired major improvements in public health. The first comprehensive study of public health was authored by Edwin Chadwick, a lawyer who became such an insufferable scold that he was forced to retire early. After typhoid struck London in 1838, the British government asked him to write a sanitation study, and Chadwick self-published the *Report on the Sanitary Conditions of the Labouring Population of Great Britain* in 1842. At a time when public health reports were stuffed with anecdotes, Chadwick was the first person to use charts and numbers. His data shows a direct link between bad living conditions, disease, and life expectancy.

In some of England's industrial cities, the working class died so young it was like there was a plague upon the people. Liverpool was the most lethal city detailed in Chadwick's report:

LIVERPOOL, 1840	Average Age of Death	No. of Deceased
Gentry and professional persons, &c	35 years	137
Tradesmen and their families	22 years	1,738
Labourers, mechanics, servants, &c	15 years	5,597

The working class of Liverpool had an average lifespan of fifteen years, which ought to be a misprint but isn't. It takes a lot of dead babies to get an average lifespan of fifteen, and Chadwick's report noted that nearly two-thirds of working-class children died by age five, along with half of middle-class children. One of the reasons the death rate was so high was that people didn't understand how to raise babies.

Britain's upper classes used wet nurses to feed their babies, but many middle- and working-class babies were fed by hand, and mothers who worked in the mills had to leave their infants at home for a twelve-hour stretch. Before cheap glass bottles and rubber nipples were sold, baby bottles were made from a hollow cow horn or a spouted pewter vessel and tipped with a nipple of cloth or leather. Fresh cow or goat milk was available in the country, but city milk was often diluted with dirty water or worse. Neither part of the feeding apparatus could be properly cleaned, so city babies were fed adulterated milk from a contaminated apparatus.

Babies who survived to eat solid food were fed pap, a mush of bread, flour, and water (the more nourishing panada included butter, milk, sugar, broth, beer, or wine). The bowls or pap boats used for feeding babies looked like spouted gravy boats, and were made of easily cleaned pottery or metal. Some pap boats were designed for babies to suck food at their own speed. But many pap boats were designed so mush could be blown into the baby's stomach directly, or used with a hollow-handled spoon to blow food into the baby. This process, gavage, is used on geese to fatten up their livers for pâté. By blowing food into a baby's stomach, a single caretaker can feed many babies in an hour, and the practice was common enough that medical texts of the day routinely cautioned against over-feeding. In 1878, a physician wrote, "allow me to urge you never to stuff a babe—never to overload his little stomach with food. . . . Many a poor child has been, like a young bird, killed with stuffing."

Working mothers wanted their infants to sleep most of the twelve-hour workday, and they wanted them to sleep at night, too. Along with blister plaster and leeches, the corner store carried popular baby tonics like Mrs. Winslow's Soothing Syrup, Godfrey's Cordial (known as "Mother's Friend"), and Dalby's Calmative. The active ingredient in these tonics was opium, which most babies found wonderfully calming. Drugged babies slept more and cried less, and their appetites were suppressed. Many a thin and wizened toddler with pinpoint pupils and an old face starved to death with barely a whimper. The use of soothing syrups was not restricted to the working class: babies of the upper classes were often addicted to opiates by their nannies, who understood the efficacy of calming cordials. And most babies were dosed with a wide variety of laxatives. Based on the four humors theory, any imbalance—tantrums, teething, stomachaches, and even diarrhea—required regular purging.

In addition to the laxatives and opiates, there were other hair-raising child-rearing practices. Children were "hardened," starting as babies, to accustom them to the cold. In the United States, Europe, and Russia, children often slept in chilly rooms with inadequate nightclothes or bedding, and small children were often underdressed to make them stronger. Likewise, babies were to be bathed daily, but as the infant grew the bathwater was to be cooler every day. In his 1829 *Advice to Young Men, and (Incidentally) to Young Women*, William Cobbett advised parents to teach them to get used to it and to sing loudly throughout the bathing to cover the cries of the child. Hardening started to fall out of favor in Europe and the United States around the mid-1800s but remained popular in Russia, where even princes and princesses went cold and hungry.

There were some peculiar ideas about child nutrition in the Victorian era, and a child's diet was very restricted. Fresh fruits and vegetables were thought to breed worms, and perhaps they did, because night soil was still used as fertilizer. Potatoes were the only vegetable that was felt to be appropriate for children, and a working-class child's diet was based on bread, potatoes, and water. Middle- and upper-class children ate bread and milk, potatoes, reheated mutton or beef, and boiled pudding made of suet and flour. "[A]fter a child is two years old and if healthy and strong, he may be allowed vegetables and a little plain pudding at dinner," wrote Dr. Thomas Allinson, a vegetarian who promoted whole-grain bread. The medical advice for a child's diet was to avoid fresh vegetables or fruits, which (along with the opiates) might explain all the laxatives.

Working-class baby and toddler diets were deficient in vitamins, minerals, protein, and calcium. A calcium deficiency paired with shortfalls in phosphorus and vitamin D often results in rickets. Phosphorus is associated with protein, a rare treat for a poor child, while the scant sunlight in the dimly lit factories and smoky cities left few opportunities for ultraviolet rays to hit bare skin and trigger vitamin D synthesis. Rickets is a disease of deprivation that leaves children with bowed or knock-kneed legs; they eventually grow up to be adults with small, painful, misshapen frames. Rickety girls grew into women with narrow, boyish hips, leading to difficult childbirth and higher mortality rates.

Rickets was common in northern cities across the United States as well as in England. In the 1870s, a quarter of all children under the age of five in Philadelphia had rickets, and by the turn of the century, more than half of the children hospitalized in Baltimore, Boston, Memphis, and Denver showed signs of rickets. The same nutritional deficiencies that bent children's bones led to tooth loss, and by the late 1800s, many working-class adults in Britain could not chew dark bread.

Poor housing, strenuous work as a growing child, and the standard sixty-six-hour workweek left people biologically vulnerable. In the United States, the well-studied textile mills of Lowell, Massachusetts, were staffed with young women who lived for a time in boardinghouses built by the mill owners. But factory boardinghouses that housed short-term workers were the exception. As a rule, textile factories employed the entire family, who lived nearby in inadequate urban housing. Children started work at the age of seven, eight, or nine, tending spindles in loud, dusty rooms that were crowded with machines. People worked long days, long weeks, and long years with no respite. There was no mystery why they died so young.

In the second half of the 1800s, the health and height of the urban working class slowly improved. Advances in food production, storage, and transportation increased urban food supplies. The discovery of vaccination and germs improved medical care, and the construction of urban water and sewer systems slowly reduced the incidence of disease.

The first major advance in food storage was canning, invented in 1810 by Nicolas Appert, a Parisian candy maker and grocer who filled glass jars with meat, vegetable, fruits, or dairy, secured the cork tops with sealing wax, and boiled the jars until the contents were cooked. Tin cans were patented the same year, and within a decade Britain's Royal Navy was feeding its sailors canned meat. Before cans, ships relied on salted or pickled meats, neither of which are shelf-stable. Suddenly meat was reliably available, easily transported and stored, and it stayed fresh for years.

William Underwood built a canning factory in Boston, Massachusetts, in 1822, and prospered. Even though the cans had to be opened with a hammer and chisel, food stored in tin-coated, lead-soldered steel containers was sold all over the world by the 1840s; canned food became even more popular after the can opener was patented in 1858. William Underwood Company cans were carried in Conestoga wagons by settlers moving west, and fed Union troops during the Civil War. Underwood canned beef, chicken, and pork, as well as lobster, oyster, and mackerel, and deviled ham (still sold) became the first trademarked food in 1870. (I tried it so you don't have to: it's like salty, pink ground cardboard.)

Butter or cheese were the only way to store milk until 1856, when Gail Borden Jr. patented his process for condensing milk by vacuum and then canning it. Condensed milk was used as a field ration for Union soldiers in the Civil War, where it greatly improved camp coffee. When soldiers returned home from war, their fond memories of condensed milk—more reliable than "fresh" milk sold in the city—made it a kitchen staple.

Cans changed food storage, and food transport was sped by steam-powered trains and ships. Fresh peas, strawberries, peaches, and tomatoes started to be sold in northern cities in the 1840s, and an efficient system of growers, railways, and retailers allowed asparagus picked in the morning to be served on city tables that night. About a million bushels of oranges and lemons a year were imported by steamship from the Mediterranean in the 1850s, and fresh milk became more widely available.

Vegetables, fruit, and milk traveled by train, but generally meat did not. Instead, herds and flocks walked to urban markets, and the farmer took the train home. Old Donny Joslin, who raised heifers and lambs, lived on the farm next door to ours in Vermont. In the 1880s, his granddaddy used to raise a flock of turkeys for the Boston market every year. Near Thanksgiving, he'd paint their feet with tar to give them little booties, and walk the turkeys 200 miles to Boston. He sold his turkeys for a city premium, and would ride the train back to central Vermont with a pocketful of cash for Christmas.

The Plains became the breadbasket of the United States, shipping millions of bushels of wheat and flour east, while the Northeast turned its attention to industry and manufacturing. More than half the population of New England lived in cities by 1860, and urban laborers bought many of their meals from vendors and street stalls.

By the 1870s, convenience foods had become part of urban life. In New York City, thousands of street vendors sold ready-made food and drink, including roasted peanuts and baked potatoes, potato pancakes, bagels, pretzels, hot dogs, sausages, pickles, pre-sliced fruit, ice cream, or oysters on the half shell. Working-class pantries might include bakery bread, canned beef, condensed milk, and store-bought jam. There were premade bases for stocks and sauces, and women often bought preserves and pickles rather than making their own. A middle-class pantry might include canned apricots, peaches, peas, and asparagus; compressed yeast; baking powder; self-rising flour; store-bought cookies and bread; and packets of instant soup.

As food storage and distribution improved, urban food prices dropped. At the same time, medical science was starting to stray from the orthodoxy of miasma. Smallpox, or *Variola*, was the first disease that was curbed. During an epidemic, smallpox was generally transmitted by air and roughly one in three patients died. Edward Jenner, the orphaned son of a British vicar, was thirteen when he was apprenticed to a country surgeon near Bristol and heard a dairymaid musing that she would never have smallpox because she already had cowpox. Cowpox is a disease with pustules that are bigger than chicken pox and smaller than the great pox, syphilis. Milkmaids got cowpox blisters on their hands from milking cows with poxed udders.

More than thirty years after eavesdropping on the milkmaids, Jenner inoculated his gardener's eight-year-old son, James Phipps, with pus from the sores of Sarah Nelms, a dairymaid with a nasty case of cowpox. James had a mild reaction, and when he was inoculated with smallpox two months later, he remained well. Jenner inoculated another twelve people with cowpox using both cow-to-person and person-to-person transmission, and later inoculated three of the cowpox recipients with smallpox. None of them became ill, and Jenner presented a paper on his experiment to the Royal Society of London in 1798. He named the process vaccination, from *vacca*, Latin for "cow."

It was a skimpy research paper, with a bare four people given both cowpox and smallpox. But the idea had tremendous resonance, and vaccination spread rapidly across England. Within two years, vaccination had reached most of Western Europe. Four years after Jenner's paper was presented, Dr. John Hogarth of Bath, Somerset, sent cowpox pus to Harvard professor Benjamin Waterhouse, who sent it to Thomas Jefferson. Starting with a fourteen-year-old kitchen slave, Jefferson inoculated everyone on his plantation before sending the cowpox exudate on to Washington as the foundation of the National Vaccine Agency.

According to miasmatics, epidemic disease was caused by impurities in the air that anyone could smell. In the case of smallpox, miasma activated poisons within the individual: people who had already been sick had nothing to fear, but the miasma would trigger the disease for the uninoculated. Vaccination fit into the current medical system, and doctors continued to balance humors by prescribing bleeding, laxatives, blisters, and emetics to help you vomit.

The Spanish colonies had been ravaged by smallpox, and in 1803—five years after Jenner's paper—the Spanish government sent an expedition to bring cowpox to its South American and Asian territories. This mercy trip used orphans as living receptacles of the vaccine. Any single individual would recover from cowpox before the ship arrived, so the captain brought twenty-two Spanish orphans between the ages of eight and ten, and infected two children at a time. When their skin vesicles began to exude fluid a week or so after the initial inoculation, cowpox was transmitted through skin contact to another pair of orphans. After leaving Spain in November, the expedition stopped to vaccinate people in the Canary Islands, Puerto Rico, the Caribbean coast, Venezuela, Colombia, and Ecuador. More than 197,000 people were vaccinated in Peru, and then the expedition pushed on to Bolivia, Argentina, and Chilean Patagonia. Looping back to vaccinate people in Cuba and Mexico, the expedition left for the Philippines with a new crew of twenty-five Mexican orphans (the first set of orphans were presumably abandoned en route). After vaccinating close to 20,000 people in the Philippines, three final children carried cowpox to China, where thousands more were vaccinated. Within a decade of its discovery, vaccination was used globally.

Meanwhile, people knew that their theory of disease was incomplete, and concluded that if smelly air could cause disease, smelly water probably did, too. Benjamin Latrobe, a prominent Philadelphian, noted in 1798 that putrid wells were the city's greatest source of disease, thanks to the miasma created by feces saturating the soil. Philadelphia, with its recurring yellow fever epidemics, became the first US city to build a public water system as a way to reduce disease. Elizabeth Drinker recorded in her diary in 1798 that a shower had been installed in the backyard of her Philadelphia townhouse. A year later, she wrote that she finally took a shower: "I bore it better than I expected, not having been wett all over at once, for 28 years past."

Before sewer systems were installed, popular history

claims that mob-capped maids would toss the contents of chamber pots into the streets. No surprise that the truth was a lot less flamboyant: people usually emptied their chamber pots into a brick-lined cesspit in the cellar. These cesspits held about a cubic yard of wastes, and often the base of the cesspit was left unlined so the urine could drain away, leaving the solids to be periodically shoveled out by professionals. In every large city, the subsoil was saturated with urine and feces that oozed through basement walls and leached down to the groundwater and into wells.

The water from city wells was soon tainted and unpalatable, and private water companies sprang up to provide piped water to private subscribers—at least in the wealthier parts of town. Up to that point, the few public sewers drained storm water from the streets. For household wastewater, neighbors would sometimes band together to dig channels in the street or to lay sewer pipe to the nearest body of water. As soon as public water lines were installed, the increased flows overwhelmed the uncoordinated private sewers and scanty municipal street drains. There were attempts to regulate the production of wastewater, including an 1844 ordinance in Boston that prohibited people from taking baths without a doctor's order. But public water-supply and sewer systems—and the white porcelain toilets, sinks, and tubs that people quickly installed—were such popular amenities that a sewer system was typically built soon after the water-supply system was completed.

Municipal water and sewer systems were built to sweep away miasma and improve the health of urban workers. As soon as there was a reliable water supply, commercial wash- and bathhouses became fairly common in the United States. In England, the construction of public bathhouses began in the

1830s, when cholera epidemics resulted in piles of diarrhea-soaked sheets that reeked of miasma. Initially laundry was the focus, but the baths allowed the working class to wash themselves as well.

By the 1850s, the miasma theory had become more nuanced. Doctors believed that a patient exuded a miasma that surrounded him and held toxins next to the skin, where they would likely be reabsorbed. Fresh air could sweep away the miasma of sickness, as could water. Baths were often prescribed as the remedy, and came in a variety of sizes and shapes. Bathing became known as hydrotherapy.

Between the 1840s and '80s, over 200 water-cure centers were established throughout the United States, with women as their main clientele. Public bathhouses catered to both men and women. The most expensive tickets provided spacious, richly furnished cubicles with towels and soap, bathtubs with lots of hot water, and space to change. The cheapest option was a dip in the public plunge pool, where you jumped in and washed with everyone else for a fee that nearly anyone could afford. The single-sex baths were naked: bathing suits were not required at most public pools until the early twentieth century. The water was changed once a week, and early baths were simply unfiltered river water. But it was warm, and for many children it was the only opportunity to drive the bone-deep cold from their bodies. These public baths and laundries were popular amenities, and by 1860, all of the largest cities in the United States had water and sewer systems built to wash the accumulated garbage and manure from their streets and to reduce the miasma that made people sick.

By the mid-1800s, fresh air was believed to kill disease. "All infection is weakened by dilution with air," wrote Dr. Anthony Thomson in 1841. To fumigate bedding, it just needed to be put

outside where the sun could shine on it. Instead of nature causing disease, nature was the cure.

Louis Pasteur, a French chemist, popularized germ theory and ushered in modern medicine. He discovered that heating beer, wine, or milk kept them from spoiling, providing a lower-temperature version of Appert's canning process. Pasteur branded and patented pasteurization in 1865, and within a few years the process was used globally.

Pasteur spent years working on vaccines for fowl cholera and anthrax. He learned how to oxidize the bacteria to make effective vaccines, but this discovery brought almost no public fanfare. Curing shitty chickens and poxy wool sorters was not considered to be much of an accomplishment.

Rabies was a disease with panache. Newspapers often published accounts of rabies outbreaks in wildlife, and the ghastly ends of people who died of it. Rabies could incubate for months, even years, providing a long period of uncertainty after an animal bite. It was always deadly, and dogs—beloved household companions—were a common carrier. The human death toll was never very high: in 1877, the worst year on record, England had seventy-nine people die of rabies, while over 50,000 succumbed to tuberculosis. In the United States, about a hundred people a year died of the disease. It was not a significant public health problem, but a rabies death often made a good story.

Vermont still has regular rabies outbreaks. We had a big boar raccoon who lived in the cupola of the barn with a lady or two, and each spring he fathered a new litter. We wouldn't see them often, but occasionally a mom would lead a line of cubs across the edge of the barnyard at dusk. With their little masks and puffy striped tails, the babies are so enchanting that you'd search for new words to describe them: adorabilis maximus, cutissimi.

One spring, the agricultural extension service told us there was a rabies outbreak affecting the county's skunks and raccoons. The next week, our big boar raccoon lurched across the lawn in the early afternoon. Raccoons walk deliberately, delicately placing their long-toed feet, and they don't expose themselves when the sun is high. That big boar coon had clearly lost his mind. Bob got his rifle and shot him. That raccoon had lived in the barn for years, but our boy, Sam, was about two years old and ran around outside all summer. The lady raccoon came out the next week, midday, stumbling along, her cubs haphazardly trailing behind her. I took Sam into the house, and Bob shot every single one. He's still sorry.

Rabies terrified everyone but Pasteur, who fearlessly kept a kennel of rabid dogs next to his lab in Paris. He used rabbits to create the first rabies vaccine, and injected infected dogs with dried, powdered spinal cords of rabid rabbits in a series of fourteen daily shots. Pasteur soon cured fifty dogs.

He was adept at publicity as well as patents, and a series of newspaper articles brought him worldwide attention. Among the first patients to arrive at Pasteur's lab for treatment were seven London bobbies bitten by mad dogs in the line of duty. Then came nineteen Russian peasants bitten by a mad wolf in Smolensk, some too mangled to walk. Sixteen of the nineteen doomed Russians survived, and Paris went wild. The peasants returned to Smolensk as heroes, and the czar sent Pasteur a diamond cross and 100,000 francs to start building what became the Institut Pasteur.

Pasteur's work showed the world that microorganisms caused disease and decay, but no one could see what he was talking about until better microscopes were built. The German trio Ernst Abbe, Otto Schott, and Carl Zeiss were the optics wizards who solved the problems of color distortion and light concentration to build compound microscopes with layers of lenses that could focus on bacteria for the first time. The whole apparatus was completed in 1872, and the next year leprosy was the first disease-causing bacterium to be identified: kudos to G. H. Armauer Hansen of Norway, where leprosy was common.

The miasma theory officially died in 1876, when Robert Koch spotted the anthrax bacterium. This bacterium is easy to identify, easy to grow, and quickly infectious. It was clear that sickness was caused by microorganisms that lived in water and air, and miasma was just smelly air. That meant clean water and air, wholesome living, and vaccination was the recipe for a long and healthy life.

Tuberculosis sanitariums, where patients sit on mountain porches breathing clean air and thinking restful thoughts to heal themselves, proliferated after the 1870s in the United States and Europe. Sleeping porches started to catch on in the 1880s, recommended as a preventative measure to improve general health. In 1909, Dr. Luther H. Gulick testified that sleeping with fresh outdoor air "increases not only the power to resist disease, but *raises the level of life itself.*" By the twentieth century, nature was recognized as an important component of a healthful, happy life.

4

Collecting Nature

A squirrel gathers and buries over a thousand nut caches every year, forgetting half of them; voles accumulate many more grass seeds than they can eat in a single winter; a Clark's nutcracker buries roughly 30,000 seeds a year in up to 2,500 locations. The urge to collect things may be the result of a genetic adaptation related to the ancient imperative of storing food for winter. But when food is plentiful, perhaps this collecting impulse goes astray. Some humans and other animals spend a lifetime collecting items that meet psychological rather than physical needs. I had a dog that collected beaver skulls, and lined up three in a row under a juniper tree. I personally have an absurd number of flower vases. Nomadic collectors could not carry much and may have accumulated animals rather than artifacts, but as soon as humans settled into houses and engaged in commerce, collectors flourished.

Intercontinental trade became commonplace in the 1600s, and collecting became popular among ordinary people. Ships from Portugal, Spain, the Netherlands, and Great Britain regularly imported goods from the Americas, Russia, Scandinavia, Africa, India, and the Far East. Advances in insurance, navigation, and shipbuilding tempered the risks involved in foreign trade, while a more sophisticated banking system smoothed the flow of goods. Starting with spices, furs, fabric, fish, and oil, merchandise from around the world was woven into everyday life.

Sailors commonly sold oddments from faraway lands to augment their wages. Shells and coins, knives, porcelain, and any number of pocket-sized collectables, along with parrots and monkeys, could be bought at any big port. The Netherlands in particular, with its burgeoning middle class, had many early collectors.

It is one of history's happy coincidences that some collectors gathered hundreds and thousands of specimens of animals, plants, and minerals. These collections of *naturalia* were little encyclopedias of nature, creating databases and pockets of knowledge that were independent of religious or academic hierarchies. People collected natural history specimens in order to understand nature.

Collectors of no great wealth or scholarly ambitions displayed their purchases in curiosity cabinets for their private enjoyment. In the 1600s, European collections included items from around the world. People who owned cabinets often wrote descriptions of each specimen, and occasionally hired artists to create dioramas.

Ole Worm, a Danish doctor, collected a famous curiosity cabinet called the Museum Wormianum. The detailed catalogue of this private museum was published in 1655, a year after Worm's death, with a title that can be translated as "Worm's Museum, or the History of Very Rare Things, Natural and Artificial, Domestic and Exotic, Which Are Stored in the Author's House in Copenhagen." Ole Worm was a debunker who showed that, contrary to popular belief, unicorn horns were actually narwhal tusks, and birds of paradise had feet. His collection, characteristic of the time, included natural history specimens mixed with artifacts, including statues, spears, bows and arrows, and a kayak suspended from the ceiling.

Early collectors had no reliable method of preserving soft tissue, and stuffed animals and birds were usually eaten by insects. The prodigious collector Robert Boyle discovered in 1660 that animal specimens could be preserved in ethyl alcohol, known as "spirits of wine." As soon as people knew that spirits of wine acted as a preservative, two-headed lambs and three-legged chickens achieved immortality and natural history collections expanded in earnest. Increasing numbers of collectors developed wonder rooms, and these collections became the early underpinnings of major public museums. Ole Worm's collection, for example, was bought by King Frederick III of Denmark and incorporated into his royal collection.

In curiosity cabinets, the specimens are arranged in no particular order. Nature, and the natural world, is a jumble. Everyone agreed that humans were at the divinely ordained apex of the animal kingdom, but there was little understanding of how the rest of the world's flora and fauna was ordered.

There was no intellectual framework for studying nature. Even the line between animals, plants, and minerals was blurred, with the belief that worms were spontaneously created in mud, or that mice could be made in twenty-one days from a few grains of wheat and a dirty shirt.

When it came to the medieval view of the world's animals, the only certainty was that there was a king. The lion was the head of all animals and the lioness usually had her own entry (though males and females were described together for most species), and the rest of the animals followed in no particular order. Animals that looked alike—lions and tigers, or dogs and wolves—were not grouped together. Instead, animals were listed alphabetically, or grouped according to how they were hunted. One system that lasted for centuries divided animals into:

Beasts of hunting
    hare, hart, wolf, and wild boar
Beasts of chase
    buck, doe, fox, marten, and roe
Beasts that afford "great dysporte"
    badgers, wild cats, and otters

There was no concept of how to order the natural world, but the hard truth was that by the eighteenth century, Great Britain didn't have many wild animals left. Wolves, bears, boars, and beavers were gone from the forests, and the sparse surviving fauna included deer, foxes, weasels and their relatives, badgers, hedgehogs, a variety of small rodents, and wildcats (which look like a large domesticated cat and can interbreed with them). Domestic animals provided the standards by which other animals were judged, based on their moral attributes.

Horses were the most virtuous, followed by sheep and oxen. Bad domesticated animals included pigs (who were greedy) and cats (sly).

The first person to propose a system for classifying plants and animals by their physical attributes was Carl Linnaeus, a Swedish botanist. He grouped mammals by teeth, teats, and toes; insects by wings; fish by fin bones; and birds by feet and beaks. He believed that Nature was an expression of God, who made each species as a separate act of creation. Linnaeus declared himself to be God's secretary, and dedicated every edition of *Systema Naturae* to the greater glory of God. "Great is our GOD, and great is his power, And his power is not to be fathomed," wrote Linnaeus on the frontispiece of the twelfth edition. The list of species has grown ever longer since then, and the twelfth edition of *Systema Naturae* was perhaps the last time all of the known species on Earth were presented in a single, up-to-date form until the 2007 launch of the Encyclopedia of Life. This online database includes every species on Earth, along with its Linnaean name and taxonomy. Linnaeus lives.

By the end of Linnaeus's life in 1778, his personal collection of naturalia included 3,198 insects, 1,564 shells, about 14,000 plants, 3,000 letters, and 1,600 books. His widow sold his collection to a twenty-four-year-old British medical student named James Edward Smith for £1,000 (worth over $200,000 in 2018, with inflation). Smith moved the collection to London, founded the Linnean Society of London, and botanized for the rest of his life.

Linnaeus provided a model of how to categorize any collection with a single, hierarchical system of classification that was easily understood. His use of physical characteristics to classify animals created a tantalizing picture of nature's bushy family tree with some unnamed creatures in it. After the Linnean collection was installed in London, the directors of the London Zoo and Regent's Park rearranged their animals to illustrate the standard vertebrate taxonomical categories. The National Gallery rehung its art to take school and chronology into account for the first time.

The Linnaean system allowed people to organize their collections of natural specimens just when empires were expanding. The United States usurped almost 3 million square miles of occupied land in North America, while England's holdings abroad increased by more than 10 million square miles. In England, the foreign flora and fauna brought back from these newly annexed lands fed an urge to enumerate and classify. The collection, naming, and categorizing of all living things became a grand national project.

Most collectors were amateur scholars—hobbyists—who often compiled and catalogued vast numbers of specimens over their lifetime. Collecting natural history specimens was a game that everyone could play. Men, women, and children; the well-to-do and the middle class; city folk and country muffins all contributed to this nationwide effort. Boys had egg collections from scaling up trees to wild nests and stealing eggs that they would carefully blow out at home; girls pressed ferns or flowers. Collections of butterflies and moths, beetles, bees and ants, shells, flowering plants and ferns, grasses, mosses, fungi, lichens, and seaweeds were all popular.

My British father collected birds' eggs as a child, and took me to the botany department at the University of Vermont to learn how to collect flowers when I was nine. You pick the flower at peak bloom, leaves included, and arrange it between two pieces of blotting paper layered between corrugated cardboard, providing a pathway for moisture to move out of the plant and then out of the blotting paper. Two wooden plates are the bread of a sandwich made of corrugated cardboard, blotting paper, and specimens, all tightened with canvas straps. Each plant specimen comes out weeks later, color intact, to be arranged on botanical mounting paper and secured with special glue. It's scrapbooking for plant nerds. With the *Peterson Field Guide*, any child can define the local flora for posterity. I mounted hundreds of specimens, with location, habitat notes, and botanical and common names for each one. I learned that by breaking natural areas down into their components and naming them, one by one, fields and forests become a personal garden. Familiarity makes wilderness seem like a group of old friends.

In Victorian times, studying nature and building a personal natural history collection was seen as an appropriate way to praise God. The study of flowers and other plants was considered to be an innocent activity by the Church, and it was socially acceptable for groups of unmarried men and women to go on botanizing expeditions on a Sunday afternoon.

People who moved from the country to the city began to romanticize nature. Plants and animals seemed exotic, and worthy of study. So little was known about the natural world that some commonly held beliefs seem truly bizarre today. Newspaper columns on natural history became forums to dispute long-standing conundrums like whether swallows hibernated underwater in the winter, or if a toad could live in a block of stone.

The classification of all living things may have been the world's first crowdsourced intellectual project, with many individuals each contributing a small part to a larger body of knowledge. The new scientific journals provided a platform where people could enumerate their finds. London's *Magazine of natural history and journal of zoology, botany, mineralogy, geology and meteorology* was launched in 1829, and became the *Magazine of Natural History* in 1838. *The Phytologist*, a botanical journal, was launched in 1841 with the intent of being the definitive source for all British plants. These journals and others allowed people to share their findings even if they lived far from London.

Collecting became a national obsession in England, and to a lesser extent in the United States and Europe. With a spreading railway network and better roads, people who lived in the city could easily visit the countryside. Developments in color printing led to machine-produced guidebooks with full-color illustrations that eased plant identification, while inexpensive tourist guides encouraged further botanizing excursions.

Meanwhile, there was a steady demand to see wild animals, and menageries were very well stocked. Up to the early part of the nineteenth century, most live animals arrived with sailors returning from trading voyages. Young wild animals were sold as local products at foreign ports, where sailors would buy them.

Accustomed to the niceties of modern zoos, I think of a menagerie as a place that might include grass. Instead, Victorian menageries in both Europe and North America were generally a series of small cages. In 1806, a traveling menagerie in England advertised a "noble Lion and Lioness, Panthers, Leopards, Hyaena, Lynx, Kangaroo, Ostrichs, and upwards of a hundred other animals and birds." In 1812, a London display included two tigers, a lion, a hyena, a leopard, a panther, two sloths, a camel, many monkeys, and a tapir. The Liverpool Zoo had lions, tigers, lion-tiger hybrids, leopards, jaguars, lynx, ocelots, margays, and several hyenas.

When wild animals are closely confined and fed inadequate

diets, they die. The average lifespan of a big cat in an English menagerie was about two years. Between 1832 and 1836, nine lions died in the Regent Park Zoo alone. As a result, many menageries had large natural history collections attached to them: animals that died in the zoo were stuffed and displayed in the attached museum. Over time, a menagerie's natural history collection could become enormous.

In the United States, traveling menageries and circuses were common, but there may have been no menageries in a fixed location—zoological gardens, or zoos—until after the Civil War. An animal that dies in a traveling menagerie is more likely to be fed to the surviving animals than stuffed and put on display, so the natural history collections amassed by Americans were relatively small.

The first comprehensive museum of natural history that was open to the public was La Specola in Florence, where the Medici displayed their collection of stuffed animals, fossils, and bones. The museum opened in 1775 in a modest, three-story building near the Pitti Palace. It still occupies the same timeworn rooms today, displaying about 5,000 animals from a collection that now totals over three and a half million specimens. Some of the stuffed animals are now extinct, like the faded Tasmanian wolf and the pink-headed duck from the Ganges, the great auk, the passenger pigeon, and the Eskimo curlew. A few of the animals had been pets, including a little stuffed hippopotamus that lived for a few years in the Boboli Gardens. Individually, many of the moth-eaten lumpy specimens look like they are in a zombie phase and will soon return to dust. But the effect of sorting the entire tree of life in a single building is to create a powerful intellectual tool. Wonder rooms made you wonder why there were so many species.

As a rule, insects consumed most stuffed birds and animals within a few years. Tobacco, spices, powdered sulfur, alum, camphor, and turpentine were all used as insecticides, and none of them were particularly effective. One technique involved painting the outside of the skin with a mixture of turpentine and camphor and the inside of the skin with a mixture of arsenic and aloe; finally, the mount was stuffed with sawdust mixed with arsenic, alum, camphor, mercury chloride (a compound of mercury and chlorine), and occasionally cinnamon to mask the scent. The resulting mount was highly poisonous, but still subject to insect damage.

In the 1700s, French ornithologist Jean-Baptiste Bécœur experimented with fifty different chemicals to determine how to keep his stuffed birds intact. He combined the four most effective chemicals—lime, arsenic, potash, and camphor—in a single bar of soap. This became known as arsenical soap, and by the early 1800s most natural history specimens were impregnated with this product and preserved. The 1902 *Encyclopedia Britannica* warned, "Like all arsenical preparations, this is exceedingly dangerous in the hands of unskilled persons, often causing shortness of breath, sores, brittleness of the nails, and other symptoms." Bécœur's arsenical soap was used until the 1980s to preserve skins and birds in collections around the world. By the dawn of the Industrial Revolution, animal specimens could be preserved indefinitely, in alcohol or with arsenical soap.

Zoological collections were usually based on stuffed animals, while botanical collections needed living plants. Better mail service made it easy for naturalists to communicate with each other, and soon citizen-botanists were trading cuttings from plants collected around the world. Colonizers had been prospecting the world for new plants since the 1600s, when potatoes, squash, tomatoes, hot peppers, and corn were brought from the New World and cultivated throughout Europe. Tobacco, coffee and tea, cacao, cane sugar, and citrus were all grown abroad and used by nearly everyone. New raw materials for local artisans included ostrich feathers and ivory, rosewood and mahogany. Amateur botanists had the possibility of discovering the next great food or material, as well as the fun of collecting foreign species.

Unfortunately, animals could survive sea voyages while plants generally did not. Plants died on ships from the salty air and lack of fresh water and light. As a rule, plants could only be imported in their dormant phase as seeds, tubers, bulbs or corms, roots or rhizomes. That is, until Dr. Nathaniel Bagshaw Ward invented the Wardian case, a terrarium that allowed live plants to survive a sea voyage. Ward lived in London and collected ferns and moths. He kept his cocoons sealed in glass jars. In one jar, a fern and a grass seed germinated in a bit of soil. He kept the jar sealed for four years, and watched the fern grow and the grass bloom. Eventually the seal failed, and the plants died.

Ward had a carpenter build a tightly closed wooden case with glass panes. When the sun warmed the air, the moisture in the soil evaporated, condensed on the glass, and dripped back down to water the plants. His ferns thrived in it, and his book *On the Growth of Plants in Closely Glazed Cases* found a steady market among the plant-collecting public.

In a Wardian case, tender young plants aboard ships at sea could be set on deck during the day. The glass protected the plants from salt spray while moisture condensed inside the case, keeping the plants watered. Wardian cases allowed live plants to be transported from other continents for exhibition in western botanical gardens and in private collections. Wardian cases also helped English businessmen smuggle tea plants from China and rubber plants from Brazil, breaking regional monopolies.

Botanical collections depend on clean air and water, but the air quality in coal-heated cities was often so poor that many plant species simply could not survive. When rain falls on coal smoke, the water combines with the products of coal combustion to make sulfuric acid and other noxious compounds. Only the hardiest species can tolerate this toxic cocktail. Thick yellow coal smoke was a feature of many northern cities. People breathed air that was too dirty to support plant life and often died of lung disease, especially tuberculosis. Particles of soot—smuts—from domestic and industrial coal fires swirled in the air and settled into a sticky black layer that coated every surface and smudged any light fabric.

Indoor air was also polluted: wood fires smoked; coal fires emitted oily, black soot; and candle smoke was often greasy. As gaslight replaced candles, the nature of indoor air pollution changed. Coal gas was made by heating coal in an enclosed oven with an oxygen-poor atmosphere and the resulting gas, also called lighting gas, was a mixture of hydrogen, methane, carbon monoxide, and ethylene with some sulfur and ammonia compounds thrown in. The gas was highly flammable and had to be purified before it was burned.

Burning gas depletes the air of oxygen and emits carbon monoxide. This was not a problem with streetlights, where the carbon monoxide could dissipate. But indoors, the built environment had become unhealthy for plants and humans alike. The swoon of a Victorian lady was more likely from a lack of oxygen due to carbon monoxide poisoning than from her tightly laced corset. The products of combustion corroded the picture wires, so pictures were hung with cords. So few plants could endure indoor living conditions that Aspidistra, a decidedly unlovely plant, became a drawing-room favorite.

Baltimore was the first US city to install gas street lighting, in 1816. Many cities followed, and by the late 1840s, gas lighting had reached small towns and even some villages. Kerosene was first distilled from coal in 1846, and quickly replaced lighting gas. The switch to kerosene was accompanied by increased reports of fires, explosions, and suffocations. Occupants of a poorly ventilated building risked dying of carbon monoxide poisoning, but buildings were usually drafty. By the 1860s, improvements in lamp designs made explosions less likely.

With bright indoor light, vibrant colors became fashionable for clothes and house interiors. In 1856, William Perkin discovered how to make dye from coal tar, a waste product. He named the new shade mauve, but instead of the pinky gray mauve of the twenty-first century, this shade was closer to hot purple, a cousin to hot pink. Emerald green, magenta, and azulene (shocking blue) followed, and each dye was bright in cotton and eye-popping in silk. Plant-based dyes are tastefully muted, and the fabrics faded during washing and when exposed to light. The new chemical dyes made nonfading bright colors and a true black that was an immediate hit with businessmen, who began to dress in predominantly dark colors so they could walk outside without getting marked by smuts.

Scheele's green, made from copper arsenite, is a bright grassy green used for everything from fabric to wallpaper and paint. Women wearing dresses of Scheele's green were poisoned directly by the arsenic in the fabric, while the paint and wallpaper poisoned people slowly through flakes and off-gassing from the wall. It was a dangerous era, and if the light-ing didn't kill you, the green dress might.

In the polluted city air and toxic household loadings of most urban environments in the United States and England, the new Wardian cases became a feature of stylish drawing rooms. Small mechanical pumps made it possible for ama-teurs to keep an aquarium for the first time, and soon the ideal was the combined aquarium and fern case. The balance the-ory explained that the ferns provide oxygen that the fish need to survive in the closed case, evidence of God's purpose on Earth.

Greenhouses became more affordable, and it was fashion-able to cultivate exotic plants. Plant specimens brought back by explorers were cloned from cuttings in private and public greenhouses and spread among aficionados across the coun-try. Hobbyists and scientists formed scientific societies that provided a forum for discussion, with separate societies for many different plant families.

In the United States, greenhouses were common on country estates owned by the upper class. George Washing-ton's greenhouse at Mount Vernon had two wings that housed slaves on either side of the growing room. Thomas Jefferson had plans for a greenhouse at Monticello, but never had the funds to build it (he overwintered plants in a windowed walk-way). Both men had plant collections from around the world and traded cuttings and seeds back and forth with their friends. Opium poppies from Eastern Europe and western Asia were planted throughout the United States. Simple opium tea made from the dried, ground pods of the orange poppies found in gardens in every town in America is as addictive and calming as OxyContin.

Charles Willson Peale, an artist with an abiding interest

in natural history, opened the first well-known museum in the United States in the new country's premier city, Philadelphia. His natural history collection was displayed in the tower and upper floors of the Pennsylvania State House, where the constitution had been written in 1787. Peale was a renowned portraitist who painted most of the Founding Fathers, and Peale's Philadelphia Museum included portraits and about 200 stuffed mammals, including bison, and more than 700 American birds posed in shadow boxes decorated with stones, sand, or branches and backed with painted landscapes. "By showing the nest, hollow, cave or a particular view of the country from which they came, some instances of their habits may be given." He exhibited the first mastodon skeleton unearthed in the United States, and chronicled the 1801 discovery with his painting *Exhuming the Mastodon*. His museum used Linnaean taxonomy to organize its specimens. John James Audubon lived near the museum, and knew it well. Peale had the largest collection of American birds in the world, and he mounted his specimens by wrapping a skin treated with arsenical soap over a wooden form, rather than stuffing the skin with fiber.

Scudder's American Museum started selling tickets in New York City in 1810. According to a history of the New York stage, it had glass cases of stuffed animals, a live anaconda, a tame alligator, a lamb with two heads, a bison, and a gallery of paintings.

P. T. Barnum acquired both Peale's collection and Scudder's American Museum in 1841. He claimed the Scudder collection totaled 150,000 objects, and that he exhibited "500,000 natural and artificial curiosities from every corner of the globe." In the United States, the largest natural history collections ended up being exhibited in the same space as the Feejee mermaid, a monkey top sewn onto a fish bottom.

The natural history collection at the British Museum had 29,595 specimens in 1848, mostly from people donating their personal collections, and by the end of the century the number of specimens of bird species in the British Museum was nearly the number of bird species in the world. In the United States, the largest natural history collections had already been sold to Barnum and used for ticket sales. As a result the Smithsonian Institution collection, which started in 1846, was based on government expeditions rather than individual contributions. The US government sponsored an expedition by the US Navy that circumnavigated the globe between 1838 and 1842, collecting thousands of animal and plant specimens. Other collecting expeditions included military and civilian surveys of the West, as well as railway and boundary surveys. These comprehensive collections of natural history specimens brought up an existential question: How on Earth did all these species come about?

Linnaeus saw each species as separately created by God. However, fossils of animals that no longer lived were part of many collections, and it was clear that some species had not survived. Did God make creatures that failed? When mastodon skeletons were identified as a different species than elephants, the first theory was that this was just a local disappearance and mastodons lived elsewhere on Earth. When Thomas Jefferson sent Lewis and Clark to the Pacific Northwest in 1806, they had specific instructions to find a herd of mastodons, and any other animals in the fossil record.

Extinction was a conundrum, as was geology. Starting in the early 1800s, it was clear that the Earth was much older than those biblically allotted six millennia. Biostratigraphy assigns a relative age to rock layers by identifying the fossil assemblages in them. It was invented by a rank amateur, William Smith, a surveyor with little formal education. He spent six years supervising the digging of the Somerset Coal Canal in southwest England, and noted that the geological layers were consistent over a wide area, and that each layer had characteristic fossils in it. He spent the next sixteen years making a geological map of England that laid out the different geological periods based on the fossils in the strata, and was so single-minded in his pursuit of fossils—and so chatty—that he was called "Strata" Smith. He published his map in 1816.

Smith was a blacksmith's son. The Geological Society of London, gentlemen all, plagiarized his map and underpriced him. He went to debtor's prison, and was eventually bailed out by a former employer. In time, Smith and his geological map were embraced by the more democratic science clubs and he was awarded an honorary doctorate by Trinity College; he eventually received the Geological Society of London's highest award, the first Wollaston Medal, and was referred to as the "Father of English Geology." To account for Smith's clearly delineated layers of long-extinct life in the rocks, it was suggested that God periodically returned and repopulated the Earth with new species.

Fossil remains and maps of local geologic layers made it clear that the world's timeline extended back into deep time. Species had disappeared from the Earth. Therefore, species had likely appeared as well. The comprehensive natural history collections, both private and public, were arranged by the Linnaean system based on evolutionary features. Charles Babbage, of adding machine fame, proposed theistic evolution in 1837 in his *Ninth Bridgewater Treatise*: God had created templates, and separate species evolved from adjustments to a basic template. A simple bear template, over time, gives you black bears, brown bears, grizzly bears, polar bears, spectacled bears, panda bears, and sun bears. Theistic evolution gave credit to God for creating a generic bear, but did not require a separate miracle for each ursine variant.

Darwin was raised in fertile ground.

Born in 1809, Darwin was sent to medical school in Edinburgh at sixteen. Several accounts record his dislike for blood and medical studies. The most useful skill he learned in medical school was taxidermy from John Edmonstone, a freed slave from Guyana in South America. Darwin quit medical school at eighteen and started studying for the clergy. He attended natural history lectures and became enamored with ground beetles at nineteen. Ground beetles are a particularly plentiful form of life—of all species on Earth, ground beetles account for a quarter of them—and Darwin was bitten by the collecting bug. Truly avid, Darwin described an incident in a letter to Leonard Jenyns that encapsulated his fervor: "under a piece of bark I found two carabi (I forget which) & caught one in each hand, when lo & behold I saw a sacred *Panagæus crux major*; I could not bear to give up either of my Carabi, & to lose *Panagæus* was out of the question, so that in despair I gently seized one of the carabi between my teeth, when to my unspeakable disgust & pain the little inconsiderate beast squirted his acid down my throat & I lost both Carabi & *Panagæus*!"

Darwin graduated at twenty-two with a divinity degree and a growing beetle collection. He promptly left on a five-year trip on the *Beagle* to collect specimens, bottling or stuffing animals as he went. He formulated his theory of evolution by the age of thirty, three years after returning from his voyage, and spent the next two decades refining and clarifying the concept before publishing *On the Origin of Species* in 1859, at the age of fifty. Instead of each niche of the biosphere being filled by an act of God, species evolved through descent with modification. Each succeeding generation is slightly different from the one before it, because some traits are beneficial and enhance the survival of an individual, while other traits are detrimental and decrease the odds of survival. Anyone who has spent time looking at a large natural history collection would question why God would possibly bother to create so many different species that are nearly identical to each other. Evolution was quickly accepted as a logical explanation of the multiplicity of life.

Darwin's theory of natural selection was more problematic. Natural selection was named to contrast with artificial selection, the nineteenth-century term for selective breeding. Natural selection is based on genetics and the differential survival of different genetic phenotypes: some traits increase longevity, and other traits do not. Gene theory was first proposed six years after Darwin's *On the Origin of Species* in Gregor Mendel's 1865 paper "Versuche über Pflanzenhybriden" ("Experiments on Plant Hybridization"), and was not accepted for another thirty years.

Compound microscopes made it possible to see germs shortly after Pasteur's germ theory explained why canning works. Natural selection is an amoral, arbitrary, nondirectional process that is not aligned with historical progress, and it's based on structures that need an electron microscope to be seen. It was nearly a hundred years after the theory was postulated before scientists could see the DNA and genes behind the theory of evolution.

Linnaean classification was based on accumulative descriptions of physical features, and was easily adapted to reflect evolutionary development. To provide a graphic representation of how species are related to each other, scientists began to build phylogenies, diagrams that show the evolutionary path of populations through generations and long periods of time. These diagrams start to look like trees: ancestral stocks branch and become two or more different species, which may branch again and again. Each branch of the family tree is called a clade: a group of organisms with a common ancestor that represents a single branch on the tree of life. The clado-gram is an elegant representation of evolution, and a simplified portrait of a complex reality.

Strangely, there is still no clear understanding of how to define a species. In 1859, Darwin wrote, "I look at the term *species* as one arbitrarily given for the sake of convenience to a set of individuals closely resembling each other." In the twentieth century, a species became a population whose members could only reproduce with each other. This is the biological species concept: over time, populations became separated forever through geography or other barriers, and when different species mate, the offspring are sterile. E. O. Wilson wrote, "The origin of species is therefore simply the evolution of some difference—any difference at all—that prevents the production of fertile hybrids between populations under natural conditions."

This definition never accounted for asexual reproduction in plants, or routine hybridization. Now that genetic testing allows scientists to sequence genomes, it is clear that different species routinely hybridize. According to DNA evidence, red wolves are a coyote-wolf hybrid rather than a separate wolf species. Bobcats and lynx are crossbreeding in Canada. Grizzly bears and polar bears have exchanged genes throughout history, and according to genomic analysis, today's pizzly bears are not a new phenomenon. *Homo sapiens* contain genetic material from Neanderthals, so hybridization played a role in our background as well. Nature is not so neatly parsed, and species are not as genetically isolated as we would like to believe.

The ultimate lesson learned through collecting is that all living things are related, and worthy. Collecting creates a personal connection with the natural world, and some childhood collectors became champions of the wilderness, including Teddy Roosevelt. Starting with a seal skull at ten years old, young Theodore "Teedie" Roosevelt started "what we ambitiously called the 'Roosevelt Museum of Natural History.'" In his autobiography, he wrote that he "collected specimens industriously and enlivened the household with hedge-hogs and other small beasts and reptiles which persisted in escaping from partially closed bureau drawers."

A generation of children who collected naturalia grew up to become adults who protected nature.

5

Selling Nature

At first, the New World was home to great flocks and herds of wild animals, and its shoreline was crowded with birds, pinnipeds, whales, and fish. Subsistence hunters had used these animals for food and clothing for millennia, and people coexisted with an abundance of wildlife. Subsistence hunters are motivated by their family's need for meat and skins, which is finite: they harvest wildlife to live. Market hunters, who kill and sell wild animals, are motivated by money. There is no upper limit to greed, and Europeans who moved to North America came from the same cultures that had already emptied Europe of wildlife.

Ownership is a cultural construct, and by the colonists' reckoning, wild animals were owned by the person who owned the land. Although no one owned wildlife that lived on common land, these animals became private property after they were killed. The immense migratory flocks and herds of the interior were not attached to any single parcel of land. This meant wild animals were free for the taking. Commercial hunters slaughtered them en masse and sold them for cash. They nearly sold them all.

Furs and skins were among the first products extracted from the New World, with colonists buying furs that had been harvested and processed by people from local tribes. A dollar is called a buck because tanned buckskins and doeskins substituted for cash. Furs were valuable, light enough to be transported by canoe, and they were a product that did not degrade over time.

When Europeans took control of the landscape, the scale of the harvest changed. New immigrants systematically slaughtered all the wild animals and processed them into products that could be sold in cities throughout North America and Europe. Hunting for market is very different from hunting for sport: the point is to kill as many animals as possible in the shortest period of time. Commercial hunters harvest animals when the animals gather together to feed, breed, or migrate, and they kill all of the animals found in an entire area. Commercial hunting usually involves a team of specialists working together, with hunters, skinners, butchers, processors, and marketers doing different tasks.

Before railways were built, the seashore was the place to harvest animals for market. Cod was dried on Newfoundland beaches by the boatload, and sold throughout Europe and West Africa, the United States, the Caribbean, and Brazil. The oils from sea mammals were another popular product. Seal, elephant seal, walrus, and whale oil could be boiled down on nearby beaches, barreled, and shipped to market to be used for lamps, lubrication, and industrial products, including soap, leather, oilcloth, and even margarine, which must have been a truly heinous substitute for lard. Baleen are the strips of keratin that hang like a curtain from the upper jaw of baleen whales, used to strain the water for small creatures like krill. In cities, baleen was sold for stays that stiffened corsets, hoops that kept skirts in a bell-like shape, light whips and canes, umbrella ribs, and hairbrush bristles.

It wasn't hard to get into the oil business back then. It required a ship, crew, and iron try pots to render the blubber into oil, along with barrels to store it in. At first, whale oil was gathered from right whales that feed and breed near shore and float when killed. Their blubber was processed at a low simmer on nearby beaches and shipped back to Europe. The North Atlantic right whale was rare by the 1700s, when the first sperm whales were processed.

Sperm whales were hunted on the open ocean. Their blubber was rendered into oil in try pots onboard over a small fire fed mostly by whale scraps. Sperm whales had an additional product: their boxy heads hold an enormous cavity filled with about 500 gallons of spermaceti, a waxy oil with physical characteristics similar to jojoba oil.

Whalers would cut off the sperm whale's head and empty the head cavity with a bucket. The spermaceti, often listed as sperm oil, was boiled and strained before being stored in barrels. Once ashore, spermaceti was chilled in the winter cold and pressed through a wool sack to separate the oil from the wax. The filtered sperm oil stayed liquid below freezing, making it an unusually useful industrial lubricant, while the wax was treated with alkali to form bright white mounds of a hard substance that feels oily but has no taste or smell. Spermaceti wax, called sperm wax, was used for fine candles, ointments, and textile finishing.

Tallow candles are smoky and smell like rancid fat. Beeswax candles are expensive. The suggestively named sperm candles provided a third option for lighting that was clean burning and brighter than tallow, but less expensive than beeswax. Whale oil, also called train oil, was boiled down from whale blubber and used in lamps and miners' headlamps.

By the 1850s, killing and processing whales was the fifth-largest industry in the United States. Records from the New Bedford whaler *Milton* provide a typical account: The *Milton* left port in 1836, and returned three years later with a net profit for the voyage of about $100,000. The owners took about $65,000, while the captain received a one-seventeenth of the profit, or $5,882; the first mate one–twenty-second, or $4,545; the boatsteerer (harpooner) one–seventy-fifth, or $1,333; and the blacksmith one–one-hundred-and-fortieth, or $714. The best-paid seaman earned $800, while the worst-paid received $571 for about three years of work, a little over $15 per month. In 1915, the total value of the New England whaling industry in the 1800s was estimated to exceed $330 million, the equivalent of more than $8.1 billion in 2018 after inflation. Fortunes were made selling nature's bounty for private gain, but not by the sailors or the hired help.

Seal oil was also a big business. Seals raise their pups in great rookeries, and were easily harvested. Fur seals were clubbed and skinned, and the pelts were salted and shipped in wooden casks. Seal oil, like whale oil, was used for lighting (for both streetlights and in homes), textile manufacturing, and leather tanning. In Newfoundland alone, sealers flensed and rendered the fat of roughly half a million seals a year between 1818 and 1862. In 1857, over 370 ships carried 13,600 people to work for the seasonal project of rendering fat Newfoundland seals into a salable product. Only cod was more important to the Newfoundland economy.

As an oil source, elephant seals (then called sea elephants) were even better than seals. They crowd onto beaches during breeding season, hauling themselves out of water for an interlude of sun and sex. They are unaggressive, unafraid, and very large. Laborers could set up their try pot on one end of the beach and systematically boil down the whole herd. The sealers lanced the elephant seals, clubbed them, stripped them of their blubber, and rendered the fat into oil on-site. Elephant seal oil was very high quality. "Clear, inodorous, and not liable to contract that rancid smell of which whale oil can never be deprived; when burned in a lamp it yields a bright and pure flame, without smoke, and without exhaling that infectious smell peculiar to most animal oils." The main thrust of elephant seal hunting lasted fifteen years. In 1846, there were seals in abundance on islands and beaches of the US West Coast, and by 1860 they were too scarce to hunt.

A single colony of 300 to 400 northern elephant seals was found in 1880 at Bahía San Cristóbal, on the coast of the Baja in Mexico, and every single one was killed. The world population of northern elephant seals dropped to as few as twenty to one hundred individuals (today, there are over 150,000).

Walrus pods were also processed for oil, as well as for tusks and a widely appreciated hide. Walrus hide was used for harnesses and shoe soles, and made a high-performance rope that was cut in a spiral from the tail to the neck in a single unbroken piece that could stretch ninety feet. An 1880 monograph on pinnipeds says that all of the rigging on Norwegian and Russian ships had been made of walrus-skin rope. In the twentieth century, walrus hide was commonly used for pads on the tip of pool cues and doctors' bags.

Whales play an important role in nutrient cycling in the ocean. A blue whale consumes about 8,000 pounds of krill a day, while a humpback will eat about 5,000 pounds of food. According to a 1998 analysis from Tokyo's Institute of Cetacean Research, whales eat an estimated 280 million to 500 million tons of food each year. The world catch of fish has topped out at perhaps 90 million tons, so in 1998 whales consumed three to six times more marine resources than humans, and their population has increased since then. (Cetaceans and humans mostly consume different species.)

Pinnipeds are also big eaters. A harbor seal may consume a bare ton and a half of fish in a year, while a male walrus (who can consume 6,000 clams in a single meal) may eat more than twelve tons of food in a year. If ocean production was a zero-sum equation, reducing the population of whales and seals should increase the amount of seafood available for humans to harvest. Instead, marine mammals change the ocean ecosystem in ways that increase fish production.

Cetaceans move nutrients from deep water into shallow water by eating krill, fish, and squid from the depths and releasing their urine and feces near the surface. According to Joe Roman, a conservation biologist at the University of Vermont who studies marine mammals, whale and pinniped poop is a significant source of nutrients for ocean ecosystems. The urine directly fertilizes the phytoplankton (the primary producers in the ocean, equivalent to grass on land), while the nutrient-rich feces are consumed by zooplankton (secondary producers, like grazers). More phytoplankton and zooplankton means more food for fish.

When whales and seals die, they usually sink to the bottom of the ocean. This is an important pathway for carbon to be exported to the deep sea, an environment usually lacking in food bonanzas. When a whale falls to the sea floor, hundreds of organisms flock to the carcass. Scavengers, including hagfish, sleeper sharks, and many invertebrates, chomp away at the whale's soft tissue, consuming forty to sixty kilograms per day. Deep-sea worms and crustaceans give way to a host of bone-munching microbes as the whale is whittled away to its component parts.

The natural life cycle of a marine mammal removes nothing from the ocean, while its existence actively sustains and enhances marine productivity. Finally, marine mammals cull fish stocks in a way that enhances school health, removing smaller, slower individuals and reducing fish numbers, lessening competition for food. (Humans prefer to take larger fish.)

Removing the top predators from an ecosystem can have unintended consequences. In the marine ecosystem, interrupting the nutrient cycles creates a top-down trophic cascade that can result in a number of secondary population collapses. Approximately 400,000 whales were harvested near the Aleutian Islands in the twentieth century, and marine biologists observed a number of marine populations collapse after the whales were gone. First Steller's sea cows disappeared, and then northern sea lion populations collapsed. Then the smallest marine mammal, the sea otter, disappeared, and the sea urchin populations (that fed the otters) exploded. The offshore kelp beds were overrun by urchins, who ate the kelp down to its holdfasts: no more kelp. The kelp forest had acted as a nursery and hiding place for commercially important fish, where they lived until they were large enough to swim in the open ocean as part of the ocean fishery. The fish stocks near the Aleutian Islands collapsed, and Alaskan fishermen went bankrupt. Nutrient cycling is an important job, and when it slows down the ecosystem becomes impoverished. Removing millions of whales, seals, walruses, and sea lions has reduced the oceans' productivity.

∘ ∘ ∘

Many of the products made from wildlife were everyday items that had international markets. Everyone agreed that doeskin made the best gloves, while buckskin was good for britches and jackets. Buffalo skins made excellent robes, and tough buffalo leather was used universally for the drive belts of industrial machinery. Every good watchmaker lubricated his clocks and watches with oil made from porpoise jaws.

Oil was one common product that was harvested from sea life, while eggs and down were others. Many seafowl gathered together to breed in great flocks on beaches, making them prime targets for humans. Eggers would go through a seabird rookery and smash every egg they found, prompting the birds to lay fresh eggs that could then be gathered all together. A bounty, from the Latin *bonitos*, is a generous gift freely provided. The bounty of nature in the New World was that instead of raising chickens to lay eggs, you could simply gather fresh eggs from seabirds. An omelet sold in San Francisco in the 1890s was more likely made from the eggs of common murres, western gulls, or tufted puffins than chickens. Photographs printed between 1850 and 1900 used albumen prints, where the albumen from egg whites is used to bind the photographic chemicals to paper. The albumen for nearly all of the photographic paper during those decades came from albatross eggs from Laysan Island near Hawaii. If you have an old photograph, you also own a bit of albatross egg.

Down was also collected from the wild. Eider ducks pluck the down from their breasts to line their nests for the ducklings. For many centuries, people collected eiderdown from wild nests without killing the ducks. The wholesale destruction of eider duck nesting grounds came at about the same time as the seals were boiled down for oil, and soon eider ducks were killed indiscriminately for down and meat. As the dense flocks of eider ducks started to disappear, people started exploiting the great auk for down. This little flightless bird lived on rocky islets from Canada to Norway, including Newfoundland, Greenland, Iceland, the United Kingdom, and Ireland. It was about thirty inches high and eleven pounds with the black-and-white coat and upright stance of a penguin, and no fear of humans. As more great auks were killed for down, their eggs became increasingly rare. Many British and European egg collectors tried to buy a great auk egg before it was too late to get one. There may have never been more than twenty breeding grounds for the great auk, and eggers made return visits to the same colony to collect eggs on consecutive days. The last auk in Scotland was killed on an island in 1844; the last auk in Iceland was killed on an islet the same year.

Until the railways were laid, hunters were largely restricted to shipping furs, hides, oils, and down. By 1910, the United States had more than 230,000 miles of rail, and wild animals from all over the country could be sold as meat.

With reliable rail transportation, the oysters that lay in shoals of millions upon millions could be harvested on the East Coast and sold in the interior. Trains transported tons of bivalves to inland towns and cities, and the increased sale volumes spurred the oyster industry to improve its tools, vessels, packing containers, and shipping. Tongs had been used to harvest oysters since the 1700s, in dugout canoes with wide, flat bottoms. As the 1800s progressed, instead of hand-harvesting oysters with tongs, people rigged dredges to drag from flat-bottomed sailboats, or skipjacks. Eventually steam engines were used on boats to pull up the dredges.

Before the railroads expanded, most oysters were canned. An article in the *New-York Tribune* from January 9, 1857, describes how oysters were made into money in New Haven: "There are the openers, the washers, the measurers, the fillers, the packers, each of which performs only the duties pertaining to its own division." According to the reporter, "The oysters are taken directly from the vessels to the places occupied by the openers, . . . who earn from $5 to $9 per week. An expert . . . will open 100 quarts per day, but the average is not perhaps over 65 quarts. The standard price is, I think, 2½ cents per quart. This work gives employment to many hundreds." The oyster shuckers were often from Eastern Europe; after the Civil War, African American women were often hired as shuckers.

From the opening room, or shucking room, the oysters are taken to the filling room. The oysters are poured into a large hopper pierced with holes, then rinsed and drained. A keg is filled with one person holding the hopper over the keg, while another measures and pours. Two or three men could fill 2,000 kegs a day.

Oysters were first canned in Baltimore, close to the oyster beds where newly freed slaves provided plenty of labor for hire. Soon the oysters were steamed before they were shucked, in twenty-bushel lots. After being steamed and shucked, the oysters were washed in cold water and sent to the fillers' table. The cans were filled, weighed, and hermetically sealed with a cap soldered over the hole. After boiling the cans in pots of water to sterilize them, the cans were cooled, labeled, and packed.

The railways allowed oysters to be sold fresh. Thousands of miles of rails were laid after 1860, and the Atlantic oyster business surged above 20 million bushels a year. Pittsburgh, Cincinnati, Detroit, Chicago, Milwaukee, St. Louis, St. Paul, and Minneapolis all enjoyed fresh oysters on the half shell. By 1870, Maryland alone produced more than 10 million bushels a year at a value of $4 million or more. Oysters were the most valuable fishery in the United States in 1880, when the first complete survey of the oyster industry showed a harvest of 22,195,000 bushels. The largest dealers shipped oysters to as many as one hundred dealers in fifty cities. From 1875 to 1890, Maryland harvested more oysters than any place on Earth.

Americans were enveloped in a great oyster craze. Oysters were pickled, roasted, fried, scalloped, and fricasseed; there were oysters in stews, stuffing, soups, patties, and puddings; oysters for breakfast, lunch, or dinner. "No evening of pleasure was complete without oysters; no host worthy of the name failed to serve 'the luscious bivalves.'"

In every town were oyster parlors, oyster cellars, oyster saloons, oyster bars, houses, stalls, and lunchrooms. New York City had over 850 oyster establishments by 1874, and by the early 1900s, New Yorkers were consuming about 500,000 bushels of oyster per season, about two meals a week of oysters for every person in the city. However, after the turn of the twentieth century, the oyster beds were depleted, oysters became linked with typhoid, and the oyster craze was over.

Moving millions of bushels of oysters from shoals to the hinterlands changed water quality and the calcium cycle.

Oysters are biological filters that remove suspended particulate matter from the water. They are filter feeders that eat phytoplankton, or free-swimming algae. As they eat, water quality improves. Generations of oysters settle on top of each other, building reefs that provide habitat for many species of fish and crabs.

Harvesting the oysters removed a significant amount of hard-bottom habitat from the bays and created a bottom-up trophic cascade. More phytoplankton was available (since oysters no longer ate it) and the food web shifted, resulting in an increase in zooplankton (which also eat phytoplankton) and their jellyfish predators. Water quality degraded, since fewer oysters means that less water was filtered. Oysters also remove nitrogen from the water, so plant growth increases when they are gone.

Finally, oyster shells contain quite a lot of calcium. Calcium is a necessary nutrient for plants and animals, originally found in sedimentary rock. Weathering and rainfall moves calcium from land into the ocean, and it is the fifth most abundant nutrient in seawater. Once an atom of calcium weathered from rocks has reached the ocean, it is commonly said to take a million years for that atom to return to land. Unless, of course, it is part of the millions of bushels of oysters harvested and sent by rail to the oyster-eating cities of the United States. The oyster harvest sped up the calcium cycle, and made ocean-based nutrients available for agricultural application.

The railways also allowed market hunters to harvest animals far from the seashore. Wildfowl that gather together to migrate or breed are well suited to market hunting, and the mass harvest of birds like passenger pigeons, geese, ducks, and curlews required only a railway system to transport the meat, and a telegraph system to let the commercial hunters know where the flocks were.

The most astonishing victim was the passenger pigeon.

Passenger pigeons were once the most populous birds in North America, numbering perhaps 3 to 5 billion birds in total that traveled in multimillion-bird flocks. It is hard to imagine the power represented by birds that travel in groups of hundreds of millions or more. Alexander Wilson, called the father of American ornithology, was in a riverside cabin when he "was suddenly struck with astonishment at a loud rushing roar, succeeded by instant darkness, which, on the first moment, [he] took for a tornado, about to overwhelm the house and everything around in destruction."

But his companions calmly replied, "It's only the Pigeons."

A Wayne County, New York, resident wrote in 1854, "There would be days and days when the air was alive with them, hardly a break occurring in the flocks for half a day at a time. Flocks stretched as far as a person could see, one tier above another."

Passenger pigeons did not appear every year. They roamed about the eastern forests in huge flocks, eating acorns, hickory nuts, beechnuts, and chestnuts; worms and insects; grains, berries, and fruit. Many nut species have indifferent harvests most years, and occasionally produce bumper crops. The roving hordes of pigeons were able to exploit these random excesses of resources. In the eastern part of the country, flocks of passenger pigeons could be found in Boston, New York City, Philadelphia, Cleveland, Columbus, St. Louis, Minneapolis, Chicago, Detroit, Toronto, and Montreal, among other places.

When passenger pigeons nested and raised their single

chick, their nesting site could cover many hundreds of square miles. The birds were so densely clustered that there could be dozens of nests in a single tree, and branches would break from the weight of them. The droppings would pile up inches deep under the trees, killing the understory shrubs and ground-cover. After a nesting season, the pigeons left behind land that was covered with broken trees and a layer of manure, primed for clearing and planting.

Passenger pigeons were not welcome visitors, as a rule. A flock of pigeons could clean out a wheat field or an orchard in just a few hours. When farmers cast their seed to plant their fields, passenger pigeons might drop by and eat nearly every grain. Seed drills became a necessary tool to protect the grain from passenger pigeons. The pigs that fed on forest mast—acorns and other nuts—had nothing to eat after the birds passed through (except pigeons: surplus passenger pigeons were often fed to pigs).

There was a benefit to having these hungry birds visit town, though. The birds were fast fliers with a well-developed breast muscle, and anyone could kill as many as they wanted. People used shotguns, of course, and could take down a handful with every shot. Some hunters used their bare hands or clubs. A flaming torch could be used to dazzle the birds with light after they had settled into their nests at night; the startled birds would drop to the ground helpless and ready to be gathered in sacks. Entire roosting sites could be set on fire, leaving heaps of scorched birds two feet deep.

Netters had astonishing hauls. At an 1851 nesting near Beekmantown, New York, netters caught 1,200 birds in a single net. During the 1878 Petoskey, Michigan, nesting, a three-person team caught over 50,000 pigeons in their nets. (Some netters used pliers to crush the skulls of the birds caught in the nets, and others would "grab a pigeon by the leg and toss it into his mouth headfirst, then chomp down on the skull.")

An adult pigeon weighed a bare nine to twelve ounces. Young pigeons, or squabs, weighed even less than the adults, but were very tender. The squabs were fed on mast regurgitated from the crops of both parents, and were sometimes so fat that they split when they fell from their nests. Pigeon pie made from squabs was a favorite, as was pigeon stew.

Jessup Whitehead's 1893 cookbook, *Cooking for Profit: A New American Cookbook Adapted for the Use of All Who Serve Meals for a Price*, provides a recipe for passenger pigeon pie that requires eighteen birds for the dish.

Pigeon or Squab Pie

Take 18 squabs, pick, singe, open down the back, draw, and divide in halves; wash and dry them and flatten with the cleaver. Pepper, salt and flour them on both sides. Melt ½ pound of butter in the baking pan the pie is to be made in, lay in the squabs and bake them light brown. Pour into the pan about 2 quarts of broth or water and continue the baking. When done sufficiently thicken the gravy, add walnut catsup or a little Worcestershire sauce and salt and pepper, cover with a short crust and bake twenty minutes longer.

Even at eighteen pigeons per pie, there were far too many pigeons to eat fresh. Most of the pigeons harvested were salted, smoked, or pickled and packed in barrels. For ship food, roasted pigeons were packed into barrels and covered with melted lard or mutton fat that congealed to form an airtight seal. The fat squabs could be rendered into oil that was used as shortening and to make soap.

By 1851, regional markets had been fully established and great nestings were few and far between on the East Coast. Pigeons nesting near Plattsburgh, New York, were harvested by at least four different companies who shared the nesting ground. "It would be impossible to give an accurate account of the whole number taken; but four companies engaged in catching and purchasing, the writer knows, forwarded to different markets not less than *one hundred and fifty thousand dozen*." That's 1.8 million birds, dressed by people paid five cents per dozen to process them.

National markets for the birds were established as the railways expanded into pigeon range. The railway station agents made it their business to telegraph the news when pigeons came to town, and professional pigeon hunters bird-dogged the flocks.

A large roost settled in southern Missouri in early 1879, and was relentlessly pursued by hunters. The birds drifted north between eight and twelve miles a day, and when the birds settled to rest, the hunters scattered throughout the tract with shotguns and coordinated their fire into the trees. The carcasses were collected in the morning and delivered to the nearest railway station. "From here shipped every day from seven hundred to a thousand dozen pigeons (8,400 to 12,000 birds), bringing into the county $600 to $800, net cash per diem. The birds are sent to Boston and New York, where they sell at $1.30 and $1.60 per dozen."

Feathers were generally collected from birds killed for meat and used to stuff beds and pillows. "In 1936, Alvin McKnight of Augusta Wisconsin related that he and his wife slept on a pigeon feather bed they received in 1877 filled with the feathers of 144 dozen passenger pigeons"; 1,728 pigeons were plucked for a single comforter.

People who harvest a million birds here and a million birds there become very skilled at killing, processing, transporting, and marketing their prey. And eventually commercial hunters will process their last million.

The second-to-last great nesting of passenger pigeons occurred in 1874. The birds arrived in Shelby, Michigan, in early April, and occupied an area twenty miles long and four to seven miles wide. The chicks arrived in two weeks, and birds passed continuously overhead gathering beechnuts and worms that might be twenty-five miles away. Locals from the small town of Shelby spent the entire day shooting to take 250 to 300 birds, but these locals were joined by 600 professional netters. One lucky netter took 1,848 pigeons in a day. In thirty days, 900,000 pigeons were shipped from Shelby, pumping $50,000 into the local economy.

The last great nesting of passenger pigeons was in Petoskey, Michigan, in 1879. The register of the Rose Hotel showed that pigeoners arrived from Maine, New York, Pennsylvania, Maryland, Virginia, Wisconsin, Michigan, Minnesota, Iowa, Ohio, Illinois, Missouri, and Texas. The pigeoners established packinghouses and wagons with teams for hauling out dead birds. Locals were hired for these jobs and were trained to trap and kill the birds. Any boy could get a job plucking pigeons, and between locals and professionals there were 2,000 people harvesting and processing pigeons. The pigeoners stretched out alongside the birds for forty miles. They killed birds from dawn to dusk, hauling out wagon after wagon of birds for fifty days, with daily shipments to Detroit, Philadelphia, New York, and many other cities. That was the last multimillion-bird flock of passenger pigeons, though the stragglers were continually harvested for the next decade or so. These gregarious birds did not successfully breed without a crowd, and the last lonely passenger pigeon died in a zoo on September 1, 1914. It's the only time that we knew the exact date a species became extinct.

Passenger pigeons spread seeds wherever they flew. Three to five billion individuals moving around their favored food may account for the predominance of nut trees in antebellum forests. Passenger pigeons moved around billions of pounds of nutrients as well. The accumulated droppings from the roosting areas acted as a nutrient reservoir for the surrounding forest. The broken branches and dead understory were fuel for forest fires, and roosting areas were more likely to burn. The patchwork of meadows and forests made by wildfires enhanced ecosystem productivity by providing a variety of habitats and increasing the amount of edge, that fruitful zone between two ecosystems. Removing billions of passenger pigeons from the landscape slowed down seed dispersal and nutrient cycling, and decreased the complexity of the forest landscape.

∘ ∘ ∘

Ducks and geese were also aggressively harvested. The punt gun was a large muzzle-loading shotgun that was developed to harvest waterfowl on a commercial scale. It was like a duck cannon, and weighed as much as 200 pounds. Punt guns were ten to twelve feet long with a bore as large as two inches that was loaded with up to two pounds of shot (compared to the ounce-plus of shot used by modern duck hunters). Each gun was tailor-made, but by definition punt guns were too heavy to hold. The recoil was so great that they had to be mounted directly on the bow of a small flat-bottomed boat, or punt. A single shot at a flock could kill fifty birds, and to aim the gun, you had to move the boat. If you used your punt gun as part of a coordinated effort, you could set off the fusillade at dawn and spend the rest of the day processing 500 duck carcasses. Punt gunning was so successful that by the late 1870s, many states banned it.

To process ducks for sale, the carcasses were gutted, scalded, plucked, and chilled in salted ice water. "A flour barrel is the best thing to ship them in. In packing keep the feet straight back and turn the head back under the wing," instructed an 1897 handbook. Crushed ice is layered on top of the ducks, with a layer of burlap on top, fastened with a hoop and the promise that "ducks dressed and packed in this manner can be shipped 400 miles."

Eskimo curlew is another migratory bird that was lost to market hunters. Like passenger pigeons, Eskimo curlews traveled in an enormous flock of millions. They migrated 6,000 miles every season between the arctic tundra of northwestern Canada to the wetlands of Patagonia in South America, areas that were rich enough to feed their multitudes. Eskimo curlews were about twelve inches long and ate berries, insects, and snails. They nested in the arctic tundra, where the short summer and long days create a local explosion of insects and calories. The outpouring of insect hatches fed the nestlings during the period when their parents were largely surviving on fat stored during their slow journey north. The whole flock, including the youngsters, then flew 3,000 miles to the east coast of Canada to fatten up in Labrador and Newfoundland. According to naturalist Farley Mowat, hundreds of thousands of square miles of heathland are carpeted with a low bush that bears juicy, pea-sized berries that ripen in July. Curlew berries (*Empetrum nigrum*) were so delicious that the curlews' modest tan-and-brown plumage would be stained all over with rich purple juice. They became "wonderfully fat," so plump that when they were shot in the air they often split open when they hit the ground. Curlews were shot in Labrador, where the guns of the 1870s could routinely kill thirty birds with a single shot. Every Newfoundland family started the winter with several barrels of curlews packed in salt or their own rendered fat. The Hudson's Bay Company packed tens of thousands of curlews in tins that were shipped to London and Montreal as a gourmet specialty item.

As a rule, curlews were safe on their 3,000-mile trip across the Atlantic from Labrador to South America unless the flock was blown onto the East Coast of the United States, where the plump little fowl were called doe-birds or doughbirds and shot until the bullets ran out. When the flock hit South America, it may have scattered and regrouped in the Argentinian pampas and Patagonia.

In the spring, the curlews went up the west coast of South America, across Central America and the Gulf to arrive in Texas in March. They fattened up on insects and snails during their leisurely trip up the heart of North America, and reached Kansas and the Dakotas in April before crossing Canada to the northwest coast, where they laid eggs and waited for the coordinated hatch of nestlings and insects.

Curlews were easy to kill, and people who lived on the Mississippi flyway liked to kill them. When the flights were heavy, hunters filled wagons with them. In 1872, the first railway carload of spring curlews preserved on ice reached New York City, where they sold for a fancy price. And that was the end of the curlews.

In southern Texas, enormous flocks of curlews disappeared after 1875. The last great flocks in Kansas were seen in 1879; curlews disappeared from Nebraska in the 1880s; the flock was gone from Labrador by 1886. It is possible that a handful of Eskimo curlews survive—a flock of twenty-three was seen in

Texas in 1981, and individuals have been sighted nine times since then, most recently in Peggy's Cove, Nova Scotia, in 2006—but the curlew nation has been gone for more than a century.

All these migratory birds have a common ecological function: they move phosphorus from the ocean to the center of the continent. The phosphorus cycle is said to be the slowest nutrient cycle: the element weathers from rocks, moves into the soil, where it feeds plants, and eventually ends up in the ocean, where it drifts to the bottom sediments that, over time, upwell to become mountaintops. These geological processes take eons, and yet every plant and animal needs phosphorus to carry out basic life functions. No surprise that there's a whole other phosphorus cycle running on air and water delivery: seabirds eat fish and fly their phosphorus inland. Likewise, salmon and other anadromous fish collect phosphorus in the ocean and move it inland to fertilize the forests. When the migratory birds disappeared, so did the flow of phosphorus that had enriched the forests and central plains.

The Rocky Mountain locust disappeared about the same time as the Eskimo curlews, with the last big swarms in 1873 and 1877. The Rocky Mountain locust used to form biblical swarms of grasshoppers that stripped lush fields down to stubble. One famed swarm in 1875 is in the *Guinness Book of World Records* as the greatest concentration of animals ever calculated: some 3.5 trillion insects weighing millions of tons covered an estimated 198,000 square miles, greater than the area of California.

The gigantic biomass of a swarm was well matched to the appetites of million-bird flocks, and these insects disappeared at the same time as the curlews and passenger pigeons were destroyed. It was thought that perhaps farmers, with their drainage schemes and flooded fields, interrupted the life cycle of the locusts and led them to extinction. Perhaps it was the loss of nutrients. Perhaps the Rocky Mountain locust was simply in its solitary phase, and swarms would form again in the right conditions. After more than a century of speculation, the Rocky Mountain locust was formally declared extinct in 2014, based on DNA evidence.

The buffalo was another species that was nearly harvested to extinction by commercial hunters. The aboriginal buffalo herds may have numbered 60 million or more. By the 1840s, the American Fur Company was buying 100,000 tanned buffalo robes a year from various Plains tribes for four dollars each, and shipping them down the Mississippi. When the railways and telegraph were laid and buffalo products could be easily transported, the harvest expanded. William "Buffalo Bill" Cody worked as a hunter for the Kansas Pacific Railway between 1867 and 1868, and killed nearly 5,000 buffalo in 18 months to feed the 1,200 men building the railroad. The men dined on tongues and tenderloins, and this interlude marked the beginning of the great buffalo sale.

The Union Pacific Railroad and its branch in Kansas crossed the western limit of the buffalo range in 1868, and railways ran from the East Coast to the foothills of the Rocky Mountains. In the next sixteen years, nearly 60 million buffalo were killed.

Market hunters killed the buffalo for hides and tongues. Tanneries paid as much as three dollars a hide for fresh hides, and twenty-five cents per tongue. Armed with powerful, long-range rifles, a single hunter could kill as many as 250 buffalo a day.

Buffalo tongues were sold in fine restaurants across the country. Buffalo leather drive belts for machinery were an industrial standard, and the bones were ground for fertilizer. Soon buffalo hunters had year-round work.

By the 1880s, as many as 5,000 hunters and skinners were involved in the buffalo trade. By 1884, the herds were gone. In Kansas, dealers paid $2.5 million to buy buffalo bones to be used in various carbon works around the country. It takes about a hundred carcasses to make a ton of bones, and the price was about eight dollars a ton. Kansan dealers bought the bones of 31 million buffalo.

The buffalo were replaced with cattle, another grazer, so the nutrient cycles were not interrupted. But the water cycle did not fare as well. Buffalo act delicately by the waterside: they walk down to drink, carefully watching out for wolves, and they leave. Cattle will spend all day in a stream, churning the riparian edge into a muddy wasteland. In drier states where public land is leased for cattle grazing, as much as 98 percent of the streamside vegetation has been stripped by cattle, degrading water quality and removing the riparian edge, the most productive fraction of the landscape.

Fish were also industriously harvested. Sturgeon, for example, were among the most common fish on the Atlantic seaboard as late as the 1850s. Then it was discovered that American sturgeon eggs made caviar that was almost as good as Russian caviar. The swim bladder of the sturgeon is used to make isinglass, which can be used for a flexible waterproof window in a surrey, to make a very pure gelatin used in desserts, and to clarify wine and beer. Females filled with eggs were particularly valued. Nets, guns, harpoons, and even bombs were used on the big spawning runs with such attention that in 1890, the harvest from the Delaware River alone was more than 5 million pounds. By 1920, sturgeon were rare.

Alligators once maintained dense populations throughout

their range, seen on the banks of every southern waterway; their sluggish forms were often mistaken for stranded logs. Alligators were rarely killed until the Civil War, when the Confederate Army outfitted some of its soldiers with alligator shoes and saddles. The demand for skins did not end with the war. In 1884, a government report on the fisheries stated, "Alligator hunting is growing less and less successful in Florida as the game diminishes in numbers. From simply being a pastime it has become a regular business, and thousands upon thousands of these creatures are now annually slaughtered for their hides and teeth. . . . At the rate the alligator family is now disappearing, not many years will elapse before the supply will be wholly exhausted."

Elegant slippers and boots, suitcases, pocketbooks, and music rolls provided a robust demand for skins. In addition, there was a steady market for live baby alligators less than six inches long that were sold as pets for home aquariums, and "for curious mementoes to be sent to distant friends."

In 1922, Karl Schmidt of Chicago's Field Museum of Natural History wrote that "steady hunting during the past 60 years, the robbing of their nest for eggs, the capture of large numbers of newly hatched young for 'souvenirs' and wanton slaughter by so-called sportsmen, have decimated the species to such an extent that few places are now left where it can still be said to be abundant."

Mammals, birds, fish, reptiles, mollusks, and even insects were eradicated from the landscape during the late 1800s. Whitetail deer and turkeys were gone from most states east of the Mississippi River. Commercial crews had emptied the shores, forests, and plains of wildlife, shipped them by rail to market, and sold them. Even many songbirds were heavily hunted for food.

The forests were stripped out as well. During the 1800s, the United States was home to the largest timber-exporting ports in the world. As with market hunters, the loggers' only real barrier was the transportation system: if there was a way to get timber to the water, an area was logged.

Until 1850, small local sawmills supplied most of the wood used throughout the United States, and the trees often came from farm woodlots or from clearing for agriculture. The industrial cutting of forests for export was pioneered in Maine, which became the world's premier timber source for about twenty years because of geographical factors that allowed trees from the middle of the state to be inexpensively transported to the coast. The western tablelands were relatively flat, creating straight rivers that were linked together with lakes. The rivers had high spring flows from snowmelt, and the granite bedrock channeled the snowmelt directly into the streams. This provided forceful spring floods that pushed the logs to the mills. Trees were cut and trimmed in late fall and winter, when snow provided a low-friction surface for horses or oxen to skid the logs to the nearest river. Once the ice melted in the spring, loggers floated the logs downstream on swollen spring flows to sawmills on the coast. The rivers brought newly cut lumber downriver, where a fleet of vessels carried it to cities on the eastern seaboard, the Caribbean, and South America. The sawmills provided off-season jobs for Maine farmers, while the lumber camps provided a market for their beans and potatoes.

Bangor, Maine, near the mouth of the Penobscot River, was the world's largest timber port in the 1830s, when a few big businessmen were vying for control of Maine's forests. They bought up whole townships, built sawmills, and competed over the construction of dams and canals, redirecting water to serve their needs. In Maine, industries based on processing the state's natural resources—including wood, ice, granite, lime, slate, and fish—created fortunes for a few businessmen, while poorly paid laborers did the work.

Technological advances allowed forests to be harvested more efficiently. Steam engines allowed loggers to cut trees farther away from water and still haul them to the riverside. With circular and band saws, trees were processed with less waste. Maine forests were soon felled, and by 1840 the seat of the lumber industry moved to upstate New York and Pennsylvania. In 1850, New York State forests produced a billion board feet a year, moving the lumber down the Erie Canal and the Hudson River. By 1860, the center of timber production had moved to the Great Lakes, but 3,376 vessels still docked at Bangor and loaded more than 200 million board feet of lumber. By 1880, the Great Lakes region dominated logging, with Michigan producing more lumber than any other state. The lumber from the Great Lakes region was sold in New York City, which became the largest lumber market in the world.

The population of the United States tripled between 1850 and 1900, reaching 76 million. Rural communities were able to use local wood, but cities used large quantities of lumber that had to be brought in from remote forests. The people who settled the treeless prairies needed wood for houses, barns, fences, outbuildings, and fuel. Farm fences had to be made of wood or stone before the invention of barbed wire in 1867, and the prairies are stoneless. By 1850, there were about 3.2 million miles of wooden fences in the United States, which is enough to build a fence to the moon (or back) thirteen times. The railways added over 230,000 miles of track in the next sixty years, using as much as a quarter of the country's total timber production.

As the distance between consumers and forests increased,

logging and milling wood became large-scale, industrial operations. Between 1850 and 1910, lumber production rose from 5.4 billion board feet to 44.5 billion board feet annually. The country's forests were cut and sold for private profit.

Forests clean the water, through filtration, transpiration, and protective streamside vegetation. When forestland is changed into farmland, the waterways carry less water and more silt, there are fewer places for animals and birds to live, and the soil is more likely to move from the land into the waterways. Half of the forestland east of the Mississippi is now used as farmland, and land that once improved water quality now degrades it.

Wild animals and old-growth forests are the embodiment of nature. When Europeans moved to the New World and built railways, they transformed nature into money by selling the animals and trees. A few families got rich and built enduring fortunes, including the Astors (furs) and the Weyerhausers (forests). But money is fluid, and will flow to the next opportunity. Natural resources are more fragile. The harvests of the buffalo, passenger pigeons, curlews, and oysters were one-time events, and these animals never returned.

The American landscape was altered by their removal; more subtly, nutrient cycles were disrupted, sometimes permanently. A plant living on the Plains is less likely to enjoy phosphorus dropped by a migratory bird. Oysters no longer filter the water in the nation's bays and estuaries, and the fisheries are lacking the nutrient boost provided by whale feces. Half of the eastern forests have been removed, and those that remain are less likely to be pocked with meadows. By simplifying our local environment and harvesting the living pathways used by nutrients that life depends on, we degraded our waterways, forests, and fields.

Those early days of easy harvest carried a lesson: without regulation, people emptied the water, land, and skies of animals. By the end of the 1800s, there were no catamounts or wolves east of the Mississippi. The eastern elk was extinct, moose had disappeared, and deer had been gone from New England forests for more than a generation. Nature was admired for her scenic beauty, but forests were not valued as habitat, and wild animals were not seen as a fundamental element of a forest ecosystem. Eastern forests remained empty scenery for more than fifty years.

6

Erasing Nature

If nature is embodied in natural ecosystems and native species, then agriculture is decidedly unnatural. Agriculture is the way we organize the environment to make food and fiber. Farmers take a piece of land and replace the existing flora and fauna with species they choose themselves. And it's almost always the same few species: according to the United Nations' Food and Agriculture Organization, twelve plant species provide 75 percent of our total food supply, and only fifteen of the 50,000 known species of animals account for over 90 percent of all livestock production. Humans and our few domesticated plants and animals use up most of the Earth's fertile habitat. There are surprisingly small populations of wild animals left in the world, and they usually live on the least productive land. Agriculture has edged nature almost out of existence. As a result, the way we practice agriculture has an enormous impact on what little nature is left.

Until recently, farming had required unending amounts of labor. Trees had to be cut and the stumps grubbed; the earth had to be de-rocked, turned, planted, cultivated, weeded, watered, and then the hard work of harvest began. Before the internal combustion engine was invented, the only practical sources of farm labor were domesticated animals and humans. Repetitive, physically demanding, and never-ending labor led agricultural societies to embrace the caste system, feudalism, slavery, and eventually automation.

In the New World, European colonists tried to re-create pastoral England with fields of wheat and barley for bread and beer, and pastured farm animals for meat, eggs, and milk. The colonists' privately owned flocks and herds needed barns for shelter, fenced grazing, and fields hewn from the forest to grow winter hay and fodder. Native Americans harvested wild animals that lived independently in the forest, but the colonists held wilderness and its denizens in low regard. Replacing ancient forests with a civilized landscape of pastures, fields, farmyards, and woodlots was seen as God's work.

From the very start, Europeans practiced two different types of agriculture in the Americas. There was subsistence agriculture, where the yeoman farmers lauded by Thomas Jefferson grew a variety of crops for their own consumption or for local sale. Families brewed their own beer, made their own bread and butter, and kept a few pigs, chickens, and a milk cow or a flock of sheep. Oxen, mules, or horses were used for power, while parents and children provided the labor. Then there was plantation agriculture, typically an international business where a resident labor force grew products that were sold abroad. The colonies had everything necessary for large-scale agriculture—a temperate climate, fertile soil, and plenty of water—but there weren't any peasants. Plantation agriculture, as practiced by Thomas Jefferson (who preferred imported wines to homebrewed beer), used enslaved people for resident labor.

For the first 300 years of European colonization, more Africans crossed the Atlantic than Europeans. The most comprehensive analysis of shipping records over the course of the slave trade is the Trans-Atlantic Slave Trade Database, edited by David Eltis and David Richardson. Ship by ship, the database includes information on almost 36,000 slaving voyages. Of the 12.5 million Africans shipped to the New World, about 10.7 million survived the Atlantic passage. Over 95 percent of the people shipped from Africa sailed to the Caribbean and South America, with less than 5 percent disembarking in North America. In total, about 450,000 Africans arrived in the United States before 1808, when importing slaves was outlawed.

From the first days of colonization, New World plantations were part of a global money web based on enslaved Africans, North American land, and European markets. Enslaved people were often mortgaged, and they worked alongside indentured servants and wage laborers to grow tobacco. In the 1600s, landowners in Virginia and the Chesapeake Bay region paid their farm expenses with loans from London bankers and delivered tobacco on consignment to the London docks.

By 1808, the total number of people who had arrived in the United States from abroad included about 450,000 Africans and 680,000 Europeans. Nearly half of all European immigrants arrived as indentured servants, typically bound for three to seven years and usually under the age of twenty-five. Indenture—a contract that binds a person to service for a specific length of time—became less common after the American Revolution, when the relative cost of transoceanic transport dropped and people could afford to buy their own boat tickets. With fewer indentured servants, slavery became more entrenched.

Tobacco, rice, indigo, cotton, and sugar plantations spread from Virginia all the way to the Mississippi floodplains. Each of these crops requires labor-intensive processing after harvest, which provided year-round work for a captive labor force. Cured tobacco, fermented indigo, hulled rice, and deseeded cotton were mostly exported to Europe; molasses and refined sugar were sold in the United States.

Enslaved people and indentured servants did the plantation handwork of tilling, planting, hoeing, harvesting, and processing, while oxen, horses, and mules provided the nation's agricultural power. Oxen—castrated bulls—were more common than horses until the mid-1800s. Oxen can pull very heavy loads, slowly and steadily, and can clear land, plow heavy soils, and break sod. A plow ox would typically work hard for seven to ten years, and then be fattened up for a few restful months before slaughter.

For thousands of years, oxen have pulled moldboard plows that cut the soil with a metal point called a share or plowshare. The curl of soil is flipped over by the moldboard, making a furrow—a *V* cut into the field with freshly over-turned earth on one side of it. This brings fresh nutrients to the surface, smothers weeds, loosens the soil, and incorporates manure and crop residue into the root zone. Plowing warms the earth in the spring, speeding germination.

In addition to plowing, oxen hauled loads. They are slower than mules or horses, and cheaper: in 1850, a yoke of oxen cost about $50, while a good team of mules could run $200 (about $5,800 today). Oxen can work well eating grass, while working horses and mules need grain to maintain condition.

Oxen are strong and their pace is measured; like mules, they cannot be rushed. Horses are much faster than oxen, and can easily be worked to death. The average lifespan of a horse is twenty-five to thirty years, today. But before the widespread adoption of the internal combustion engine, the average working life of a horse was as low as three and a half years. The horse's speed and its willingness to be overworked made it the preferred source of power in the early days of the Industrial Revolution.

The *Aid Book to Engineering Enterprise Abroad*, published in 1878, provides an engineering analysis of the lifespan of a working horse:

> In London, a two-horse car, running 70 miles per day, usu-ally requires ten horses, each horse thus having 14 miles of work. But to maintain this service, eleven horses are pro-vided so as to allow for occasional rests. But where the cars are light and the gradients very favourable, horses are worked 16, 18 and even 20 miles per day. . . . The London General Omnibus Company, by careful selection of their horses, and proper treatment, raised the working-life of the animals from three and a half years to five years.

Enslaved people were routinely worked to death as well.

In total, about 680,000 Europeans and 450,000 Africans had arrived in the United States before the first census was taken in 1810. That year, the census counted almost 7.2 million total Americans, including 3 million white men, 2.78 million white women, and 1.2 million enslaved and 200,000 free people of African descent (the US Census did not count Native Americans until 1860). It was a time of bad nutrition, rampant disease, deadly childbirth, and harsh upbringing. If the survival and reproductive rates for slaves were equal to those of other early Americans, then we can calculate how many people of African descent should have been living in the United States in 1810. With comparable longevity and reproduction, there would have been about 3.8 million African Americans in 1810. Instead, the census counted 1.4 million African descendants. By 1810, this country was already missing 2.4 million black people.

Plantation economics were unforgiving, and plantation agriculture was a rich man's occupation. At a time when field labor cost up to $10 per month plus room and board, an enslaved person cost about $1,000. Slaves were an expensive investment. In Louisiana, the sugar plantations were funded by mortgage-backed bonds guaranteed by the state and sold to investors in Britain, Europe, and even New York; the bonds paid 5 percent interest, and the work was so brutal that the average lifespan of an enslaved man on a big sugar plantation was seven years. A seminal 1958 study of antebellum economics showed that a single enslaved agricultural worker who bore five children for sale over thirty years earned her owner nearly 7 percent on his capital investment. Plantation agriculture wasn't all about the crops. Instead, agricultural profit margins were slim (as they are today), and plantation profitability was often based on selling slaves. As Thomas Jefferson wrote, a "woman who brings a child every two years is more profitable than the best man on the farm."

Thomas Jefferson's experience as a plantation owner illustrates the point. Jefferson inherited his 5,000-acre plantation, Monticello, at the age of twenty-one. When he died in 1826 at the age of eighty-three, his lifetime of agricultural enterprise had created debts of $107,000, equivalent to about $2.5 million in 2015. These debts were paid after his death by auctioning off his land, buildings, and slaves. In the end, Thomas Jefferson's heirs sold humans to pay for his French wines.

Labor and power—how to get the work done—is one intractable problem with agriculture, and soil fertility is another. The narrow profit margins for slave-grown commodities led landowners to exploit the fact that the new country was land-rich. Instead of spending labor and money to maintain soil fertility by adding organic matter and rotating crops, slaves carved new fields out of the forest whenever the soil became depleted, usually every ten to twenty years. By the early 1800s, much of the new nation's farmland was nutrient deficient and eroding. Overgrazing, poor crop rotation, and scant fertilization had worn out the fields.

Crop rotation may sound esoteric, but every farmer sees that a field planted annually with the same crop gives a smaller harvest every year. Pests settle in and multiply, and without precise fertilization, it's easy for soil micronutrients to become depleted. When a field grows a different crop each year, last year's insects hatch to find the wrong food, and the exact menu of necessary nutrients changes annually, allowing the soil to replenish itself.

Since the Middle Ages, Europeans have practiced a three-year rotation where one year a field is planted in rye or wheat (for bread), the next year in barley or oats (for beer or porridge), and the third year the field is left fallow, or unplanted. Most farm animals were slaughtered in the fall, because there was too little feed to support a herd through winter.

Charles Townshend, the elegant Second Viscount Townshend, popularized a new system of land management in the 1700s: instead of leaving fields unplanted every third year, "Turnip" Townshend (so-called because that was his favorite topic of conversation) advocated a four-crop rotation between wheat for bread, barley for beer, turnips for cattle, and clover to add nitrogen to the soil and for grazing. This system allowed livestock to be kept year-round and increased the amount of manure available for fertilizer. By adding nitrogen and organic matter to the soil with manure, and by planting nitrogen-fixing crops like clover, crop yields increased along with the farmer's herds.

Fertilizers include manure, seaweed, or other nutriments, or land can be planted with clover and other legumes that have little nodules on their roots containing symbiotic bacteria, called rhizobia, that fix nitrogen. When the plant dies, nitrogen in the nodules is released into the soil, making it available to other plants. Legumes fertilize the soil, and when they're included in a crop rotation, there's no need for a fallow year.

The benefits of fertilizer, crop rotation, and a legume cover crop were understood when the East Coast was first plowed, but land was abundant and there was no obvious need to conserve it. In addition, there was no scientific body of knowledge to help people farm.

In 1760, the first book of agricultural advice in North America was published in Boston: *Essays upon Field-Husbandry in New-England as It Is or May Be Ordered* by Reverend Jared Eliot. He advocated using fertilizer, planting legumes, plowing deeply, and ditching the lowlands to make fields. The next American book of agricultural advice, also written by a clergyman, was published thirty years later: Reverend Samuel Deane's *The New England Farmer; or, Georgical Dictionary: Containing a Compendious Account of the Ways and Methods in Which the Important Art of Husbandry, in All Its Various Branches, Is, or May Be, Practised, to the Greatest Advantage, in This Country* helped the new nation's farmers meet the demands of an expanding marketplace.

Agricultural production was bumping along until 1815, when Mount Tambora erupted. This Indonesian volcano was the most explosive event in human history, creating an enormous sun-obscuring plume of ash that circled the Earth at the equator in a matter of weeks. The plume then drifted towards the poles, cooling the Earth for three years. Tambora's layer of volcanic ash darkened the sky, average global temperatures fell between 3°F and 6°F, and rainfall patterns changed dramatically.

Global cooling was an agricultural catastrophe. The year of 1816 became known as the "Year There Was No Summer." Frosts and floods killed crops throughout the northern hemisphere, and many people went hungry. In Vermont, 1816 was remembered as "Eighteen-Hundred-and-Froze-to-Death," the year that people ate groundhogs and nettles. There were killing frosts every month, and people left New England in droves for the promised lands of Ohio and Pennsylvania. Across the Atlantic, the Rhine River rose nine and a half feet above its usual level, leaving whole villages under water. In July 22, 1816, the *Times* of London reported that in Germany, "hopes of a very fine harvest have been almost ruined. The loss in hay, corn, tobacco and pulse is incalculable." On August 2, 1816, the *Times* reported from the Netherlands that "indescribable misery has taken place, so that the lower classes of people have been obliged to feed on herbage and grains."

The worldwide failure of agriculture in the cold, dark years after the eruption of Mount Tambora spurred interest in agricultural science. In 1818, agricultural knowledge was codified in the *Farmers' Almanac*, a handbook printed in Morristown, New Jersey. It told farmers when to plant which crops and how to cultivate and fertilize them. People were eager to adopt scientific practices, and quickly embraced both the *Farmers' Almanac* and the reverends' agriculture books from the 1700s.

Fertilizer is part of our national mythology: schoolchildren are taught that Squanto showed the Pilgrims how to plant each corn hill with three fishes, so the corn would grow strong. This story is likely apocryphal, but perhaps it's so widely known because it speaks to the bone-deep human urge to increase crop yields. Fertilizer is like pixie dust that might grow giant vegetables, and long before Miracle-Gro swept the market, every gardener believed in the possibility of a perfect soil amendment. Manure is one of the oldest, easiest fertilizers except that it has to be mixed with a carbon source (like yard wastes or animal bedding) and composted before it can be used as a soil amendment. The pile heats up as the manure breaks down, and then the pile needs to be inverted so the wastes and weed seeds are uniformly sterilized. Over the years, Bob has composted mountains of cow manure, horse manure, and sheep manure, turning the piles neatly with a tractor bucket. (This year, the manure from a flock of forty sheep is scheduled for delivery in April.) Composted manure is an old favorite, but fertilizer goes by fashion as well. Volcanic dust, water from the bottom of a pair of seventy-gallon tanks stocked with carp, beneficial bacterial brewed up in the next town and sold by the gallon: I've tried them all, because the exact combination of supplements to make your plants flourish is always a bit of a mystery.

The three main macronutrients in any fertilizer are nitrogen, phosphorus, and potassium. At the time Mount Tambora erupted, nitrogen sources included blood, fish, and manure; phosphorus from rock phosphate, bones, fish, and seaweed; potassium from greensand, kelp, and ash. Agricultural science promoted these fertilizers (still popular today, and I have sacks of most of them), but the favorite product was South American guano.

Guano (from the Quechua *wanu*) is the accumulated feces of seabirds, bats, or seals that is aged and ready for direct application. The social behavior of these animals creates guano in huge, concentrated, ever-increasing piles. Made almost entirely of nitrogen, phosphate, and potassium, guano is an ideal fertilizer.

Peruvian guano has been used as a fertilizer for centuries. Garcilaso de la Vega wrote in the 1609 *Royal Commentary of the Incas*, "They use no other manure but the dung of sea birds, of which large and small varieties occur on the coast of Peru in such enormous flocks that they seem incredible to anyone who has not seen them." The Humboldt Current carries cold, nutrient-rich Antarctic waters up the Peruvian coast that feeds shoals of anchoveta, an anchovy relative. For thousands of years, millions of cormorants, pelicans, and boobies ate anchovetas and shat on a chain of coastal islands, where the extremely dry climate preserved millions of tons of bird feces. The largest reserves of marine phosphorus in the world were piled into mesas more than 150 feet high on the Chincha Islands off Peru's southern Pacific coast.

Alexander von Humboldt, the Prussian naturalist and geographer, was the first European to promote guano. He was in Peru taking temperature measurements of the soon-to-be-named Humboldt Current, and often went down to the piers where guano was being unloaded. Humboldt brought samples of guano back to Europe in 1804, and turned them over to "the best analytic chemists of the day." His widely read essays on the efficacy of fertilizing with guano resulted in a guano boom. As Gregory T. Cushman wrote in *Guano and the Opening of the Pacific World*, thus began the world's guano age. Representatives from Britain's Antony Gibbs and Sons formed a joint venture with the Peruvian government in 1841, and soon about 300 ships laden with guano were leaving Peru every year.

The Peruvian government used convicts, indentured Chinese, and kidnapped Polynesians to mine their guano islands. The first group of seventy-nine indentured Chinese workers arrived in 1849, and eventually more than 100,000 indentured workers were imported from China to harvest Peruvian guano. The Peruvians and Chileans nearly depopulated Easter Island and Tongareva, kidnapping whole villages and forcing them to live and work mining bird feces on the Chincha Islands.

Peru's guano boom lasted from 1840 to 1870, with 12 million tons of guano shipped to Europe and North America, valued at $500 million. In 1877, A. J. Duffield noted that "it is only in Peru that we find an epoch of Gold and Silver juxtaposed with an Age of Manure." European-style agriculture's dependence on guano deposits faded after 1909 when Fritz Haber developed the Haber-Bosch process of industrial nitrogen fixation. Today, ammonia-based fertilizers are responsible for feeding perhaps one-third to one-half of the Earth's population.

Fertilization and crop rotation are simple ways to increase crop yields, but reducing the labor required to run a farm took machines, invention by invention. Until Jethro Tull's seed drill was invented in 1701, a field had to be sown with the seeds scattered by hand and the ground harrowed to cover the seeds, or hand-planted with a few seeds put into a small hole and covered, hole after hole after hole (stoop labor at its finest). A seed drill efficiently plants the seeds and covers them to a specific depth, ensuring that more seeds sprout. It takes far less labor than hand planting, and seed drills became common in the 1800s. In modern-day Vermont, a single seed drill is shared by the whole neighborhood.

As plants grow, it is useful to hoe between the rows to kill weeds and loosen the soil, and Jethro Tull's horse-drawn hoe was the first time a field could be cultivated with horses instead of humans. Grain was harvested with scythes, and then threshed in a labor-intensive process of beating the harvested grain to separate the grain from the stalks, and to separate each grain from its protective husk, or chaff. Grain was threshed with a tool made of two sticks of wood with a hinge in the middle, unchanged since Roman times. A man could flail seven bushels of wheat, eight of rye, fifteen of barley, eighteen of oats, or twenty of buckwheat in a day.

For 2,000 years, about a quarter of all agricultural labor was used for threshing with everyone wielding the same stupid flail until Andrew Meikle's steam-driven thresher, patented in 1788, became common in the 1800s. Thomas Jefferson owned three threshing machines by the time he died, and ordered one of Meikle's threshers from London in 1792. It took nearly a year to arrive and was eagerly awaited. In a letter to James Madison, Jefferson wrote,

> I expect every day to receive from Mr. Pinckney the model of the Scotch threshing machine. . . . Mr. P. [Pinckney] writes

me word that the machine from which my model is taken threshes 8. quarters (64. bushels) of oats an hour, with 4. horses and 4 men. I hope to get it in time to have one erected at Monticello to clean out the present crop.

In the 1800s, new farm machines reduced the need for both power and labor. A hundred bushels of wheat required 300 labor hours in 1800, 50 labor hours in 1900, and 3 labor hours in 2000. Farming became much more efficient, and better transportation allowed crops to reach local markets. When Jefferson ran Monticello, it cost less to ship a crop to Europe than to move it thirty miles inland. Transportation slowly improved with turnpikes, canals, and finally railroads. First, the turnpike network of privately owned and operated roads expanded rapidly in the early 1800s. Water transportation improved when canals connected different river systems. The Erie Canal, completed in 1825, connected the Great Lakes to the Hudson River and allowed lumber, coal, and hay from the entire Great Lakes region to be barged to New York City. The Illinois and Michigan Canal connected the Great Lakes to the Mississippi River in 1848. Finally, railroads superseded the canal system and trains generally brought crops to market in the second half of the 1800s.

Both land and population expanded dramatically. The 1803 Louisiana Purchase and the subsequent destruction and eviction of Native American tribes from Florida to Minnesota brought vast tracts into European-style cultivation. To farm the newly depopulated land, the federal government issued 160-acre lots to about 400,000 families through the Homestead Act. The railroads were deeded millions of acres of public land, and to sell it they provided low fares from Europe to coax hundreds of thousands of farmers from Scandinavia,

Germany, and Great Britain to immigrate. The number of farms in the United States tripled between 1860 and 1905, from 2 to 6 million.

Since then, the amount of cultivated and grazed land in the United States has held steady. Almost one in every five acres in the continental United States is plowed as cropland, and an additional two in every five acres are grazed as rangeland. Native plants and animals are excluded from land used for cultivated crops like vegetables or grains. Orchard crops like fruits or nuts can have native vegetation under the trees, and grazing land for cattle or sheep can be shared by a variety of native plants and animals. Eating grass-fed meat, fruits, and nuts can support native ecosystems, but eating vegetables or grain generally does not. Instead, our chosen plants and animals have replaced nature in nearly every river valley and on the most productive land. Much of the land reserved for wildlife is desert scrub and steep mountains.

The expansion of farmed land was accompanied by a second wave of agricultural improvement. Land grant colleges date back to 1862, when Abraham Lincoln signed legislation that granted each state public land to fund colleges of agriculture and the mechanical arts. Since then, every state has a center of agricultural expertise. The extension service started in the 1880s with the intent of providing an agricultural expert for every county in the United States.

The extension service gave local farmers access to the latest advances and varieties, and it still works well. Today, if your plants or animals are hit by an outbreak of disease, the extension agent will tell you who else is affected and explain your treatment options. You can bring in insects, damaged fruit, or diseased leaves and have your problem diagnosed. You can bring in your soil for analysis, get the test results explained, and have the appropriate amendments for your acres laid out like a shopping list. The extension service still provides every citizen with a personal agricultural consultant, no appointment necessary and no bill, in nearly every county. My agent is a local hero; he'd blush if he knew how much people truly appreciate his guidance. I have questions for him every year, and they're always answered.

It is difficult to grow things well, and takes both information and hard work. Bob planted an orchard in Vermont on a west-facing slope above the house. We planted a total of 160 trees on twenty-five-foot centers, filling less than three acres. He got the trees from David Fried, a nurseryman who was making a big effort to propagate old-time varieties of apples. David spliced twigs from heirloom apple trees gathered from abandoned orchards onto a cold-hardy Russian rootstock, making sturdy northern trees. According to him, certain varieties prefer to be planted together; some were good for the crest of a hill; and some varieties needed to be planted in a location with less wind.

The trees arrived bare-root and we had to get them into the ground as quickly as possible, so there was a long checklist to be completed before they came. We needed 160 holes, but learned that when you pile soil from the hole onto the ground, too much dirt is lost in the grass to refill the hole. Bob got a stack of burlap bags from Green Mountain Coffee Roasters to pile the dirt on, one per hole. The trees had to be top-dressed with compost, so he got a truckload of horse manure and turned the pile twice before the trees arrived. We bought a hundred pounds of black rock phosphate and a hundred pounds of Jersey Greensand.

The trees were laid out on a twenty-five-foot grid that sprawled over three small slopes interrupted by two swales.

Bob paced out the orchard and marked each hole with a stake, a task done with such concentration that twenty years later, he can still pace out twenty-five feet to within a few inches. Each tree needed a hole roughly a foot in diameter and a foot and a half deep, so we hired a man to dig them and leave a pile of soil neatly mounded on burlap beside each one.

The adult size of a tree is based on the rootstock, and you can choose any variety in either dwarf, semi-dwarf, or standard size. The rootstock determines a tree's cold tolerance, and how quickly it grows. We chose standard trees, hoping to maximize the yield per acre.

The trees arrived in bundles of a dozen whips with bare roots, wrapped in burlap that had to be kept moist. Each tree had a squiggled taproot of less than a foot, and a slender whip above that was no more than four feet high. For planting, each hole got a handful of Jersey Greensand, a handful of black rock phosphate, and two cups of a locally made organic fertilizer. Adding a little soil and some water to the hole allowed us to mix it into a slurry, and then it was a two-person job: one person holding the tree in place, and the other filling the hole with soil and water, building up the soil around the tree until the hole is filled. When the whip is straight, upright, and centered in the hole, you form a ridge of soil and grass around the edge of the hole to hold water in place, and move on to the next tree.

From that day on, the biggest problem was keeping the young trees watered. Bob bought a 300-gallon tank for the back of the truck, with a hose attached to the tank. He watered each tree once a week for their first summer and fall, and once a month through the winter and the next year.

There was no need for a deer fence in that location. Instead, mice were the tree-killers. They would scamper over the top of the snow, and stop by each whip to girdle the trees by eating the cambium layer, often six or eight inches above the ground. Each whip had a screen around its spindly little trunk from about an inch underground to a foot or so aboveground to protect it from mice, and later to protect it from being stripped by the weed whacker when cutting the grass low around each tree. Finally, Bob painted each tree's little trunk with white latex paint on the south side, because the winter sun on dark bark can be so hot that the bark splits open, wounding the cambium layer.

You couldn't believe how fast those trees grew. Pruning is serious business, because you cannot alter a tree's eventual height, but you can determine its shape. The natural shape of an apple tree does not maximize fruit production, and the purpose of pruning is to help the tree form a strong framework. The first pruning, the winter after the whips took root, was to ensure that each tree only had one leader and to cut the whip to stimulate the growth of the remaining buds, encouraging branching.

The second winter pruning is to reduce any legginess. You cut branches that are too vertical and one branch of every forked limb. The young trees grow quickly, and require steady attention to guide them into the open, strong-limbed shape that will produce the most fruit. Your goal as a pruner is to allow each tree to express its true nature. Pruning is tough.

There's nothing easy about this project. You have to choose your crop, varieties, and soil amendments, then you source materials, figure out the labor, and pay attention for years to make a profit. And then the pests descend.

With larger fields, more farms, and monoculture—the practice of raising a single crop in an area—pests and diseases flourished. The Colorado potato beetle, indigenous to a small region in the southwestern United States, spread to cover about

3 million square miles of North America. Pests multiplied, and hunkered down.

Organic pesticides have been used since the 1600s when rotenone, extracted from the roots of several tropical and subtropical plant species, became popular in Europe and the United States for controlling caterpillars. Pyrethrums, called Persian or Dalmatian Insect Powder and made from imported chrysanthemums, were dusted on aphids and caterpillars. Tobacco extract was used to control ants and lace bugs, and it works (if you want to get rid of an ant's nest, boil up a pack of chewing tobacco in a big pot of water, and pour the tobacco tea on the nest).

Toxic inorganic pesticides debuted in 1867 with the invention of Paris green, a mixture of arsenic and copper sulfate. This was the beginning of chemical warfare against crop pests, and many other compounds followed. It was also the peak of horse labor. There were 25 million horses and mules in the United States in 1910, more than one for every four US citizens. One-quarter of all cropland was used to grow hay and oats for horse feed.

Horses were replaced function by function. Streetcars replaced horse-drawn omnibuses by the 1900s, cars took over for the horse and buggy next, and motorized trucks finally hauled more freight than horse carts in the 1920s. Tractors had been invented decades earlier, but were too big and costly for farmers to buy: they weighed more than an elephant and were nearly as expensive.

Henry Ford introduced the Fordson in 1917, a smaller, cheaper tractor for the masses. Round after round of new technologies followed. Power lifts, rubber tires, and diesel engines eventually made tractors more practical than horses. Every tractor displaced about five horses, and it was not until the 1940s that tractors provided more horsepower than animals.

Cultivation was confined to the East Coast for the first 200 years of settlement, wearing out the soil, but in the 1800s, millions of immigrants took their oxen west and plowed the Plains. By the 1900s, mechanization reduced the need for farm labor, horses replaced oxen, and 60 percent of all land was used to produce food. Since then, our footprint on the landscape has remained the same, but we produce much more food per acre, and feed about 10 million indolent horses today instead of 25 million hardworking horses a century ago.

We have taken the best three of every five acres for domesticated plants and animals, and left much of the rest as forestland. But to make the country safe for cattle and sheep, we killed nearly all of the large predators, everywhere. Grizzlies and black bears, mountain lions, lynx and bobcats, wolves, coyotes, badgers, and wolverines were almost eradicated. When you remove the apex predator from an ecosystem, populations of their corresponding prey species multiply, with unpredictable outcomes. When wolves were returned to Yellowstone, they hunted for elk and deer along the river's edge. The grazers no longer stripped the riparian vegetation, so young adult beavers had places to hide during those vulnerable months when they leave their home ponds to set up dams of their own. The wetlands multiplied and more water was retained in the valley, increasing the land's productivity. In Yellowstone, wolves raised the water table. Apex predators reorder an ecosystem in unexpected ways.

I wish I could say that agriculture and nature have maintained an uneasy truce since the early 1900s, but that would be incorrect. Removing predators across the continent upended natural ecosystems. Nature was rearranged, and has not been restored.

7

Conserving Nature

People loved scenery in the 1800s, and they liked looking at it in large groups. Niagara Falls had been attracting tourists since the early 1800s, and by the 1860s there were six different rail lines bringing an annual influx of 60,000 visitors. A suspension bridge provided a splendid view, and there were many grand hotels in the nearby village: Cataract House, Empire House, International Hotel, Vedder, American Hotel,

Monteagle Hotel, and Niagara Park Place (boasting reading rooms, billiards, a soda fountain, and a bar). In the next decade, Niagara Falls became the greatest tourist attraction in the Americas, with over 100,000 visitors a year.

The falls were splendid, but the surrounding area was a huckster's dream. In 1860, William Dean Howells described Niagara Falls as a place where "peddlers hawked their wares, and sideshows erected at every vantage point were filled with freaks assembled from all over the world, so that the vicinity of the cataract had taken on the aspect of a colossal carnival." (He admired the five-legged calf in a nearby tent, offered as a secondary wonder.)

Mark Twain wrote of "competing hackmen, aggressive salesmen, and Indian craftsmen soliciting tourists in shops, in front of hotels, and even throughout the sloped banks of the Park." As a final insult, locals built high fences around much of Prospect Point so tourists had to buy a ticket to see the waterfall. Americans appreciated natural wonders, and were adept at making a profit from them. But the area surrounding Niagara Falls showed that privately managed vistas were soon ruined.

California, like New York, was the site of natural wonders that were widely admired. California became a state in 1850, and two remarkable natural features—the giant sequoia groves and Yosemite Valley—were publicized soon thereafter. The American public learned about the sequoias from a hunter who was hired to supply meat for the employees of the Union Water Company, a mining outfit in Calaveras County (neighbor to Mark Twain's jumping frog). Augustus T. Dowd was tracking a wounded bear when he stumbled across a grove of giant sequoias in the spring of 1852. A June 1852 article in the *Sonoran Herald* described the Bunyanesque groves, and was soon reprinted in San Francisco's *L'Echo du Pacifique* and other newspapers across the country. By July 23, 1853, news of the giant sequoias had crossed the Atlantic and was printed in the London *Athenaeum* (oddly enough, seeds from sequoias and redwoods had arrived decades earlier). The largest tree in the north grove (which now includes about a hundred trees in Calaveras State Park) was named the Discovery Tree, and was cut down in 1853 to make a dance floor. Five men worked for more than three weeks to fell it. It was 1,244 years old.

Yosemite Valley had been known to fur traders since the 1840s. In 1855, British immigrant and soon-to-be journalist James Hutchings organized an expedition to visit the valley that included Thomas Ayres, an artist known for his Gold Rush drawings. They took the natives' trail into the valley, and stopped at what became known as Inspiration Point so that Ayres could sketch the view that became the first published drawing of the valley. In July 1856, Hutchings's report of the trip appeared in the first issue of *Hutchings' Illustrated California Magazine*. He described Yo-ham-i-te Valley for the world, and told the story of how the Yo-ham-i-te Indians had been removed from the region. The same year, Thomas Ayres exhibited a series of paintings of Yosemite in New York City.

The world took note. New York publisher Horace Greeley visited in 1859, and reported in 1860 that "the Yosemite Valley (or Gorge) is the most unique and majestic of nature's marvels."

A band of admirers of the valley started agitating to preserve Yosemite as a state park. Landscape architect Frederick Law Olmsted, temporarily living in California, was an advocate for Yosemite. In 1860, eastern clergyman Thomas Starr King moved to San Francisco and visited Yosemite, where he was spiritually moved by its splendor. He preached a series of sermons on Yosemite in San Francisco, and published letters about it in the *Boston Evening Transcript*. Author Fitz Hugh Ludlow (best known for *The Hasheesh Eater*) went on a Yosemite expedition in 1864 with a group that included Albert Bierstadt, an artist of the Hudson Valley School who worked in oils. In an article in the June 1864 issue of the *Atlantic Monthly* titled "Seven Weeks in the Great Yo-Semite," Ludlow claimed that Yosemite "surpassed the Alps in its waterfalls, and the Himmal'yeh in its precipices."

These men and others proposed that Yosemite Valley and the Mariposa Sequoia Grove be reserved by Congress for the public. President Abraham Lincoln, eager to tie the country together, signed a bill on June 30, 1864, that gave Yosemite Valley and the Mariposa Grove to the state of California "for public use, resort and recreation"; the two tracts "shall be inalienable for all time." It was common for the government to protect wilderness for the elite, but this was one of the first times that a government protected wilderness for the people.

After the Civil War, the United States started to build national institutions. Along with state colleges and the agricultural extension service, there were national banks, a National Academy of Sciences, a national Department of Education, and a national commissioner of agriculture. Reserving Yosemite for the state of California had created a context for national parks, and Yellowstone, with its hot springs and geysers, was a spectacular site.

Mountain men and trappers had written of Yellowstone for decades—steaming rivers, petrified trees, and boiling mud—but these reports were believed to be tall tales. Three private explorers took an expedition down Yellowstone River in 1869, and an 1870 expedition included the surveyor-general of

Montana and a US Army detachment of six soldiers. Lieutenant Gustavus Doane, whose finely pointed mustachios extended beyond his ears, wrote a carefully detailed report.

In 1871, a geological survey sponsored by the government resulted in a multimedia report by Ferdinand Hayden that included paintings by Thomas Moran and large-format photographs by William Henry Jackson. These reports and letters from many supporters convinced Congress to protect the region. In Hayden's report to the Committee on Public Lands, he wrote that if the bill did not pass, "the vandals who are now waiting to enter into this wonder-land, will in a single season despoil, beyond recovery, these remarkable curiosities, which have required all the cunning skill of nature thousands of years to prepare." Yellowstone National Park, the first reserved land in the United States and one of few in the world, was created on March 1, 1872, when President Ulysses S. Grant signed the Act of Dedication.

Sport hunting and fishing were popular upper-class activities in Europe and the United Kingdom, but the United States had a long history of subsistence hunting by the general population. Generations before Henry Ford built his first Tin Lizzie, Samuel Colt's revolver was manufactured on an assembly line using interchangeable parts. Colt was a master marketer. He commissioned western artist George Catlin to make a series of paintings of men posed with a Colt gun, and used the paintings in newspaper advertisements. He gave revolvers to prominent world citizens, including shoguns in Japan, the king of Siam, the Russian czar, and British government officials.

The gun business boomed during the Civil War, and when it was over the new arms industry kept making guns. Hundreds of thousands of rifles and revolvers were sold, and deer, elk, moose, bears, wolves, mountain lions, bobcats, and turkeys were hunted out of many states.

When Yellowstone became national property, senators were concerned that hunters would empty the park. The *Congressional Globe* has Rhode Island senator Henry B. Anthony's statement: "We do not want sportsmen going over there with their guns." And Nebraska senator Thomas Tipton knew hunters as well: "I think if . . . we allow the shooting of game or the taking of fish without any restriction at all, the game will soon be utterly destroyed. I think, therefore, there should be a prohibition against their destruction for any purpose, for if the door is once opened I fear there will ultimately be an entire destruction of all the game in that park."

From the start, Yellowstone Park banned hunting and tried to move the Indians out. Wilderness was, by current definition, unoccupied land. Members of the Shoshone, Crow, Bannock, Blackfeet, and Nez Perce tribes had traditionally lived at Yellowstone either year-round or seasonally. At first, park laws limited their territory but allowed hunting rights. Then their hunting rights were revoked, and eventually their access to Yellowstone Park was cut off entirely. By 1880, all Native American tribes had been officially banished from Yellowstone, although some quiet hunting continued. The US Army patrolled the region, keeping the wilderness safe from poachers, squatters, and Native Americans alike.

On the other side of the continent, the Adirondack Mountains of northern New York were being recognized as a natural treasure. The name *Adirondack* originated as a Mohawk word for the Algonquin people, "Barkeaters" (it's an insult). J. T. Headley's 1849 book, *The Adirondack; or Life in the Woods*, sold 10,000 copies in fifteen years, and according to the *New York Times*, "his vivid and spirited sketches of wild life has drawn general attention to the vast untrodden wilderness of New-York State, until what was then an enterprise to be undertaken with toil and labor, is now within the reach of every summer traveler. Ladies now visit the Adirondack country in considerable numbers."

William Henry Harrison Murray's 1869 wilderness guidebook, *Adventures in the Wilderness; Or, Camp-Life in the Adirondacks*, promotes wilderness for its beautiful scenery and "health-giving qualities." Stagecoach lines and a railroad followed, and by 1875, there were more than 200 hotels in the Adirondacks.

The town of Saratoga Springs, with its numerous mineral springs, was developed as a spa town. There were many grand hotels, including the Grand Union Hotel. According to an advertisement in 1871, "This establishment is by far the largest and most complete hotel in the world, and with its various buildings, cottages, lawns, groves, and promenades, occupies seven acres of land comprising nearly an entire block of the town . . . four hundred large and airy rooms on the first and second floors. . . . The banqueting room . . . has ample and sumptuous accommodations for 1,200."

The Adirondacks were a vacation spot for the middle class. The upper crust enjoyed the area as well, and bought vast tracts of the Adirondack forest in the late 1800s. Much of this land is still wild today. There were about forty sprawling estates built in the Adirondacks by industrialists of the Gilded Age. The Vanderbilts, Rockefellers, and Marjorie Merriweather Post (who built Trump's Mar-a-Lago in Palm Beach), the Guggenheims, Webbs, and many others built great camps of native materials on thousands of forested acres.

A great camp typically included a main house, boathouse, guesthouses, workshops, caretaker's cabins, vegetable gardens, stables, livestock, barns, and even schools for staff children. Frederick Vanderbilt hired artisans from Japan to "Japanize" his cabins and dressed his maids in kimonos. Mining magnate Adolph Lewisohn, a man with great ambitions about how much he would accomplish during his vacation, brought a retinue that included a chef, valet, barber, secretary, stenographer, golf caddy, chess partner, and separate tutors for French, voice, and dancing.

In 1864, when Olmsted, Central Park's designer, was politicking to preserve Yosemite, the *New York Times* proposed making the Adirondacks "a Central Park for the world." It is unsurprising that the owners of vast tracts wanted the rest of the region preserved, and there was a powerful constituency for forest protection. Maine and the Great Lakes region had already been clear-cut, and by 1885, a new state constitution declared the park "shall be forever kept as wild forest lands." It remains the only constitutionally protected forest in America.

At 6 million acres and more than 2,500 lakes, Adirondack Park is the largest park by far in the lower forty-eight states. Native Americans had been expelled from Yosemite and Yellowstone, while the Americans (some of whom had political clout) who lived within the boundaries of the Adirondack forest region were allowed to stay. This suggests that wilderness was defined as empty land in the western states as a tool to move indigenous people off public land. People whose ancestors had lived in the Adirondacks no more than a few hundred years were grandfathered in, while people whose forebears had lived in Yellowstone for thousands of years were required to leave. Towns and villages have remained part of the Adirondack wilderness ever since.

By the Romantic ethos of the era, urbanites needed to

sojourn into the wilderness for spiritual restoration and to encounter nature individually. They did it en masse. Railways provided middle-class access to wilderness vacations not just at Niagara, but also in the Poconos of Pennsylvania, the Catskills of New York, and the White Mountains of New Hampshire, where huge rectangular wooden hotels were filled with city folk. Often larger than a hundred rooms, some hotels had their own railway depot. Visitors brought trunks and maids to commune with nature for the season.

Nature was appreciated as beautiful, healthful, and euphoric. Naturalist John Muir's prose on Yosemite is enough to make you blush: "Drinking this champagne water is pure pleasure, so is breathing the living air, and every movement of limbs is pleasure, while the body seems to feel beauty when exposed to it as it feels the campfire or sunshine, entering not by the eyes alone, but equally through all one's flesh like radiant heat, making a passionate ecstatic pleasure glow not explainable."

Nature and wilderness were also used for entertainment: starting in 1883, Buffalo Bill brought the Wild West to eastern cities and Europe. The show featured hundreds of cowboys and Indians, horses, mules, and steers, as well as live buffalo, elk, deer, moose, and bears. It was wilderness on tour. The Wild West show ran for thirty years and toured Europe eight times. Buffalo Bill—William Cody—was one of the most recognized Americans of the age, seen by millions on a single tour.

The middle and upper classes enjoyed wilderness for the beautiful vistas, healthful living, entertainment, and spiritual enlightenment. Wilderness was also the source of lumber, and of wild animals sold for meat, fur, and feathers. These two competing uses started to clash in the late 1800s. The US population doubled between 1870 and 1900, from 38 to 76 million. Rail miles quadrupled to roughly 200,000 miles of track. And feathers became fashionable.

The widespread use of feathers across the industrialized world—and fashion on this scale—was a wholly new phenomenon. *Godey's Lady's Book* was a wildly popular monthly magazine that included a hand-tinted fashion plate and a sewing pattern with every issue. It standardized fashion trends across the country. The new middle class had more purchasing power, and ready-made clothing and pre-dressed hats were available for the first time.

Department stores were new, too, and British designer Charles Worth was the first clothing manufacturer to sew his brand labels onto clothing. By the 1880s, dresses from the House of Worth were sold through an international network of department stores. Women's magazines multiplied, as did catalogue-based mail-order clothing. So when feathers became fashionable, it was on a scale that had been previously unimaginable. Feather-topped hats, for example, were featured in the Sears, Roebuck catalogue and mailed from coast to coast.

Feathers and whole birds were embraced with great enthusiasm. Not only the plumage, but also the wings, heads, and stuffed bodies of birds were everywhere. Hats were commonly crowned with any number of plumes, and feathers were sewn together to make fashionable fans and cuffs. In 1872, a British book of commerce reported that "a new and very pretty ornamental application of feathers is that of the entire head and plumage of some birds for fans and fire-screens; and the brilliant heads of many of the humming-bird family, mounted as necklets, ear-pendants, and brooches, form a novel species of jewellery."

Women enjoyed wearing local feathers. In 1886, ornithologist Frank Chapman took two late afternoon walks through the uptown shopping districts, and tallied the stuffed birds that he saw on women's hats. In a letter to the editors of *Forest and Stream* (now *Field & Stream*), Chapman listed a total of 173 birds of forty different species, including three bluebirds, two red-headed woodpeckers, nine Baltimore orioles, twenty-three waxwings, three scarlet tanagers, an Acadian owl, and a green heron. Women adorned themselves with the mating plumage of snowy egrets, the wings of sparrows and terns, the head of an owl, or a whole stuffed grackle topped off with a couple of warblers.

The feather market was global, with feather auctions held in Paris, London, and New York. The industry was centered in London, where four auction houses sold feathers in bulk. A single order of feathers by a London dealer in 1892 included 6,000 birds of paradise, 40,000 hummingbirds, and 360,000 East Indian birds. When a single sale in 1897 included the skins of 80,000 parrots and 1,700 birds of paradise, William H. Hudson, a representative of the Royal Society for the Protection of Birds, claimed they would have covered much of Trafalgar Square "with a grass-green carpet, flecked with vivid purple, rose and scarlet."

Birds of paradise, with their foamy flank plumes, were just one of the commercially valuable species harvested abroad. There were many others. Toucans and macaws, condors and albatross, scarlet ibis, marabou stork, and hundreds of other exotic bird species were sold in the London feather auctions. Between 1901 and 1910, over 14 million pounds of foreign feathers were imported to the United Kingdom at a cost of nearly £20 million. These enormous values and weights included hundreds of thousands of featherweight hummingbird skins that sold for a bare two pence each.

Local birds were also popular. Seabirds—the wings of "white gulls"—were especially prized. Excursion trains delivered hordes of hunters to the killing grounds, and London dealers paid a shilling for each wing. In the United States, *Good Housekeeping* magazine reported in its 1886–1887 winter issue that a plumage hunter killed 40,000 terns on Cape Cod in a single season; likewise, Cobb Island along the Virginia coast yielded 40,000 seabirds to a New York businesswoman who sold them to a hatmaker for forty cents each. The new rook rifle made killing easier: it was almost noiseless, and allowed a hunter to destroy most of a gull, tern, heron, or egret rookery at a single go.

The egret trade was particularly unfortunate.

During the mating season, an egret develops long dorsal plumes and spreads these thready feathers like a peacock's fan. Since their salable feathers are breeding plumage, the birds had to be shot as they nested. Without parents, the babies—which are fluffy and beaky and undeniably cute—starve to death, each leaving behind a hank of down, a sharp yellow beak, and two twiggy legs.

There was endless demand for egret feathers in both Europe and North America from the 1890s onwards. In 1903, the long gauzy plumes, or aigrettes, sold for $32 an ounce while gold cost a mere $20.67. And it took just four to six mating egrets to make an ounce of aigrettes. The 21,528 ounces of aigrettes sold over a nine-month period in London that year may have been the plumage from 129,000 egrets, and by the turn of the twentieth century, the Everglades' egrets were teetering on the brink of extinction.

These birds were unprotected against the pull of a global market, and the mental framework for the destruction of native wildlife had already been established: like the passenger pigeon and the buffalo before them, plumage birds were expected to disappear into the maw of commerce.

Instead, citizens united to save the birds. It was a two-step process. In the February 11, 1886, issue of *Forest and Stream*, editor George Bird Grinnell announced the formation of the Audubon Society. He urged the public to rise in opposition to the killing of birds for the millinery trade and appealed to women to take the lead in opposing the practice. "The reform in America, as elsewhere," he wrote, "must be inaugurated by women, and if the subject is properly called to their notice, their tender hearts will be quick to respond."

George Bird Grinnell grew up in Brooklyn, and his family lived for a time on the former estate of John James Audubon, where he was taught by Audubon's widow. He graduated from Yale in 1870 with a degree in zoology. As a graduate student, Grinnell spent years out west studying the buffalo and the Native Americans. He was known for his respect of tribal elders. The Pawnee called him "White Wolf" and eventually adopted him, as did the Blackfeet, who called him "Fisher Hat." Grinnell was hired as the naturalist on army expeditions to the Black Hills in 1874 and the new Yellowstone Park in 1875. The report from the Yellowstone expedition includes an attachment by Grinnell that documents poachers taking buffalo, deer, elk, and antelope for hides.

His time in Yellowstone led to many magazine articles on conservation and the American West. Grinnell, who finished his PhD from Yale in 1880, was an expert on Indians and buffalo. He went west nearly every summer, and was the editor of *Forest and Stream* magazine from 1876 to 1911. That's where he met Theodore Roosevelt. Grinnell's review of Roosevelt's 1885 book, *Hunting Trips of a Ranchman*, included the line "we are sorry to see that a number of hunting myths are given as fact, but it was after all scarcely to be expected that with the author's limited experience he could sift all the wheat from the chaff and distinguish the true from the false." When Roosevelt, offended, came by to argue his point of view, he found that Grinnell was deeply knowledgeable and shared his interests. They became fast friends with the shared conviction that market hunting had to stop or the country's native species would go extinct. Given the recent excesses of market hunters, this was a reasonable fear.

Grinnell and Roosevelt founded the Boone and Crockett Club in 1887, dedicated to the restoration of America's game. The club's mission was "to promote manly sport with the rifle" and "to work for the preservation of the large game of this country." The Boone and Crockett Club can claim the earliest North American usage of the term *fair chase* in the fifth article of its constitution, adopted in February 1888.

Fair chase was a new concept. At the time, popular hunting techniques included driving game with fire, shooting animals that were floundering in snow, and hunting with a pack of dogs that herded deer into a lake where they could be taken by boats. Rather than the satisfaction of an all-out slaughter, fair chase allowed animals to escape and be hunted another day. This was a huge shift in how educated Americans viewed wildlife.

Roosevelt and Grinnell did their best to explain fair chase to the public. Roosevelt, who authored forty-five books if you include his compilations of speeches and letters, wrote about hunting and fair chase in his 1893 book *The Wilderness Hunter*. Grinnell's *Forest and Stream* magazine and the Boone and Crockett Club's Acorn book series on hunting explained how hunting was about the experience rather than the harvest.

Grinnell and Roosevelt edited the club's publications and

worked on legislation to save the buffalo. The world's last herd of *Bison bison* was sequestered in Yellowstone and being poached to oblivion. Thanks in part to the lobbying of the Boone and Crockett Club members, the 1894 Yellowstone Game Protection Act saved the park's animals, timber, minerals, "natural curiosities [and] wonderful objects" from harvest, and the buffalo from near-certain extinction.

Gifford Pinchot, who became part of this crowd, was the grandson of a lumber baron. He grew up on the East Coast and graduated from Yale before he went to Europe to study forestry. He returned to the United States in 1890 when he was twenty-five, and was dismayed by the way the forests were being plundered. Presidents and governors were giving land away willy-nilly to railroads, developers with new town plats, mining conglomerates, and timber syndicates. Pinchot's grandfather had already processed Pennsylvania's forests into board feet.

When Pinchot returned from Europe, he went on a forest tour of the United States. He hiked in the San Francisco Mountains above Flagstaff, Arizona, where the Hopi kachinas live in the summer. He visited Yosemite and saw the redwoods and sequoias, and the rain forests of the Pacific Northwest. Pinchot returned to New York and hung a shingle: "CONSULTING FORESTER." He was one of the few foresters in the United States at that time.

Gifford Pinchot met John Muir on a hike in upstate New York in 1892. Muir, or "John of the Mountains," was a national treasure by then, an elder statesman and guru of the wilderness. A Scotsman by birth, Muir arrived in the United States at the age of eleven and kept his brogue all his life. After almost losing his sight in an accident, Muir went traveling and ended up in Yosemite in 1868. He stayed there for six years, working mostly as a shepherd. He would generally hike alone, going into the mountains with "only a tin cup, a handful of tea, a loaf of bread, and a copy of Emerson."

Muir believed that God is revealed through nature, and that humans are part of an interconnected world. "Everybody needs beauty as well as bread, places to play in and pray in where nature may heal and cheer and give strength to the body and soul alike." Muir felt a spiritual connection to nature, and his articles, written in passionate prose, made him famous. He wrote about Yosemite and Mount Rainier, about Alaska's Glacier Bay and Arizona's Petrified Forest and Grand Canyon; he championed the General Grant Grove and Sequoia national parks.

Meanwhile, wilderness was becoming scarce. The 1890 census showed that the frontier—an area where the population density was less than two persons per square mile—no longer existed. A year after the Oklahoma Land Run, Yosemite became a national park, the frontier was officially closed, and it was becoming obvious that if the remaining forests were not protected, they would be cut and sold.

In 1891, Congress passed the Forest Reserve Act, which allowed the president to set aside publicly owned forestland. The first public forest was the Yellowstone Park Timberland Reserve, and by 1893, President Benjamin Harrison had created fifteen forest reserves containing 13 million acres. President Grover Cleveland added two forest reserves totaling 5 million acres. From there, President Woodrow Wilson established a system that unified the parks, and almost every president since then has added to the total.

Muir and Pinchot both loved the forests and opposed clear-cutting. But Muir was a Romantic, like Henry David Thoreau, while Pinchot was utilitarian. Muir wanted to preserve the wilderness, and valued nature for its spiritual and transcendental qualities, while Pinchot valued forests for their trees. In 1898, Pinchot became head of what would become the US Forest Service and a leading spokesman for the sustainable use of natural resources for the benefit of the people. "The object of our forest policy is not to preserve the forests because they are beautiful or because they are refuges for the wild creatures of the wilderness but for the making of prosperous homes. Every other consideration comes as secondary."

Grinnell became president of the National Parks Association, which favored preserving the parks rather than cutting them. The Boone and Crockett Club lobbied to preserve wilderness for aesthetic reasons rather than profit. "When we try to pick out anything by itself, we find it hitched to everything else in the Universe," wrote Muir.

The rush to preserve some national forestland before it was all cut was successful. However, the large mammals had been hunted out and the birds were disappearing. Grinnell's new Audubon Society had faded away by 1895, and the wearing of feathered hats was as common as ever.

Enter the ladies. Harriet Lawrence Hemenway was a Boston Brahmin, daughter of the Lawrence, Massachusetts, fabric mill family and wife of philanthropist Augustus Hemenway, who inherited a shipping fortune. In early 1896, she read a heartrending article about plume hunters in southern Florida, and the wreckage of the egret nesting grounds. She asked her cousin Miss Minna B. Hall to tea, and they went through the social register—Clark's Boston Blue Book—together. They made a list of their most fashionable friends, and a series of afternoon tea parties changed history.

They urged their friends to not wear feathered hats. "We sent out circulars," Hall later recalled, "asking the women to join a society for the protection of birds, especially the egret. Some women joined and some who preferred to wear feathers would not join." These ladies were busy. In a letter in the April 18, 1896, issue of *Forest and Stream*, Hall wrote, "I enclose a circular of the Massachusetts Audubon Society, just started here. . . . The purpose of the society is to discourage buying and wearing for ornamental purposes the feathers of any wild bird, and to otherwise further the protection of our native birds."

About 900 women joined this upper-crust feather boycott, and Hemenway and Hall organized the Massachusetts Audubon Society the same year. Soon there were Audubon societies in more than a dozen states; their federation would eventually be called the National Audubon Society. Within a year, women around the country were rallying to protect America's birds.

In Kansas, the *Topeka State Journal* wrote on May 8, 1897, "If you can accomplish the complete disuse of bird plumage as a decoration of women's apparel our beautiful birds will once more become numerous." The October 24, 1897, issue of the *Chicago Daily Tribune* asked women to save wild birds from extinction by pledging that "they would not wear birds or bird plumage of any kind except ostrich plumes on their hats." Ostrich plumes, the editor explained, can be gathered without torturing or killing the bird.

In 1900, just four years after the Back Bay ladies started planning their strategy over Earl Grey and lapsang souchong, the conservative congressman John F. Lacey of Iowa sponsored the Lacey Act, a bill that required that game birds have regulated legal hunting seasons and bag limits, and allowed hunting for sport and food but not for sale. Nearly twenty years after the complete slaughter of passenger pigeons, curlews, and buffalo, it became a federal crime to transport game or birds killed in violation of any state law: the fine for knowingly transporting poached wildlife was $500, and the fine for buying poached wildlife was $200. Commercial hunting was finally outlawed.

It was just in the nick of time. America's game species were already gone from most of the eastern states, and when Roosevelt became president in 1901, he knew that wildlife would disappear without protection. President Roosevelt created the first national wildlife refuge on Pelican Island in Florida in 1903, hoping to protect egrets and other birds from extinction by plume hunters.

He helped create the US Forest Service in 1905, and appointed Pinchot to lead it. By the end of his presidency in 1909, they had established the first wildlife refuges and national monuments, added to the forest reserves, and increased the number of national parks. In total, Roosevelt protected nearly 230 million acres of land.

Americans liked hunting, and resented the Lacey Act of 1900. New government regulations that dictated where and when they could kill wild animals were un-American. The Florida Audubon Society hired two wardens who were deputized by the state, but when a plume hunter killed warden Guy M. Bradley in 1905, a sympathetic jury acquitted his murderer. In 1908, Columbus G. McLeod, the second game warden, went missing; his body was never found. Later that year, Pressly Reeves—a third Audubon employee—was killed in South Carolina. Three deaths in three years led the New York legislature to pass the Audubon Plumage Law in 1910, outlawing the plume trade; other states followed, and feathered hats faded away.

The Migratory Bird Treaty Act of 1918 outlawed market

hunting and forbade interstate transport of birds, a landmark in American conservation that made it "unlawful to pursue, hunt, take, capture, kill, possess, sell, purchase, barter, import, export, or transport any migratory bird." The rest of the world followed. Great Britain's Plumage Act of 1921 banned the sale of most plumes, and New Guinea protected all of its species of bird of paradise in the 1920s, ending more than four centuries of selling bird skins.

Meanwhile, women cut their hair in the 1920s, and the elaborately plumed platforms of the previous generation slipped out of fashion. Modern women wore slouch hats and cloches. Birds that survived the global slaughter continued to go about their lives, building nests and raising chicks year by year. The forests had been saved . . . sort of.

8

Nature in the City

Cities were famously dirty. As city populations increased, so did the wastes generated within city limits. Human wastes were stored in cesspits and removed by horse-drawn wagons, but the volume of manure produced by horses drawing those wagons (and all the other city horses) dwarfed the volume of human wastes. Joel Tarr, an American expert on urban horses and their manure, figures that each working city horse produced about twenty-two pounds of manure a day and several gallons of urine. In 1880, New York City and Brooklyn were home to about 1.7 million people, with roughly one working horse for every ten people. That's more than 3.4 million pounds of horse manure, every day, often deposited directly onto the street along with a flood of piss. With scant funding for street cleaning, the wastes that accumulated along the streets of rich neighborhoods were often dumped in the poorer sections of town.

In 1900, there were well over 3 million urban horses in the U.S., and those city horses deposited enough manure to breed billions of flies, each one a potential vector for disease.

In the United States, cities often made an effort to clean their streets during an epidemic, since it was believed that miasma caused disease and horse manure was miasmatic. But as a rule, people tolerated large piles of manure lining both sides of the street. Some cities allowed private contractors to collect the manure and sell it for fertilizer, but they typically neglected to collect other kinds of rubbish, leaving the streets less clogged but not clean.

Horse manure was reused on farm fields outside city limits, and other urban wastes were regularly recycled: ragmen collected and sold old clothing, while tinkers repaired and resold old pots and pans. But city folk did not generally compost their organic wastes. Instead, they dumped it into the street where it was eaten by feral pigs. Charles Dickens wrote of New York's urban pigs in 1842: "Two portly sows are trotting up behind this carriage, and a select party of half-a-dozen gentlemen hogs have just now turned the corner. . . . They are the city scavengers, these pigs." Pig feces smell remarkably like human feces. These were added to the horse manure, and streets turned into cesspools when it rained. Ladies trailed their skirts in fetid slop. Cities had no parks, there was nowhere to stroll, and nature was restricted to horses, scavenging pigs and goats, and their ordure.

Living amid all these wastes was deadly. Cesspit contents leached down into the groundwater and contaminated wells, increasing the likelihood that people would catch one another's diseases. In addition, Judeo-Christians preferred to be buried in sanctified ground, so most churches and synagogues were flanked with small graveyards. Over time, these burial grounds were filled with layers of rotting caskets and putrefying bodies that slowly dripped down into the groundwater, a source of potent organic compounds that made water from some city wells taste ghastly. The overfilled city graveyards were unlovely, and thought to be pestilential.

Death was a familiar event in the 1800s. Incomes were rising, but child mortality rates remained stubbornly high. Most people were nursed at home, died in their own bed, and the wake and funeral were held at home as well. Elaborate rituals provided solace and guidelines for people to process their grief. Mourning protocols dictated how people dressed, behaved, and decorated their houses after a family member died.

A black wreath was hung on the front door, black bows were tied around doorknobs, and the doorbell was muffled. Curtains and shades were drawn, shutters closed, and the mirrors in the house were covered with black fabric. Black bunting could be used to decorate fireplace mantels, window frames, shelving, doors, and especially the bedroom of the deceased. The clock in the room where the death occurred was stopped, and restarted after the burial. White stationery with a black border was used for death announcements and funeral invitations as well as personal correspondence (the wider the border, the deeper the mourning). Death portraits and masks were popular. An 1848 advertisement in the *Boston Directory* reads, "Our arrangements are such that we take miniatures of children and adults instantly, and of DECEASED persons, either in our rooms or at private residences. We take great pains to have Miniatures of deceased persons agreeable and satisfactory, and they are often so natural as to seem, even to Artists, in a quiet sleep." Hair from the dead (and the living) was artfully arranged into jewelry, corsages, or elaborately framed wreaths.

A widow's ensemble was precisely defined. During the first year, a widow in deep mourning wore a Victorian version of a corseted burqa made of dull black cloth (ugly and uncomfortable). She did not leave home without full black attire (untrimmed but for the black ribbons on her underwear) and was shielded behind a weeping veil of impenetrable black crêpe; she was allowed to attend church services but little else. During the second mourning, as long as nine months, dresses were made of dull black cloth, but they could have trim. The black veil could be flipped back to expose the face and jet-black jewelry or hair brooches were permitted. Half mourning, the third stage of grief, lasted from three to six months, and widows could wear gray, lavender, mauve, or violet in addition to black, and all types of adornments.

In total, a widow would mourn for her spouse for as long as two and a half years, but could remarry after completing the first year of deep mourning. Widowers had simpler rules, with a man showing his grief in the width of his armband. Children dressed in white with white ribbons to mourn their siblings (by the rules, siblings wore mourning attire for six months). Men and women wore mourning cockades and badges both to the funeral and for months after. These dress codes allowed friends and strangers to identify the details of a bereavement without asking.

This was a society that dwelled on death, and when the cholera and yellow fever epidemics of the 1820s and '30s arrived, cities needed thousands of new burial plots for the corpses. Urban churchyards were already packed. The solution was to dedicate garden cemeteries outside of city limits. No one wanted to linger in the moldering churchyards, but a country site where the wonders of nature were a backdrop to thoughts of the next world was a welcome innovation.

In Boston, the Massachusetts Horticultural Society bought 174 acres of land that they hoped would rival Père Lachaise Cemetery, the first garden cemetery of 110 acres in the heart of Paris, consecrated in 1804. Mount Auburn Cemetery, the first garden cemetery in the United States, was consecrated in 1831. It was designed to provide city dwellers access to pathways, ponds, and lavish landscaping.

Garden cemeteries had long, winding paths that looped around hills and ponds, creating serendipitous views and unexpected surprises. In contrast with traditional churchyards, these graveyards provided naturalistic landscapes, picturesque settings, and space for contemplation as well as interments. Historian David Charles Sloane wrote that rural cemeteries were seen as gardens of graves, or resting places where the public would visit to solemnly contemplate mortality. Carriages drove slowly on the winding roads, orienting passengers towards the cemetery's internal ponds and hills. Visitors were embraced by nature. Tombstones became more elaborate, carved from granite, marble, and bronze, and deeply incised to last for generations.

The church burying ground gave way linguistically to the graveyard. One of the definitions of *yard* is a piece of land used for cultivation, a garden or field. A graveyard is a place where monuments grow. *Cemetery* is from the Greek *koimētērion* (κοιμητήριο), a sleeping place, and the garden cemetery movement encouraged the slumbering dead to enjoy a bit of nature.

∘ ∘ ∘

Boston's Mount Auburn Cemetery was popular among locals and visitors alike, and many garden cemeteries were built in the next decade. Green-Wood Cemetery in Brooklyn, Laurel Hill Cemetery in Philadelphia, and dozens of others were used for strolling and picnicking, and visiting garden cemeteries became a major tourist activity.

These cemeteries were the first public landscapes, and they were used like public parks. The first big public park in the United States that wasn't full of graves was New York's Central Park, established in 1857 on what soon became 778 acres of land that was owned by the city (after using eminent domain to buy out about 1,600 African Americans and Irish immigrants).

Garden cemeteries had already established the public's preferred picturesque, naturalistic landscape, and the chief innovation in the design for Central Park was to have separate pathways for pedestrians, riders, and carriages; the transverse traffic is concealed in sunken roadways that are screened from the park with shrubbery.

Landscape architecture, where traditional gardening is combined with city planning, was a phrase first used by Frederick Law Olmsted, who imposed nature's curvilinear scenery on a rectangular urban grid to build Central Park. That was his first project, but he clearly had a knack for it and eventually built parks that paid attention to nature in cities across the country. From the US Capitol Building to Berkeley and Stanford with hundreds of projects in between, Olmsted followed the patterns of nature instead of planting straight rows of trees and blocks of plant material.

Olmsted was born in Hartford, Connecticut, in 1822 and stopped school at the age of fifteen. Instead of going to Yale, he learned surveying as an apprentice to a civil engineer; kept books for a dry-goods company in New York; and sailed to China on a merchant ship. At twenty-two, Olmsted managed a farm bought by his father in Staten Island, where he planted a pear orchard and changed the road from straight to meandering to improve the views. He took a six-month walking tour of Europe and the British Isles in 1850, where he visited orchards and private estates, parks, and scenic countryside. This trip was the inspiration for his first books, *Walks and Talks of an American Farmer in England* volumes one and two, which sold well.

The success of his books on British farming led the editor of the *New-York Daily Times* to send Olmsted south to report on slavery. Olmsted traveled intermittently in slave states between 1852 and 1854, and produced many columns and three books. He was not a fan of the institution.

Olmsted's first opportunity to create a space to foster social democracy came in 1858, when the design that he submitted with Calvert Vaux for New York's Central Park won first prize. Olmsted had seen beautiful landscapes in England and had done some landscaping on his farm on Staten Island. But in reality, his first landscape project was Central Park. The curious part is that although he had no experience, his philosophical understanding of the role that a park could play in a city was profound. Olmsted's intent was to create public spaces that were enjoyed by the poor as well as the rich, and his vistas were designed to create relaxation. His simplified landscapes remove distractions and demands on the conscious mind. He wanted to democratize nature and make its healing powers available to everyone.

"It is one great purpose of the Park," he wrote, "to supply to the hundreds of thousands of tired workers, who have no opportunity to spend their summers in the country, a specimen of God's handiwork that shall be to them, inexpensively, what a month or two in the White Mountains or the Adirondacks is, at great cost, to those in easier circumstances."

The Civil War was launched before the park was finished, and Olmsted was appointed executive secretary of the US Sanitary Commission (later the American Red Cross). He had a hard war. Olmsted supplied the Union Army with medical supplies and supervised the care of the wounded, a gruesome job. He had a mental breakdown, resigned, and then moved to California to manage a mining estate where, Zelig-like, he helped draft legislation to reserve Yosemite Valley and the Mariposa Sequoia Grove.

Olmsted believed that nature healed the individual and helped civilize society. In Yosemite, he saw the power of scenery. According to Olmsted, "The enjoyment of scenery employs the mind without fatigue and yet exercises it, tranquilizes it and yet enlivens it; and thus, through the influence of the mind over the body, gives the effect of refreshing rest and reinvigoration of the whole system."

To Olmsted, landscape and social reform were inextricably combined. When his Central Park design partner, Vaux, asked him to return to New York City so they could work together as landscape architects, Olmsted bought a ticket east. Over the next thirty years, they designed more than 100 public parks, 200 private estates, 50 residential communities, and

40 college campuses. Olmsted believed that every site has unique ecological and spiritual qualities, and that people wanted "a simple, broad, open space of clean greensward, with sufficient play of surface and a sufficient number of trees about it to supply a variety of light and shade. . . . We want depth of wood enough about it not only in hot weather, but to completely shut out the city from our landscapes."

For Olmsted, nature was not a substitute God, but a way to serve the public and private needs of people; nature was not a philosophical construct but a physiological requirement for a happy life. Since Olmsted believed that nature was necessary for happiness, he held that democracy could not succeed without public parks and access to nature.

I grew up near Shelburne Farms, a typical Olmsted project from the late 1880s. The owner, New York financier William Seward Webb, had bought all or part of twenty-nine farms to assemble a 2,800-acre parcel for an estate on the shores of Lake Champlain. The farms he bought were similar to those that once blanketed Vermont, built along straight roads with pastures outlined by stone walls, each property self-sufficient with its own woodlot, grazing, hayfields, orchard, barn, farmhouse, and outbuildings. Eventually he acquired almost 4,000 contiguous acres.

Olmsted had all of the barns and farmhouses torn down, the stone walls dismantled rock by rock, and the dirt roads and their ditches erased. Olmsted's plantings and designs were site specific: "Plant materials should thrive, be non invasive, and require little maintenance. The design should conserve the natural features of the site to the greatest extent possible and provide for the continued ecological health of the area." In many sites, that meant restricting his plant lists to native species. In Shelburne, he planted tens of thousands of trees, shrubs, and underbrush, using all native species (except for two non-native tree species: Douglas fir and Colorado spruce). His plant lists included most of the trees native to the Northeast: birches, basswoods, ashes, oaks, hickories, chestnuts, elms, and willows, along with thousands of native pines, hemlocks, and firs. His intent was to restore the land to what it might have been two hundred years ago, but better.

The main road curves through an expansive meadow, then rises up through a stretch of deep woods. The lake, great house, and barns are revealed and disappear as the road curves. The forests and meadows are placed to create views that beckon you to go farther. Olmsted's design directs movement through the landscape, leading you along without you being aware that you're being led.

The landscape looks natural, and today the clumps of 140-year-old trees seem as though they were always there. "Fine specimen trees of the old spontaneous growth are to be preserved," wrote Olmsted, who saved every large tree he could. Trees and shrubs were planted back from the gracefully curving roads with species grouped in an apparently random way.

He planted shrubs by the thousands: alders, swamp azaleas, blueberries, black and red raspberries, thimble berries, elderberries, buttonbushes, pussy willows, wild roses, viburnums, witch hazels, and others that had been gathered from the wild by local nurseries. He also ordered native vines, including bittersweets, clematis, and wild grapes. Olmsted used common wildflowers, like goldenrods and asters, and fancy wildflowers like twinflowers and trailing arbutus.

At the time, landscape theory recognized three types of vistas: beautiful, picturesque, and sublime. The German philosopher Immanuel Kant defined sublime as the "infinite, dynamic, and fearsome qualities of nature." The Hudson River School was all about the sublime. Beauty, found in boxwood hedges and formal gardens, was the result of proportion, utility, or perfection. Human mastery over nature was seen as beautiful. Picturesque—Mount Auburn's style—is something in-between. A picturesque landscape is worthy of being included in a picture: "a picturesque view contains a variety of elements, curious details, and interesting textures, conveyed in a palette of dark to light that brings these details to life."

Historian Charles Beveridge described Olmsted's work as a balance between beauty and the picturesque. He always had a large open meadow in his parks, an element of grace that acted on you subconsciously as an antidote to the city. This was the smoothness and flow of the pastoral. This was beauty. The picturesque was the rough, shaggy ruggedness of the landscape planted with native species. The sublime—"the childish playfulness and profuse careless utterance of nature"—was something Olmsted believed was impossible for humans to create.

Olmsted designed city parks with a backbone of native plant species throughout the United States more than a century ago, when gardens everywhere were planted with rhododendrons and petunias. When you make a garden with native species or their cultivars, those fancified cousins with flashier colors or bigger flowers, then native birds and insects (including fabulous creatures like hummingbirds and bumblebees) will make a point of visiting your garden. Olmsted created habitat refuges in cities around the country.

∘ ∘ ∘

When we built in the high desert, Bob decided that he was done with lawns, and sold his mower. The high desert is a tough landscape. If you don't water it—if you leave the land to nature—you get a sagebrush–juniper complex in a hundred years, but in the first decade or so, it's just bare ground with a few sprigs. Seeds are everywhere, though, and if you water this dry ground you get weeds and a broad variety of alien and native species that require more water than is naturally available. The only quick way to get native landscaping in the high desert is to grow the plants in pots, and then transplant, mulch, and water them for a year until they get established. When the new transplants' roots are growing and the plants start to get bigger, you weed the entire area and reduce the amount you're watering. It's a nightmare.

Olmsted's trick was to simplify the landscape, using larger numbers of fewer species to create sweeping pastoral views. I chose a short list of deep-rooted native grasses, from Indian grass, switchgrass, and big bluestem with roots that run eight to ten feet into the ground to little bluestem with five feet of roots (compared with a bare two to six inches of roots for Kentucky bluegrass). Unless a plant has an extensive root system to gather moisture from the soil, a few hours of a hot, dry wind can suck all the moisture out of a young transplant, and the wind can blow for days. To survive here, plants need to start with a substantial root ball. When a gallon-sized pot of grass is transplanted and mulched, the hot wind can blow and the plant will be able to gather enough moisture to keep itself alive.

Native grasses are finicky to grow from seed, but big plants are expensive. I went for the cheap third option and bought deep plugs for about a buck apiece. The plugs, at fifty plants per flat, have grooves down the side of each cell to encourage the roots to grow straight down. Each plug is a solid bunch of vertical roots about two inches long, and they are sent by mail just when the roots reach the bottom of their little cell, before they start looping around. If you transplant them into pots the day they arrive, they grow incredibly quickly.

It was a two-year project. I started with 200 plugs of grasses potted up into gallons, but most of them didn't have enough root structure to be transplanted into the ground that fall. Potted plants freeze-dry in Colorado's sunny winter days if they aren't babied, so I overwintered the grasses with a truckload of mulch mounded around the pots, and watered the whole area once a month during the cold. The next spring, I lined up the big grasses and transplanted another 1,000 plugs of grasses and wildflowers into four-by-four pots for their first phase. I did all my transplanting at a friend's greenhouse, and she kept my small pots inside and watered them daily until the cold weather had passed. I grew another thirty shrubs using naturally seeded sprigs from my next-door neighbor's native shrubs. (I later added another 200 sweetgrass because the first twenty-five did so well, making a total of about 1,400 plants.)

A cold spring killed an easy 10 percent of the babies, and the plants took months to develop their roots. They were ready to go into the ground in waves, each with a handful of high phosphorus and potassium fertilizer to stimulate root growth. I had hoped they'd be able to live without mulch, but no such luck: the first week, they wilted and needed water three times a day. We put a mound of mulch around each plant, and they perked up five truckloads later. The game plan was to water the plants very deeply once a week, to drive their roots downwards. This meant that the weeds were going to grow like crazy, with plenty of water, plenty of sun, and fertilizer leaching from the transplants.

It was a terrible job. Each transplant has its own ring of mulch, and the weeds in-between had to be pulled before they flowered. The yellow clover was the worst. It's a pretty non-native that grows on disturbed land, three feet tall with a root shaped like a little person with three or four long legs. If you do a bad job pulling out the root the first time, it grows into an octopus, each arm stronger than the next.

That summer, I spent one day a week weeding with a friend, a giant strong man whom I paid $20 an hour and an excellent lunch (around here, that's good pay). When we were done for the year, he said that he would never, ever weed for me again. Ever.

It was done, though. The next year required nearly no watering, so the plants grew as they were intended to and the weeds were slow to develop, and manageable. The third year, some of the grasses and wildflowers I originally planted have disappeared and others have multiplied. The area has filled in and is on a virtuous cycle where the natives rule and there are very few weed seeds left. The landscaping fades seamlessly into the old-growth sagebrush—Olmsted would cheer— and it uses almost no water. It's the prettiest garden I've ever built, but there is nothing simple about establishing a natural-looking landscape.

o o o

About the same time that Olmsted was building his parks, the city's horse-drawn wagons, carriages, and omnibuses that stopped at any place along their route were disappearing. First came the gasoline-powered trucks and electric trolleys with defined stops; subways and streetcars followed. When the horses went, so did their manure, and cities became much, much cleaner.

Electric streetcars were introduced in 1887. They traveled at twice the speed of a horse-drawn carriage and required a significant investment. Tracks were usually laid by private businesses. Between 1890 and 1907, the total distance of streetcar tracks in American cities increased from less than 6,000 miles to more than 34,000 miles. The construction of these new streetcar lines allowed suburbs to grow.

The great historian Sam Bass Warner pointed out that railroad suburbs grew up around rail stations like little villages, while streetcar suburbs formed continuous corridors of single-family homes. Developers built subdivisions on a grid that was often an extension of the plan of the parent city. The houses were generally built within a five- or ten-minute walk from the streetcar line. The homes often had neither stables nor garages, because the whole community depended on the streetcar.

Streetcar companies extended the range of the commuter and opened fringe land for residential development by reducing the time and cost of traveling into the city. People wanted to live in nature with a lawn, house, and garden, spurring suburbanization. In the United States, cities had started installing massive public water and sewer systems in the 1860s, and most urban households had water faucets by 1880. About one in three urban households had toilets by that time, while two-thirds of all city residents shared public toilets or outhouses. When the streetcar lines were laid, tax-funded city water and sewer systems extended their services to the new lots, while services like telephone, gas, and electricity were provided by private businesses.

In practice, this meant that every suburban house had a flush toilet. The ideal of living in a place where nature presses in on you becomes even more attractive when coupled with modern plumbing. Any small house in the suburbs was healthier than a city apartment with a shared toilet.

The Ford Model T arrived in 1908, and allowed a broad spectrum of households to move to the suburbs. The automobile was adopted by upper-middle- and upper-income households, while the middle and working classes continued to use streetcars that generally became public utilities, adding buses, elevated trains, and subways to expand their routes.

Olmsted is often credited for the first American lawns. His 1869 design for Riverside, a Chicago suburb, included a lawn for every lot. Soon it was taken for granted that every suburban house was surrounded by a bit of nature. The inner city was dedicated to commerce and slums, while commuters mowed their lawns in the outer suburbs as their children played in nature. Along with suburban greenery, these new suburbs embraced a different concept of childhood.

The role of childhood had been debated for centuries. In theory, work was good for children since "idle hands are the Devil's playthings." Queen Victoria's husband, Prince Albert, spoke for many people when he argued in 1857 that a working man's children were "part of his productive power, and work with him for the staff of life; the daughters especially are the handmaids of the house, the assistants of the mother, the nurses of the younger children, the aged, and the sick. To deprive the labouring family of their help would be almost to paralyse its domestic existence." It was also well established that children could be an indispensable source of family income. There were moral and financial reasons to support child labor.

Children worked for lower wages than adults, and they didn't organize or argue. Child farm labor was standard practice for most of human history, and child factory labor was a natural extension of a child's obligation to help the family. However, people were starting to see childhood in new ways. Jean-Jacques Rousseau's *Émile, or On Education*, published in French in 1762 and in English the following year, laid out a Romantic view of childhood. Rousseau never raised a child: his five offspring (with his housekeeper) were each dropped off at the nearby foundling hospital where they most likely died of neglect. His fictional son, Émile, is raised amid nature and allowed to follow his natural curiosity. Émile's virtue flowered, resulting in a well-adjusted adult who is also a good citizen.

Original sin dictated that children were small devils in need of correction. Rousseau saw children as uncorrupted and pure with natural freedom, creativity, and spontaneity, little tabulae rasae with the malleability to be formed however you wanted. William Wordsworth (who raised five) saw children as especially close to God. The aristocracy and middle classes embraced these Romantic views of childhood.

This new view of childhood as a special stage of innocence and learning saw the flowering of children's literature. *Little Women*, *The Adventures of Tom Sawyer*, and *Adventures of Huckleberry Finn* were published in the United States; *Heidi* was published in Switzerland; *The Adventures of Pinocchio* in Italy; *Alice's Adventures in Wonderland*, *Treasure Island*, *Kidnapped*, and *The Jungle Book* were published in Great Britain. The Victorian middle and upper classes emphasized the role of the family and the sanctity of the child, an attitude that has remained dominant in western societies, while the children of the lower classes endured grinding poverty and hard work.

Not surprisingly, people started to have smaller families when childhood became more valued. As a rule, city women had smaller families than country women, and wealthy folk have long had fewer children than poor folk. But after 1850, all of the different demographic groups—white, black, city, country, rich, poor—started having fewer children. A woman in 1800 was likely to have more than seven children, while in 1900 the average woman had 3.5 children.

The steep drop in fertility started before the Civil War, before the country was largely urban or industrial. In fact, the fertility rate in the United States began to decline before mortality did.

In an urban environment, children are more expensive to raise and less useful, particularly after child labor laws were passed, while the growth of industrial employment increased the value of education. In addition, there were significant advances in birth control. All of these factors reduced the birth rate.

Today, people routinely plan their pregnancies. In the 1800s, women tried to reduce the number of accidental pregnancies. The rhythm method was useless because the recommended "safe" days were the wrong days. Douching can reduce the likelihood of conception by 50 percent, and modern studies show that withdrawal can be 80 percent effective, or even higher. A sea sponge soaked in vinegar with a string attached was another method that worked relatively well. Instructions on the use of silk condoms were found in the bestselling, much translated "On the Use of Night-Caps—Seven Years Experience on the Practicability of Limiting the Number of a Family, by the Best Known Methods; Including Some Valuable and Novel Information, Never Before Published; Addressed Exclusively to Married Couples by a Married Man (with six children)," published in 1844.

Newspaper advertisements for birth-control devices and drugs to induce abortion (or "relieve female irregularities") were common. Contemporary estimates of mid-nineteenth-century abortion rates in the United States suggest that between 20 and 25 percent of all pregnancies in the United States ended in abortion, and information on how to successfully end a pregnancy was readily available. Bestselling lay medical guides included William Buchan's *Domestic Medicine*, published in 1784, with pages of various remedies for an "obstructed flux," and Peter Smith's *The Indian Doctors Dispensary*, published in 1812, which tells readers how to discreetly become "regular."

Charles Goodyear, an American inventor, heated sulfur and natural rubber to make flexible, stretchable, durable vulcanized rubber in 1844. Natural rubber latex is made from the sap of the Brazilian rubber tree, and as soon as it was vulcanized, condoms could be made from latex instead of silk or intestines. Rubbers were produced in large quantities by 1860. They were cheap and could be rinsed and reused. In addition, primitive latex diaphragms, cervical caps, and weirdly shaped "womb veils" could be worn without your husband's knowledge, and were available by mail. Douches made with rubber hoses and bags were better than the vaginal syringes they replaced. Finally, a reliable spermicide became available in 1885, when you could buy pessaries made of lumps of cocoa butter with some quinine mixed in, providing a greasy barrier and spermicide in one.

Birth control was one way to reduce family size; another was to abandon your children. American legal ideas about children were inherited from the English Poor Laws under the principle of *parens patriae*, where the state is the ultimate parent of all children. By the mid-1800s, there were hundreds of thousands of homeless children to care for in the United States, and there were many private and public solutions to the problem of child abandonment.

Foundlings were babies given up by their mothers, and the first foundling home in the United States was established in 1856 in Baltimore, Maryland. By the early twentieth century, most large cities had at least one foundling home (where mortality rates were often over 90 percent). Orphans were children who had lost one or both parents, or a child who was forced out or abandoned because of overcrowding, a more capacious definition than we use today. Poorhouses, county almshouses, and orphanages housed both foundlings and orphans, while runaways lived on the streets. More than 600,000 men died in the Civil War, increasing the number of stray children. In New York City alone, the number of children in almshouses and asylums tripled.

One solution to overcrowding in orphanages and poorhouses was to ship the children west as farm labor. Between 1854 and 1929, over 200,000 abandoned children were shipped west in so-called orphan trains. The children were advertised in advance of the train's arrival, and the locals would come to the station to pick out a likely child.

With compulsory schooling, children changed from being an economic asset to a liability. From kindergarten through college, children need protection, food, and guidance. Schooling creates an extended period of nonproductive nonadulthood. And when the emphasis of childhood shifted from work to learning, childhood became a time of joy. Factory-made dolls and organized sports, smaller families, child labor laws, and the construct of childhood as a time of play and exploration led to nature study and summer camp, where city children experience nature.

Massachusetts was the first state to enact compulsory school attendance in 1852, and children between eight and fourteen were required to attend school at least twelve weeks a year. By 1918, every state required that school-age children attend school, and nature study was taught in most public schools.

The nature study movement believed that God is revealed

in nature. Romantic and sentimental, the curriculums included Florence Holbrook's books of myths, nature spirits, and fictional Indian stories and Anna Botsford Comstock's *Handbook of Nature Study*, which sees nature as the best context for educating children: "study nature, not books."

Louis Agassiz, a Harvard University zoologist, created nature study in the 1870s. Agassiz believed that natural history needed to be taught from "the direct observation of natural phenomenon rather than learning about the outdoors from textbooks." He'd give graduate students a preserved fish and ask them to contemplate it deeply.

Nature study advocates believed that studying nature could reveal scientific truths, make students love nature, and bring joy to an industrialized world. According to the nature study model, nature itself was the rightful source of both the scientific thinking and ethical values that made a modern citizen.

Comstock's *Handbook of Nature Study*, published in 1911, was close to 500 pages and grew to almost 900 pages in subsequent editions. It is divided into four parts: "How to Teach Nature Study," "Animals," "Plants," and "Earth and Sky." Birds are the first topic of study in the animal section. Here, Comstock reminds the teacher that studying birds is more than naming birds, and the real purpose is to understand the bird's life. Using a notebook to record their observations, students answered questions like: On what date did you notice the first arrival of robins in the spring? Does the robin begin to sing as soon as it comes north? What is the color of the beak? What is the color of the tail feathers? Later questions cover singing, nest building, eggs, young, and finally observations over the summer break.

The Boy Scouts and Campfire Girls embraced nature study,

but the movement was more widespread. By 1915, "14 states required elementary schools to teach nature study, and 23 states issued outlines for nature study instruction. A 1921 survey said '1905 to 1915 saw the incorporation of nature study outlined in the Course of Study of almost every state in the union.'" So many people participated in nature study that children, rural schoolteachers, and middle-class families became a source of ardent conservationists.

Aldo Leopold and Rachel Carson, writers/scientists both, were taught nature study as children, and their work was profoundly influenced by their early exposure to nature journals. Nature was seen as a moralizing force, an antidote to industrial society, a crucible of democratic citizenship, and a place of respite and beauty.

9

Rearranging Nature

Water is both reusable and infinitely divisible. It can be shared any way you want, and recycled again and again. When you look at how easily this resource is moved and measured, it seems unconscionable that there isn't water for wildlife. The history of water rights allows for my agricultural water and your municipal water, but a fish that lives in a stream has no right to water at all.

Nature relies on the water provided by rainfall and

snowpack, while agriculture requires specific inputs of water at certain times during a plant's life cycle. There is too little rain in most western states to support domesticated plants and animals, so nearly every lake, river, stream, pond, and underground aquifer is diverted into a network of ditch systems. Without irrigation ditches, the crops and livestock in most of the western United States would not survive.

Laws determine how we share water, and water laws vary from state to state. East of the Mississippi River there is generally enough rainfall to grow crops, and surface water can only be used by the people living next to a river, lake, or pond. This riparian ("riverside") system requires that a landowner who diverts water put it to reasonable use for a household, livestock, gardens, irrigation, industry, or recreation. Most riparian states use permits to make sure that upstream landowners' water use doesn't affect the rights of downstream landowners.

West of the Mississippi, there is generally too little rainfall for unirrigated agriculture. Water laws are critical in this region, but the existing legal system is based on an accident of history. Miners settled the region first, and they needed water to develop their mining claims. Their fierce competition for this scarce resource was ultimately settled with money, and a set of laws that favored the mine owners. Those laws have endured, resulting in a deeply irrational system.

My Jack London–ish vision of mining includes men wearing Levi's panning for gold nuggets in gravel-bottomed rivers and men wielding pickaxes in underground tunnels to break up ore. These Norman Rockwell versions of placer and hard rock mining had disappeared by the early 1860s, when industrial-scaled mining processes funded by great companies bought out the small operators. Industrial placer and hard rock mining both depended on poorly paid workers and vast quantities of water.

Placer miners (from *placel*, Spanish for "sandbank") remove minerals from the fine-grained mud, silt, and sand deposited in the streambed by flowing water. Rather than sifting gravel with a pan, cup by cup, hydraulic mining—hydraulicking—uses high-pressure water jets to sluice alluvium by the cubic yard.

A holding pond is built above the stream, and a system of hoses and nozzles shoots high-pressure water at the streambed to wash the mineral-bearing deposits—along with the hillside—down and through huge sluice boxes similar to wooden troughs with ridged bottoms that catch the gold. This process, where gravity separates the minerals from the slurry of water and sediment, dates back to Roman times. Hydraulicking was first used in California in 1853.

A placer deposit lies on the surface of the Earth and is easy to get to. By assaying samples, you can calculate the value of a deposit at a certain location before you start mining, making it practically risk-free compared to hard rock mining's invisible veins. But in the arid West, it took enormous sums of money to develop the water-delivery system.

An account of hydraulicking from 1905 explained how to set up a placer mine: First, a complete set of samples are assayed to chart the quality and extent of the deposit, and with a little solid geometry you can estimate the total value of the site. Then the price of the water system is calculated, including the cost of constructing "flumes, pipe-lines, and ditches from one to one hundred miles in length, and in doing so it may be necessary to tunnel mountains, span chasms, siphon across valleys, bracket flumes to the side of the cliffs, build reservoirs and dams, and finally, settling dams." According to a 1901 publication by the Institution of Civil Engineers, "In California, the water had to be brought . . . hardly ever less than 25 miles, and sometimes as much as between 100 and 290 miles, to do the work." It was not unheard of for companies to spend a million dollars for their water system, roughly $27 million in 2017 dollars.

Millions of tons of earth were washed into the rivers that flowed into the Sacramento Valley, and the river's valuable streamside habitat, the riparian zone, was inundated with silt. The faster flows of mountain streams carry suspended sediment, but when the stream reaches the valley and floodplains, the water slows and the silt drops out. Upstream hydraulicking raised the riverbeds downstream, broadening the rivers and increasing the extent of spring floods.

The water used by the early miners was diverted before there was any law up in those high mountains, often by ditch companies on a first come, first served basis. When there wasn't any more water to divert, tough luck. Ditch companies sold the water by the miner's inch, the rate of water flow through a one-inch hole in a two-inch-thick plank with a head of six inches. The amount of water in a single miner's inch varies by state, from a low of 31,000 gallons a day in Southern California to Colorado's robust 40,000 gallons a day. Water was sold in huge quantities, and the mines used it limitlessly. California's North Bloomfield hydraulic mine used over 15 billion gallons of water in 1879, a year's water for a modern city of 400,000. According to the report of the state engineer of California, over 92 million cubic yards of debris from hydraulic mining was dumped into the streams between 1879 and 1881.

It's hard to imagine how much earth was moved by these miners. By the mid-1880s, the California Gold Rush yielded perhaps 344 tons of gold (worth around $14 billion in 2018) and washed the mountainsides into the valleys. They sluiced away the equivalent of eight Panama Canals of high mountain soil, and dumped it onto the floodplains, making the valleys more fertile and the mountains less so.

Water was the critical element that separated gold from silt in placer mining, and separated gold from its host rock in hard rock mining. In the nineteenth century, a hard rock miner in a tunnel would break the ore into fist-sized pieces with a pickax and then bag the rocks and pack them out by burro to a stamping mill. There, the rocks were smashed into gravel by water-powered stamps. It took four to ten tons of water to stamp a ton of ore, so hard rock mining, like placer mining, was a water-dependent process.

Mines weren't usually adjacent to a stream, so there was no way to apply the riparian system used by eastern states. When the mining companies first started diverting water, miners figured that the person who diverted water from a river first has the right to continue using that water. But if that person stopped using their water, they lost their rights to it: you can sell your rights to the highest bidder, but you can't hold onto rights you don't use. When Colorado became a state and the law came to those high mountain mines, water courts regularized this concept as prior appropriation based on priority. The most senior rights have the highest priority and get their water first during dry years, while those with junior water rights get none.

The reason why this matters is that this system of water rights has endured. West of the Mississippi, the right to use water from a stream, river, or lake is still private property that can be bought and sold like a car or house. Each water right has the original date that water was first diverted, the amount, and the location where water must be extracted from the river. If you don't own a water right, you can't take water from a stream or river no matter where you live or if your animals are dying of thirst—and if you own a water right, you can take water from that stream or ditch and live in Timbuktu, provided you take it every year.

If you own water rights, there is little reason to sell them unless you sell the land, and some individual ranches have more water rights than small cities. In addition, there is no impetus to conserve water. If you do not use your entire allotment, you technically—legally—can lose the right to use it. Even if there is a better way to use the water, the owner of the original water right has the right to use her water any way she pleases, no matter how wasteful it may seem. Many ranchers use the same irrigation techniques as their grandparents because there is no reason to adopt a more efficient system. Most arid states use prior appropriation to distribute their water; most wet states use riparian rights; and some states (including California and Oklahoma) use a hybrid system that combines both riparian and appropriative rights.

∘ ∘ ∘

It takes a surprising amount of infrastructure to live in dry country. One of our neighbors has their own well, and another has drilled four dry holes over the years. We drilled for water, but came up dry. The bill was $10,000, and Bob's comment was that it would have been more fun to make a campfire of $20 bills. People who don't have wells have to haul their own water, so we bought an 1,800-gallon cistern and a pump. The concrete cistern is buried near the drive and filled by a hose from the truck. We bought a 350-gallon tank that sat on the back of the pickup truck, but when the tank was full, the weight was too much for the one-and-a-half-ton truck. Bob had the suspension system beefed up by installing larger shocks and welded a steel bar onto the back of the truck bed so the tank wouldn't come through the back window. There's a water station in Durango and another in Ignacio, both twenty minutes away, where you can fill a water tank with town water. Water is cheap—a $20 punch card is good for four loads—but the loaded truck is dangerous to drive because the water weighs more than a ton, so the truck is slow to stop and the tank is quick to slide into the cab. I never once picked up a load (I'm a sketchy driver), and after two years, Bob finally retired from water hauling this spring when the driveway was too muddy to manage without chains. We have water delivered once a month now, by a man whose knuckles are tattooed HARDWORK. He's a single dad who takes $100 cash for an 1,800-gallon load. It's a bargain.

In cities and suburbs, people use drinking water on their landscaping. In the country, westerners often have completely separate systems for house water and irrigation water. Our water rights on the ditch an eighth of a mile down from our house are substantial and the ditch rights date to 1893, so in dry years that ditch will get filled first. We get water from a spur of the Morrison ditch system that carries water from the Vallecito Reservoir, about ten miles away as the crow flies but much farther by ditch.

Our rights, which came with the land, give us 7,200 gallons a day between May and October, but it's not easy to use that water. We had to build a pond to store it, and a distribution system to move it around. Once the pond was filled, it was just the beginning. Bob rented a trencher that had two handles like a rototiller and a chain-linked rotating blade that dug a four-inch-wide trough about two feet deep. He laid a trench from the pond to the greenhouse and another that went up the hill and around both sides of the house. He installed a smaller pump at the pond, wired it to the same electrical line that powers the greenhouse, and laid a one-and-one-fourth-inch line in the trenches that fed seven spigots, including one in the greenhouse, one in the lower field, two on both sides of the house, and one in the back.

The pond is cleverly designed, with a beach for the deer to drink and a steep backside where we dump weeds and scraps. Bob seeded it with a native mix calibrated for this altitude and watered it daily for an entire growing season. He transplanted six clumps of cattails from the ditch, and the next year the entire shallow end was crammed with cattails from rhizomes lying dormant in the swale. The frogs came on their own, and the pond is full of native fish from the river that were pumped there as minnows. We're hoping a pair of ducks will settle on the pond this summer because their wastes make a biofilm that will help seal the bottom. Owning shares in a ditch gives you water rights, but it takes a lot of work to use the water.

∘ ∘ ∘

When the rivers run low in dry years, states that use prior appropriation make sure that the people who own senior rights get their water. If a senior right holder makes a call on the river to claim the water they own, the upstream junior rights holders have to stop diverting water until the downstream senior rights are fulfilled, and the ditch walker will make sure this happens. In dry years, some people can grow crops and some people can't.

The system of prior appropriation is not about sharing water; it's about permanently securing the most water you can use on your land. It's an acquisitive system, and early ranchers and farmers soon owned rights to most of the surface water in the West. Cities grew after that time, and the only way for these latecomers to get water was to either change the laws or to increase the amount of water that was available to appropriate. The answer was dams, and lots of them.

Dams had been built in the United States for as long as the settlers used waterpower for mills, and the Atlantic salmon have been blocked from many East Coast rivers for centuries. The Atlantic salmon that recently spawned in the Connecticut River are thought to be the first breeding pairs in the river since the Revolutionary War.

Until 1902, dams were relatively small structures built by private investors. Then Congress passed the Reclamation Act. In time, the Bureau of Reclamation built dams nearly everywhere it could, and it didn't shy away from large projects. The dams increased the amount of water that was available for withdrawal in the western states, providing drinking water for cities while preserving the system of prior appropriation for ranchers. But agriculture was changing.

After the buffalo were exterminated, immigrant farmers grazed cattle on native grasslands until the end of the 1800s. The prairie soil was held in place by the root systems of native grasses that often extended ten, twelve, and even twenty feet deep. When wheat farming expanded west, farmers plowed up the sod and planted wheat, an annual grass that dies at the end of the season.

Horses were replaced by tractors and then larger tractors. Power was provided by internal combustion engines rather than muscles, so truly massive tillers and combine harvesters could be used. During planting season, tractors worked around the clock, plowing more and more land. These farmers were the first agriculturalists not confined by the limits of animal strength, shifting their relationship with labor and nature, and they unwittingly ruined their land.

Fewer horses meant fewer perennial hayfields to feed them and less manure to top-dress the fields, reducing the amount of organic matter in the soil and the acreage under grass. Farmers usually grazed their livestock on the fields after harvest, leaving the soil with no vegetative cover during the winter. The same fields were cultivated year after year, pulverizing the earth into a fine dust that did not clump like healthy soil. This powdered soil was ready to be swept away.

The wheat farmers of the Great Plains were among the most successful farmers in the nation until the autumn of 1931, when the rains stopped falling. The winter wheat crop failed, leaving the soil uncovered during the spring winds. The dust storms started in early 1932 when sixty-mile-per-hour winds kicked up dust clouds two miles high. There were fourteen dust storms in 1932, and thirty-eight in 1933. These storms brought boiling clouds of dust, miles high, carrying millions of tons of soil. Sometimes the middle of the day was dark as night.

Farmers kept plowing and sowing their bone-dry fields, but the rain never came. And it was unusually hot. In 1934, temperatures in Vinita, Oklahoma, were over 100°F for over a month, culminating in a hellish day of 117°F. Women would hang wet sheets in the windows to catch the dust. The bread would get so dirty that women kneaded their dough in a bureau drawer covered with a cloth with two holes cut in it to stick their hands through. Meals were eaten as soon as they were ready, and pitchers were no longer used: water and milk had to be stored in screw-topped Mason jars. During a storm, people would wear handkerchiefs over their faces and coat their nostrils with Vaseline; afterwards, housewives swept up buckets of dust that had seeped through gaps in the sashes and sills. Children were particularly susceptible to dust pneumonia, when the alveoli in their lungs filled with soil, and chickens smothered on their roosts. Hungry and thirsty range cattle were blinded when dust mixed with tears and glued their eyelids shut.

By the time the drought was over, 100 million acres of grasslands had been scoured. The area of greatest damage moved around. The years 1935 to '36 were the worst, when an estimated 850 million tons of topsoil were swept from the southern plains. "The soil is the one indestructible, immutable asset that the nation possesses," wrote the federal Bureau of Soils in 1909, "the one resource that cannot be exhausted, that cannot be used up." The bureau was as surprised as everyone else when drought came in the 1930s, and the newly plowed topsoil blew away.

On April 2, 1935, a storm blowing dust from the Plains darkened the skies of Washington, DC, as the director of the Soil Erosion Service testified to a congressional committee about the need for a national program for soil conservation. Less than a month later, the Soil Conservation Service was created in the Department of Agriculture to promote farming practices that conserved the soil and provided farmers with seeds, equipment, and expert advice as well as food aid, social assistance, and jobs programs. Every county of every state already had an agricultural extension service office staffed with experts who provided free agricultural advice, and that network was used to reduce wind erosion.

Laissez-faire capitalism does not work for agriculture, because farmers will ruin their land trying to make a living. A common argument today is that ranchers don't need regulations because no one understands better how important it is to protect their land, but history shows otherwise. The 1935

Soil Conservation Act provided subsidies for farmers who planted native grasses and trees. "It will *pay* farmers, for the first time," said White House adviser Rexford Tugwell, "to be social-minded, to do something for all instead of for himself alone." The US Forest Service planted 200 million trees on farms from North Dakota to Texas to provide shelterbelts. Contour plowing and no-till farming were adopted across the Dust Bowl. The Department of the Interior hired soil scientists whose research showed that cattle should not be grazed on harvested land, and that stubble shouldn't be burned. It hired agronomists to help farmers adopt new practices. Everyone participated with the hope that it would help the land hold the water, and it did help. There just wasn't very much water to hold.

Farmers needed government help, and the commodity markets date from the decadelong drought of the Dust Bowl era, as do crop insurance, the concept of the government paying farmers to fallow their less-productive lands, and the requirement that farmers participate in soil conservation activities. Soil and water conservation districts were a conduit for projects, education, and social pressure. These programs, like the extension service, are still a major aid to American agriculture. Farmers caught in regions ruined by dust storms made use of New Deal programs, including the Drought Relief Service, Federal Emergency Relief Administration, Federal Surplus Commodities Corporation, Works Progress Administration, and Civilian Conservation Corps. Some of the farmers were able to hang on until the fall of 1939, when the rains finally returned.

About 2.5 million people abandoned the region after losing their crops, livestock, and often their land. People whose great-grandparents arrived in Conestoga wagons drove away with everything they owned tied down to the bed of their truck. The Great Depression and the failure of dryland—unirrigated—agriculture was a socio-ecological crisis that launched fifty years of dam building. After the prolonged drought of the 1930s, it became a national goal to provide farmers with reliable sources of irrigation water.

Dams allow people to manage rivers for their own benefit. All of the major rivers in the United States were dammed again and again for irrigation, flood control, electricity generation, transportation, and for cities and industry. From the Tennessee Valley to the Central Valley of California, dams, levees, canals, and ditches allowed the Army Corps of Engineers to manage the landscape to meet human needs. Farmers, cities, and factories all had a say in how water was used but nature, the red-headed stepchild, was barely considered.

The Dust Bowl region recovered by the early 1940s, and grew bins of wheat for the war effort. The fifties, like the thirties, was a dry decade and farming based on groundwater became common. The Ogallala Aquifer underlies most of the former Dust Bowl, and when people figured out how to fix car engines to pump well water, this aquifer started to be used in earnest. The center pivot irrigation set-up was developed in the 1950s, and soon crop circles were farmed from Texas to the Dakotas.

Irrigation projects did not benefit farmers equally. Large landowners with large machines enjoyed substantial economies of scale, so megafarms proliferated as smaller farms went broke. Today, more than a quarter of the irrigated land in the United States is watered by the Ogallala Aquifer. Groundwater, like surface water, is regulated by the states, and each state follows a different doctrine.

Today, irrigation and thermoelectric power both use about

115 billion gallons of freshwater per day; the public water supply is another 42 billion gallons, and that accounts for about 90 percent of water use in the United States. Much of the electricity in this country is generated by thermoelectric power plants that burn fossil fuels to heat water that turns to steam and spins a steam turbine that drives an electrical generator. But the water used to cool thermoelectric power generation is mostly returned to the water body it came from, while return flows from irrigation are generally about half of the initial diversion, though they can vary widely. This makes irrigation the largest consumer of water by far, using 80 to 90 percent of the water in many arid states. During drought years, city residents are begged to conserve while the agriculturalists, who have a giant share of the water pie, are not asked to change their patterns of water use. Power, money, and politics have resulted in farmers flooding desert fields with water to grow crops.

By the 1960s, nearly all of the water in western states had already been allocated with rights that could be bought and sold. Many western rivers are over-appropriated, with more water rights owned than there is water flowing between the banks. The water system was settled except for the unfortunate fact that tribal water rights had never been addressed.

Tribal peoples were moved onto reservations and told to practice agriculture. Therefore, the US government surely must have intended for those reservations to have water. The precedent was set in 1908 (*Winters v. United States*) that a reservation's water rights are based on the date that the reservation was established, whether or not the rights were ever claimed, and the quantity of water they are owed is the amount needed to irrigate the reservation's irrigable acreage. Since the tribes were forced onto reservations before the ranchers established their herds, native water rights generally predate most other water rights in the West.

The tribes have had the law on their side since 1908, but it was the Indian Gaming Regulatory Act of 1988—the federal law that governs gambling on Indian territory—that changed water history. Indian gaming revenues were $100 million in 1988, and after 2009, the annual cash flow has been over $27 billion. One result of the gambling windfall is that tribal councils hired lawyers and sued for their water rights. Cases that had been filed in the 1960s and were still disputed a generation later have finally been resolved.

The standoff over Native American water rights lasted so long because there is no extra water in the system. It could have been the end of privately owned water rights based on first come, first served, but changing the system would have created winners (who previously had no access to water) and losers (the present owners of water rights). Politicians in western states are often ranchers who own water rights, and the problem was eventually resolved by providing money to build more dams and reservoirs, enlarging the water pie yet again.

In 2010, officials in New Mexico settled a 1966 lawsuit involving four Native American pueblos and non–Native American residents in northern Santa Fe County for 4,000 acre-feet of water and over $175 million for storage and distribution. The Crow tribe's 2010 settlement was for $460 million to rehabilitate their irrigation system and build a water distribution system with a reservoir that holds 300,000 acre-feet. The Blackfeet tribe settled their case with Montana in 2016, securing tribal rights of more than 800,000 acre-feet—enough water for a city of 800,000 to 1.6 million people—along with almost half a billion dollars for storage and distribution. Colorado's Southern

Utes and Ute Mountain Utes got 62,000 acre-feet from the Animas-La Plata Project, which ended up costing about half a billion dollars. The Navajo Nation got 81,500 acre-feet and $200 million for infrastructure. One acre-foot equals about 326,000 gallons, enough water to cover an acre of land one foot deep. An average California household uses between one-half and one acre-foot of water per year for indoor and out-door uses; households that haul water use much less. These are just a few of many tribal water settlements that, after generations of litigation, have finally been resolved.

Nature depends on water as surely as humans do, but until recently the needs of the natural world were barely considered when it came to water management. When dams are used to generate electricity, for example, the river's flow was routinely determined by consumer demand rather than the needs of riverine species. Politics rather than science continues to determine how water is allocated, and the private ownership of water rights in regions where water is scarce makes the system very resistant to change.

The Colorado pikeminnow lived throughout the Colorado River basin, and was historically a gigantic fish that grew up to six feet long. It was the river's top predator, and migrated as far as 200 miles to spawn in favorite canyon beaches. But the pikeminnow depends not only on unimpeded passage to its spawning sites, but also on large spring flows from snowmelt and a steady base flow. Today, the adults rarely exceed two or three feet because the rivers are too puny to support them.

Before big dams were built, a river's flow was high in the spring and dwindled throughout the year. Many western rivers are much smaller than they once were, and a river's flow is nearly always determined by humans rather than nature.

Dams usually skim off the high spring flows for storage, a

useful tool for flood control that fills a reservoir to provide water for human use later in the year when flows are low. Removing high spring flows changes the environment for every creature that depends on the river and floodplain. The riverbed is no longer shaped by big water. Farther downstream, the spring floods no longer replenish nutrients by depositing silt on the floodplain. Floodwater no longer seeps down to recharge aquifers, and the active floodplain narrows along with the river channel, reducing riverine habitat.

During irrigation season, the flows in many western rivers are skimpy. The Rio Grande runs so low that the silvery minnow, a little three-and-a-half-inch-long fish that was once the base of the food chain, is going extinct because diversions have reduced this mighty river to a weak and shallow stream. All the big fish are already gone, and there's too little water left in the river to support a minnow.

The National Inventory of Dams, a public database that includes information on every dam in the country, lists over 45,000 dams under twenty-five feet high and another 45,000 dams over twenty-five feet high, including 1,687 dams over one hundred feet high, truly massive constructions that change the entire watershed by slowing the flows upstream and altering water temperature and chemistry for dozens of miles downstream.

Water that sits in a reservoir stratifies, with lower oxygen content and lower temperature water at the bottom of the reservoir, along with higher organic content and higher concentrations of heavy metals. In addition, water evaporates in a reservoir, increasing the concentration of salts and minerals. In a desert climate, evaporation from Lake Powell and Elephant Butte Lake is estimated to exceed a tenth of the dam's capacity every year.

Below a dam, the water is typically colder, saltier, and carries less oxygen than water upstream of the dam. Dams serve as sediment traps, and the clean water released below a dam can cause river downcutting, and may decrease the amount of sand available for the shoreline. With enough dams, a fast-flowing, cold-water river can be transformed into a sluggish, warm watercourse punctuated by placid lakes. The ecological complexity of the ecosystem disappears along with the native plants, fish, and insects characteristic of cold rivers, and species that live in lakes take their place. This shift can decrease the river's ability to assimilate wastes.

In addition to changing the chemistry of water downstream, dams block species from moving upstream, and dams prevent some fish and mollusks from reproducing. Anadromous species that breed in fresh water and grow up in the ocean, like sturgeon and salmon, are often unable to reach their spawning grounds; eels that breed in the ocean and grow up in fresh water are also blocked. As more dams were built, fish runs dwindled and sometimes disappeared, as did many species of freshwater mussels whose life cycle includes a larval stage living on the gills or fins of a fish. This hitchhiking allows the offspring of a parent mussel stuck in the mud to travel to another part of the river. When fish species were changed by dams, many species of mussels were unable to complete their life cycle.

North America is blessed with the greatest temperate freshwater biodiversity on Earth. Its streams are a biological treasure. Fish, mollusks, crayfish, amphibians, damselflies, and snails are especially varied in the New World, but our dams and diversions have taken a toll on freshwater biota. Freshwater species are uniquely threatened in North America, where the extinction rate for freshwater fauna is five times that of land animals.

Since 1900, 123 freshwater species have been listed as extinct in North America, and hundreds of species of fish, mollusks, crayfish, and amphibians are considered imperiled. Nationwide, nearly 30 percent of fish species are at risk of extinction, along with almost half of the crayfish species and about 70 percent of the nation's mussel species. The culprits are dams, sedimentation from construction, runoff from mining and agriculture, municipal and agricultural pollution, channelization and dredging, and the introduction of alien species with a special shout-out to zebra mussels, a proud member of the continent's freshwater biota since 1988.

According to scientist Tierra Curry at the Center for Biological Diversity, the southeastern United States is a hotspot of unparalleled aquatic biodiversity for temperate freshwater species. There are 493 species of fish, 330 crayfish species, at least 269 species of mussels, and 241 species of dragonflies and damselflies, as well as more amphibians and aquatic reptiles than any other region. All things considered, the southeast has the richest aquatic fauna of any temperate area in the world.

Alabama may be the richest state in the union for freshwater species, and in a state that harbors so many species, each river is a particular gem. The Cahaba River, for example, is home to 125 species of fish, 50 species of mussels, and 15 species of crayfish in a modest 190 miles. This extraordinary diversity is coupled with extreme endangerment.

The Coosa River is the site of the greatest modern extinction event in North America. Thirty-nine species went extinct after a series of seven dams was built, providing electrical power to most of the state. And this is where the complexity of these water-management issues becomes clear. It's easy to point out that losing thirty-nine species in a single river is bad. But bringing electricity to much of Alabama's rural population was good. I'm sorry those snails and mollusks no longer exist, but the lakes that took their place are filled with freshwater fish that are often dinner, including largemouth, spotted, striped, and white bass; bluegill; crappie and other sunfish; catfish; and walleyes. Reasonable people could prefer a watershed filled with fish to a handful of native snails and mussels.

Until the 1970s, destruction was seen as an inevitable by-product of progress. But the fact is that minimum flows can be enforced and fish ladders can be installed. Dams can be removed. This story ends well, I promise, but it's going to take a few more chapters.

10

Poisoning Nature

When species started to disappear, it was clear that nature wouldn't survive without legal protection. It was all the more clear when air and water pollution intensified.

For most of human history, air and water pollution was a fact of urban life. Cities heated by wood or coal have always had a heavy layer of smog. When cities use coal to power industrial processes, the air is even dirtier. Worst of all are cities that host smelting and steelmaking plants, where tons of air pollutants are released in the process of generating the tremendous amount of heat needed to melt ore.

Extinction and pollution have long been seen as side effects of civilization. Tucked into that assumption is the concept that naked self-interest is the guiding principle of human society, and two corollaries: some people's rights matter more than others (so the factory owner's right to make money trumps the workers' right to good health), and nature and animals have almost no rights at all.

Until the twentieth century, the effects of coal smoke were generally local or regional. Pittsburgh, one of whose smokestacks is shown at the start of this chapter, provides a good example. The Smoky City sits where the Allegheny River and the Monongahela River join together to form the Ohio River flowing northwest out of Pittsburgh and then southwest to the Mississippi. The city's long flirtation with air pollution began in 1762, when a seam of bituminous coal was found on the south bank of the Monongahela River. Bituminous (soft) coal has a high sulfur content and releases sulfur oxides during combustion, while the nitrogen in coal is released as nitrogen oxide. Once coal smoke goes up the stack, these gases react with the moisture in the atmosphere and create sulfuric and nitric acids that reach the ground as acid rain, damaging crops, buildings, and waterways. In addition, nitrogen oxides combine with volatile organic compounds to form ozone or smog.

It's handy to have a local source of fossil fuel, no matter how polluting, and by the 1840s Pittsburgh was one of the biggest cities west of the Allegheny Mountains. In the *Atlantic Monthly*'s January 1868 edition, journalist James Parton described the city of 230,000 as "hell with the lid taken off." "The town lies low," he wrote, "as at the bottom of an excavation, just visible through the mingled smoke and mist, and every object in it is black. Smoke, smoke, smoke—everywhere smoke."

Many people saw Pittsburgh's dark haze as a sign of productivity, health, and prosperity. In 1866, Parton wrote, "The Pittsburgher insists that the smoke of bituminous coal kills malaria and saves the eyesight. The smoke, so far from being an evil, is a blessing, and it destroys every property of the atmosphere that is hostile to life." In the 1800s, the acids and carbon in coal smoke were believed to be powerful disinfectants. Local newspapers advertised "pure mountain air and healthy coal smoke" without a trace of irony.

When Louis Pasteur's bacteriology killed the miasma theory, a major justification for coal smoke disappeared. In addition, anthropologists argued that coal smoke blocking the sun was creating a rickety underclass with heritable physical and mental defects, degrading the American gene pool. By the 1900s, coal smoke was no longer celebrated.

Pittsburgh was a steel town. The first steel mill opened in 1875, and by 1911 the city was producing half the country's steel. In the 1940s, air quality was so bad that on days when the wind didn't blow, the midday sun was blacked out by coal smoke. Photographs from that time show downtown streetlamps lit at noon, with neon signs glowing through the haze.

The city established the Bureau of Smoke Prevention in 1941, and posted its first smoke-control ordinance (with a five-year delay in implementation due to World War II). The ordinance gave two choices: smoke reduction by using "smokeless fuels including anthracite coal, natural gas, or fuel oil instead of bituminous coal" or, if bituminous coal was used, the furnace had to be fired with mechanical stokers rather than men with shovels.

When Mayor David L. Lawrence was elected in 1946, he promised to clean up the city. "I am convinced that our people want clean air. There is no other single thing which will so dramatically improve the appearance, the health, the pride, the spirit of the city." Over the next four years, more than half of the households in Pittsburgh started heating with natural gas instead of coal, and Pittsburgh's sky lightened. Manufacturers switched fuels as well, and coal-burning locomotives were replaced with diesel-electric trains. According to environmental historian Joel Tarr, the United States had 35,000 coal-burning locomotives in 1950, and by 1954 there were only 350. Steamboats changed from coal to diesel, too, in one of the fastest technology shifts in the nation's history. This was a big boon to air quality.

Donora lies twenty-seven miles south of Pittsburgh, nestled in a valley backed by a steep ridge. Like Pittsburgh, it was a steel town: Union Steel built a rod mill in 1901 that became American Steel and Wire, the largest wire factory in the world. Donora Zinc Works first opened in 1915 as a subsidiary of U.S. Steel, and soon nearly all the greenery within half a mile of the plant was dead.

Both plants used soft coal and gas for fuel. Zinc Works was a modern plant designed with interrelated production processes to produce cleaner smelter smoke, and the plant's products included zinc, sulfuric acid, cadmium, and lead. The first step Zinc Works used to extract zinc was to roast the zinc-bearing ore, releasing sulfurous fumes. These fumes were reacted with nitrogen oxide to form liquid sulfuric acid, an industrial chemical with a robust market. (Removing sulfur from the smokestack reduces the amount of sulfuric acid raining down nearby: this process was developed by smelters in California and Tennessee in response to lawsuits over air quality.) Next, the roasted ore was mixed with fuel and smelted down into molten zinc. Zinc ore often contains other metals, including cadmium and lead. Both of these metals have lower melting points than zinc and go up the smokestack in the smelting process. Some of the cadmium and lead dust was collected using electrostatic precipitation devices originally designed for Montana copper smelters, but the rest went up the smokestacks and settled out over the town.

Webster lies about two miles downstream from Donora, across the Monongahela River. In the 1920s, Webster farmers sued the smelter for lost crops, orchards, and livestock and ruined topsoil, fences, and houses (which I assume means exterior paint). After long legal battles to discredit the claims, Zinc Works lost the case and started mitigation. They gave farmers tons of crushed limestone to neutralize the acids in their newly infertile soil. The smelter furnaces were adapted to burn more cleanly, and the company carried out fifteen years of air-quality sampling.

A common strategy used by western smelters was to build smokestacks as high as 600 feet to disperse the noxious gases over a wide area. In Donora, people lived in a bowl surrounded by a 400-foot ridge, and the smokestacks were a mere 150 feet high. In certain weather conditions, the smoke settled onto the town and stayed.

Before cars were common, people had to live within walking distance of the factories they worked in, even smelters, and Zinc Works was surrounded by residential neighborhoods. Donora was home to 14,000 souls, 5,000 of whom were employed by Zinc Works and American Steel and Wire.

In agricultural Webster, people had nothing to lose from suing Zinc Works. In industrial Donora, no one wanted to make trouble over the town's air quality.

On Tuesday, October 26, 1948, a stinking fog enveloped the small industrial town and stayed on the ground for five days. The dense, yellowish, irritating smog was the result of an unusual weather inversion—a pocket of warm, stagnant air—that acted like a lid on the valley, holding in sulfuric and nitrogen dioxide, hydrofluoric acid, carbon monoxide, and other poisonous gases.

The mills were still pouring out smoke on Friday evening, although the local hospital was crowded with residents gasping for breath. The phones of the eight local physicians were ringing off the hook, and fire department volunteers went house to house and administered oxygen to those unable to breathe. Board of Health member Dr. William Rongaus led an ambulance on foot through the murky streets to transport the dead and dying to the hospital. The first floor of the Donora Hotel became a secondary medical center. The funeral homes were so full that the hotel basement was used as an overflow morgue.

Gossip columnist Walter Winchell broadcast news of Donora's deadly air on his national Saturday night radio show, and U.S. Steel's lawyers ordered that the plants be shut down by six a.m. Sunday. By the time a rainstorm cleared the air at noon, twenty people were dead and 600 had been hospitalized. Most of the deceased had lived in the neighborhood flanking Zinc Works.

In the end, 7,000 people in Donora were afflicted with respiratory problems, and the town had elevated mortality rates for decades. Local newspapers accused Zinc Works of killing townspeople, while others argued that the smoke came from home heating and trains as well as commercial and industrial processes. What was needed, they said, was a smoke ordinance like Pittsburgh's.

The first response of the US Public Health Service was to announce on Tuesday morning that the disaster was just an "atmospheric freak." When the final report on the incident was released in 1949, the Public Health Service claimed that the deaths were due to fumes from a variety of sources, bad weather, and preexisting respiratory and heart disease. The first National Air Pollution Symposium was held in Southern California that year, and Donora was presented as "not an industrial accident but the victim of uniquely severe and enduring weather." More than a hundred residents filed lawsuits against U.S. Steel totaling $4.5 million in claims, but the company swore that the smog was an act of God. U.S. Steel settled the lawsuits filed against it for $256,000, or roughly $12,800 per corpse, and never admitted responsibility for the disaster.

In the United States, we share the air, waterways, and wildlife as a common resource. No one owns these commons, so people exploit the environment for private gain. And they go too far. Everyone enjoys the health benefits from clean air and water, while a few individuals profit from polluting our commons. Everyone benefits from robust salmon runs, while a few profit from canning factories. The powerful few are able to create private wealth by exploiting our common resources, while the powerless lose nature's many benefits. Environmental goods, including clean air and water, are areas where government intervention can increase efficiency.

Before the mass deaths in Donora, the federal government's response to air pollution was to support state and local health departments. The Bureau of Mines conducted federal air pollution studies for the Department of the Interior, and air-quality ordinances were passed city by city. Los Angeles' smog reduction program started in 1947, and more than a billion dollars was spent on mitigation in the next decade. St. Louis and Pittsburgh banned the use of soft coal. The year after Donora's accident, Allegheny County passed its first smoke-control ordinance and established the Bureau of Air Pollution Control. Oregon and its smelters became the first state with an air pollution–control agency in 1951, and New York City's Department of Air Pollution Control was organized in 1952, when they started taking twice-a-day measurements of sulfur dioxide.

The next year, New York City experienced a temperature inversion from November 12 through 21 that put a lid on the city's pollutants, and sulfur dioxide readings spiked. Mortality data analyzed after the incident showed that the death rate in New York City was elevated from November 15 to 24. According to statistical analyses, smog killed between 170 and 260 people.

In the midst of the smog incident of 1953, an article in the *New York Times* titled "What Makes Smog? Cities Do Not Agree" laid out the problem. No one knew what smog was, or how to fix it, and they didn't know until later that people were dying from it. The air pollution–control director for Los Angeles County claimed smog was the result of "smoke, charred paper, dust, soot, grime, carbon, noxious acids, fumes, gases, odors or particular matter or any combination thereof." Maybe so. As with gun control today, it was obvious that a city-by-city approach to air pollution was killing people.

The Air Pollution Control Act of 1955 established the federal government as the ultimate arbiter of air pollution control, a significant first step. The act provided for "research and technical assistance relating to air pollution control" and authorized the surgeon general to research air pollution and educate the public about how to prevent air pollution. The states were left in charge of prevention and control with no way for the federal government to punish polluters.

Water pollution, like air pollution, is an old problem. Rivers, lakes, and streams have been used to carry away human wastes for centuries in the United States. In addition, industrial wastes were disposed of in the waterways as well. Butchering, tanning, and dyeing were notoriously dependent on the waterways for waste removal, and as industrialization intensified, so did the volume of wastes in the rivers and streams.

Rainstorms can deposit an enormous amount of water on a city in a few hours, and cities without a drainage system will have stagnant pools and periodic flooding. To keep the streets clear of water, cities built storm drains that shunted urban rainwater into the nearest waterways. When the flush toilet was adopted in the 1880s, cities expanded their existing drainage systems to accommodate bathroom wastes as well. Rather than collecting feces in a pit in the cellar and periodically hiring someone to cart them out of town, wastes were flushed into the nearest waterway. Their lingering odor was banished from the home, and the combined sewer—so called because it combined storm and sanitation flows—became the gold standard for municipal sewer systems.

A tsunami of sewer construction took place between 1880 and 1910, and the sole purpose of a sewer at that time was to transport sewage and storm water to the nearest body of water. There was no expectation that waterways would be swimmable or drinkable, and there was no thought of wastewater treatment. Many decades later, combined sewers became a curse when wastewater treatment plants were built: whenever it rains, wastewater plants are overwhelmed by the combination of raw sewage and storm water, and dump the untreated excess into the receiving waters. But when city sewer systems were first laid, that was the point. The sewage went into the waterways, and most cities had multiple lines that led directly to the local river or lake.

At the time, Boston was the country's leader in wastewater management. Boston's sewage had originally drained directly into the harbor, leaving the mudflats reeking so strongly in warm weather that the affluent decamped to summer residences on the North Shore. In 1876, the state legislature approved the construction of the Boston Main Drainage System.

The city of Boston built a seven-and-a-half-foot-tall brick conduit that ran 150 feet below sea level under Dorchester Bay and out to Moon Island, a distance of a mile and a half. Four 50-million-gallon storage tanks were built out of granite blocks and a twelve-foot-diameter outflow pipe ran 600 feet into the ocean. By 1884, the sewage from eighteen cities and towns was piped to Moon Island in Boston Harbor and collected in tanks. Rather than pumping sewage into the harbor around the clock, Boston sewage was judiciously released to sea on the outgoing tide.

From the point of view of the waterways, there are two types of wastes: organic matter from plants and animals and everything else. As long as there is enough oxygen in the water to support life, then the microscopic organisms that live in running water will break down the animal or plant matter and use it as food. If the wastes are inorganic or poisonous, then the running water will dilute them. The understanding at the time was that dilution is the solution and all rivers run to the sea, so there was no need for restraint when it came to dumping wastes into the waterways.

This policy contaminated the drinking water for cities

downstream, creating a public health hazard. The solution was to build water treatment plants that used sand filters to clean the water and added chlorine to create safe drinking water. We polluted the waterways and used technology to make clean water for the cities.

The only regulations on a river were related to navigability, and any river running through an industrial city was polluted to a degree that is unimaginable today. The Rivers and Harbors Appropriation Act of 1899 prohibited the disposal of solid wastes in navigable waters that might impede boats, but did not address industrial and human wastes. Those were dumped with impunity.

Pittsburgh, the Smoky City, was the poster child for air pollution, and the Cuyahoga River was the avatar of water pollution. It famously burned in 1969, leading to the passage of the Clean Water Act. But there had been fires on the Cuyahoga since the 1800s.

This slow, winding river (*Cuyahoga* is from the Mohawk word *Cayagaga*, "crooked river") meanders about eighty-five miles through northeast Ohio to Lake Erie. Cleveland, at the mouth of the Cuyahoga River, was home to twenty oil refineries before the end of the Civil War.

Before cars, gasoline was an unusable fraction of refined crude oil that had to be disposed of. Refineries often dumped it directly into the waterways. John D. Rockefeller, who owned the largest refinery in Cleveland, wrote in 1881, "We used to burn [gasoline] for fuel in distilling the oil, and thousands and hundreds of thousands of barrels of it floated down the creeks and rivers, and the ground was saturated with it, in the constant effort to get rid of it." There were no federal regulations against dumping petroleum products in the river, and a rarely enforced city ordinance carried a $10 fine.

In addition to oil refineries, the Cuyahoga was lined with steel mills, chemical plants, paper mills, and other industrial facilities. The Cleveland sewer system piped its wastes directly into Lake Erie, where it joined the industrial wastes dumped into the river by Akron and Cleveland factories. When city residents complained about the smell and taste of their tap water, Cleveland moved its intake pipes farther into Lake Erie, away from the pollutants carried by the Cuyahoga.

Thanks to all of the refineries spilling oil and gasoline into the Cuyahoga, it was "so flammable that if steamboat captains shoveled glowing coals overboard, the water erupted in flames." The first big fire on the Cuyahoga may have been lit in August 1868, when sparks from a passing tugboat ignited an oil slick. In response, the Cleveland newspaper *Plain Dealer* called for oil refiners to stop dumping oil into the river: "Along the whole length of the river, under the wharves and even under the warehouses there are deposits of this flammable stuff, and in some places to the thickness of several inches." The flammable river was a problem that threatened waterfront properties and shipping.

During a spring flood in 1883, a boiler house standing in high water lit an oil slick created by a leaking refinery tank. The *New York Times* described the enormous fire racing along a creek that joined the Cuyahoga just before it reached downtown, moving towards Standard Oil's massive Cleveland refinery. Several tanks exploded and buildings burned, and only the valiant efforts of firefighters and Standard Oil employees saved the plant.

Fires on the Cuyahoga continued to burn in the twentieth century. In early 1912, gasoline leaking from a Standard Oil cargo ship was lit by a spark from a tugboat, igniting a sheet of fire on the river that burned five tugs and a yacht. "Without warning," the *Plain Dealer* reported, "a shriveling blast of blue flame from the water beneath them wrapped the dry dock in fire." In the end, three dry docks burned and five men were incinerated.

In 1922, there was another inferno near the same spot as the 1912 fire, and Congress passed a joint resolution for an international conference on maritime oil pollution. The "fire hazard created by the accumulation of floating oil on the piles of piers and bulkheads into harbor waters [was] a growing source of alarm." The modest Oil Pollution Act of 1924 prohibited maritime oil discharges but did not address industrial discharges or inland waterways.

The Cuyahoga flared again in 1930. In 1936, the river burned for five days, and an article in the *Cleveland Press* about the river's flammability identified the solution: fire tugs! Five years later when a river fire caused $7,500 worth of damage to an ore carrier, the problem was again defined as a lack of fire tugs. Another fire burned on the river in 1948, and the local Chamber of Commerce suggested regular river patrols to clean up oil slicks and other potential hazards.

In May of 1952, leaking oil from the Standard Oil Company facility formed a two-inch-thick oil slick, "the greatest fire hazard in Cleveland." According to the *Cleveland Press*, the slick spanned the river in some places. With so much available fuel, it was only a matter of time before the next conflagration. On November 1, 1952, the Cuyahoga started burning near the Great Lakes Towing Company's shipyard. The resulting five-alarm fire destroyed the Jefferson Avenue Bridge, the shipyard, and three tugboats. There were no deaths because the shipyard was closed on Saturday afternoon, but losses were estimated to be between $500,000 and $1.5 million.

Local officials and some captains of industry worked

together to reduce the risk of river fires. Refineries tried to limit their spills and boats were commissioned to remove oil-laden debris from the river. In 1957, the Army Corps of Engineers claimed the Cuyahoga was in "exceptionally good" shape because all local docks were accessible for shipping season. No mention was made of the fact that the river was unswimmable, undrinkable, and fishless for forty miles from Akron.

The Cuyahoga was not the only burning river in the country. According to John Hartig's *Burning Rivers*, fires on the Chicago River were community events, and spectators gathered on bridges to watch them. In the Rouge River, rafts of thick, oily sludge and feces regularly caught fire before they drifted into the Detroit River and then Lake Erie. The Buffalo River in upstate New York burned in the 1960s, and a tugboat on Pennsylvania's Schuylkill River was destroyed when an oil slick on the river's surface caught fire.

These rivers weren't just carrying petroleum products and feces. After World War II, the types of wastes that were disposed of changed significantly. Dow, Monsanto, and DuPont were manufacturing plastics, polychlorinated biphenyls (PCBs), and inorganic pesticides, such as dichlorodiphenyltrichloroethane (DDT). Thousands of new compounds and wastes from these industrial processes were discharged directly into the air and water. These new chemicals overwhelmed the rivers and streams that had previously been challenged by organic discharges.

Some of these materials were toxic, some were nonbiodegradable, and some of them bioaccumulate in the environment, moving up the food chain in ever-increasing concentrations. Humans are at the top of the food chain, so chemicals that bioaccumulate matter to all of us. Unlike earlier versions of air and water pollution, these chemicals were invisible.

In the 1960s, the American public became aware that some contaminants have global reach. Eighty-six nuclear bombs were exploded aboveground at the Nevada Test Site in the 1950s, releasing radioactive material into the atmosphere. Spread by the wind, the radioactive material blanketed the United States. A national network of radiation monitoring stations, which collected data between 1951 and 1958, measured thyroid doses of radioactivity as a function of age at exposure, region of the country, and dietary habits. They found that a person who drank milk had seven times more radioiodine in their thyroid than a person who drank no milk, and a person who drank goat milk had twenty-five to fifty times the exposure. Beware the lactating mammal.

Atom bomb tests alarmed the public in the late 1950s, when people learned that radioactive waste was falling on their backyards. Linus Pauling won the Nobel Peace Prize in 1962 for trying to stop aboveground testing of nuclear weapons, and the ban the bomb movement continued to spread. In 1963, many countries ratified the Partial Test Ban Treaty that prohibited the atmospheric testing of nuclear weapons.

DDT, like radioactive fallout, was invisible and persistent. DDT's fatal flaw is that its breakdown product, 1,1-Dichloro-2,2-bis(p-chlorophenyl) ethylene (or DDE), interferes with calcium deposition in bird eggs, leading to thin, fragile eggshells, and fish-eating birds carried particularly high concentrations. Species including peregrine falcons, eagles, hawks, and pelicans laid eggs with shells too thin for the parents to brood without breaking them. At a time when cities used broadcast spraying of DDT to control mosquitoes, it was clear that several bird species would disappear without federal regulations.

The thinned eggshells were an unexpected side effect of DDT, but pesticides and radiation were both known killers. PCBs were both invisible and unexpectedly dangerous.

PCBs are manufactured chemicals that are colorless to light yellow oily liquids or resin-like materials; they are often mixed with mineral oil. These mixtures are incredibly stable with no smell or taste. They are resistant to fire, pressure, temperature, electricity, and water. They do not change chemically, making them an ideal material to insulate big electrical transformers. PCBs have also been used in flame retardants, varnishes, waxes, sealants, glue, hydraulic fluids, lubricants, adhesives, and the inert fraction of pesticides. They were sprayed on dirt roads to keep the dust down. PCBs are useful because they do not break down.

PCBs were first manufactured in 1929 by the Swann Chemical Company, which later became part of Monsanto. As electrical networks multiplied during the first half of the twentieth century, companies that made transformers, like General Electric and Westinghouse Electric Corporation, became major purchasers of PCBs.

PCBs are fat soluble and accumulate in living organisms. Like DDT, they enter the food web and bioconcentrate (absorbed from water and accumulated in tissue to concentrations greater than those found in surrounding water) in fats. Phytoplankton absorb PCBs, and the zooplankton that eat phytoplankton store the PCBs in their lipids. The little fish eat the zooplankton, the bigger fish eat the little fish, and each step of the way the PCBs are conserved in their fat. PCBs have a long half-life, so they accumulate with age. The organism's lifetime body burden keeps increasing year by year. In addition to bioconcentration, PCBs also biomagnify with concentrations increasing in tissue as it moves up the food chain.

Small amounts of PCBs circulate in the blood serum and are excreted through feces. The other way PCBs are cleansed from the body is through egg-laying (for fish and birds) or lactation (for mammals).

As it turns out, PCBs mimic hormones and disrupt reproduction. The problem with hormone mimics is that both estrogen and testosterone actively control our physiology at very low concentrations, and are used throughout the animal kingdom. The same molecule that controls my fertility controls a bird's fertility, and a beetle's. PCBs have been linked to altered sexual development and behavior in numerous animal studies. In humans, PCBs affect sperm motility, endometriosis, the length of the menstrual cycle, the duration of lactation, and the volume of breast milk (and that's just the reproductive changes we know about).

Humans get their PCBs from eating fish, and women discharge PCBs from their bodies by nursing. When a woman begins lactating, her fat stores are mobilized to efficiently excrete lipids, and the mother transfers her burden of pollutants to her newborn. In the United States and other industrialized countries, PCBs are present in breast milk at about one part per million. According to the limits set by the World Health Organization, an American baby takes in five times the allowable daily intake for an adult. In 1981, one study showed that 93 percent of breast milk samples exceeded the US Food and Drug Administration's limit for newborn exposure to PCBs. The levels of PCBs in the breast milk of Europeans and North Americans are generally higher than those of women in developing nations.

PCBs are a dioxin-like substance, and people who are exposed to large amounts are often afflicted with chloracne, a debilitating set of skin eruptions that include blackheads, whiteheads, cysts, and pustules. Since PCBs remain stored in fat for years, chloracne is chronic. It takes at least two or three years after exposure to recover, and sometimes as long as fifteen to thirty years. The more subtle harms caused by PCBs were not understood for decades, but the acute response for the workers was apparent by 1933, when twenty-three out of twenty-four workers had chloracne.

In 1937, seven years after the first PCB factory opened its doors, the Harvard School of Public Health hosted a one-day meeting on the problem of systemic effects of certain chlorinated hydrocarbons, including PCBs (then called chlorinated diphenyl). Representatives from Monsanto, General Electric, and the US Public Health Service were there, and from a brief report on the one-day conference, it is clear that the dangers of PCBs were understood and widely known. It "is certainly capable of doing harm in very low concentrations," they wrote. There was "no doubt as to the possibility of systematic effects."

Monsanto was the sole manufacturer of PCBs, producing about 1.5 billion pounds before they were banned in 1979. The first manufacturing plant was in Anniston, Alabama (the state with the greatest diversity of freshwater species); the second was in Sauget, Illinois, across the Mississippi River from St. Louis. The town of Sauget was initially named Monsanto, and it was a company town. At that time, city government (which in this case was Monsanto) set the environmental regulations, taxes, and fines. No one will be at all surprised that Monsanto dumped PCBs into the waterways for decades, and both areas became Superfund sites. A world without water quality regulations is a dangerous world to live in.

People knew that PCBs were toxic and that direct contact caused chloracne, but they did not understand how persistent PCBs were until 1966, when Swedish scientists measured PCBs in human hair, birds and their eggs, fish, and pine needles. Their research, coming after Rachel Carson's *Silent Spring* on the dangers of DDT, was widely publicized.

In 1968, a scientist at UCLA Berkeley, Dr. Robert Risebrough, found PCBs in fish and birds from Puget Sound down to Baja California and Central America. Risebrough's paper, "Polychlorinated Biphenyls in the Global Ecosystem," was published in *Nature* in December 1968, the same year that PCB-contaminated rice oil sickened the residents of a Japanese town. Subsequent studies showed that in addition to affecting reproduction, very low levels of PCBs can impair the immune, endocrine, and nervous systems.

An internal document from General Electric in October 1969 titled "PCB: An Industry Problem?" details how the persistence of PCBs might affect the company. General Electric's Industrial Power and Capacitor Department purchased about 10 million pounds of PCBs a year, probably more than half of GE's total usage. Of that 10 million pounds, 9 million pounds went out in product. The rest? Some was returned to Monsanto, some was hauled away by a "New Jersey scavenger," and some was sent to the town dump. That's a million pounds a year of PCBs released into the environment from a single plant.

In total, the global production of PCBs was about 1.4 million tons. Roughly two-thirds of this is in landfills or in electrical insulators, with the other third deposited in coastal and ocean sediments. Pollutants entering the deep sea accumulate in the food chain, and deep-sea organisms regularly have higher reported concentrations of PCBs than surface-water species. PCBs have already affected the reproduction of sea lions and seals. Beluga whales are known to be contaminated with astonishingly high levels of PCBs. In the late 1980s, some researchers believed that it was entirely possible that, as more PCBs reach the oceans, all large sea mammals could disappear.

The invisible threats of DDT, radioactive fallout, and PCBs have affected people, animals, and plants around the world, in New York City as well as in remote, pristine locations like the Arctic. But there was another thoroughly modern insult to the waterways that was distressingly visible. The newfangled detergents worked better than ever, but the waterways foamed and turned green. There was nothing subtle about the change in water quality after detergents replaced soap.

Soap has been made since the Pyramids were built, from mixing alkaline ashes or lye with fats that form long hydrocarbon chains with a salt on the end. Soap traps the greasy dirt on your clothes in a little ball with oil on the inside and the water-loving part of the soap molecule on the outside, easily washed away. Procter & Gamble started making soap in Cincinnati in the 1840s, when it was the meatpacking center of the United States. Procter & Gamble used slaughterhouse byproducts—tallow and lard—to make candles and soap that it shipped on steamboats down the Ohio River to the Mississippi and then on to New Orleans. The company had huge contracts during the Civil War to supply the Union troops with soap and candles. After the war, people started to switch from candles to oil lamps, and by 1876, the company's soap production exceeded its candle production for the first time.

Their response was Ivory® soap. Instead of tallow or olive oil, this soap was made of cheap coconut and palm oils. It was white; it lathered but remained solid; it floated, thanks to the air in it; and it lasted longer than other soaps. Procter & Gamble promoted Ivory nationwide and became a multimillion-dollar company.

In 1931, Procter & Gamble started a fifteen-year research effort to develop a synthetic detergent that worked in hard water. The calcium, magnesium, and iron ions in hard water have always foiled soap by binding with it and creating soap scum that sticks to fabric. Tide®, the first heavy-duty detergent, was released in 1946 along with the automatic washing machine. Detergent is a two-part molecule, like soap, that allows water to break up oil and grease and float away the dirt. But attached to the hydrocarbon-salt chain is a sodium tripolyphosphate molecule that ties up the metals in hard water, so it all can be rinsed away. The resulting heavy-duty detergent doesn't leave a residue on fabric. By the early 1950s, Tide had captured more than 30 percent of the laundry market, and it has been the number one selling laundry detergent every year since.

Phosphate detergents are generally nontoxic, but after your clothes are clean, most of the wastewater and its detergents are released into the waterways. The surfactant in the detergent causes foam to form, and the phosphate builder makes the foam stable.

Long-lasting, stable foam is a bad addition to the waterways. The phosphorus in detergents was even worse. Algae require phosphorus, nitrogen, and carbon to grow, and there is usually plenty of carbon and nitrogen in water. As a result, phosphorus is typically the limiting nutrient for algal growth. This means that the amount of algae in the waterways depends on the amount of phosphorus in the water, and detergents contained a lot of phosphorus.

Freshwater scientist Christopher Knud-Hansen noted that the new laundry detergents contained about 7 to 12 percent phosphorus. By 1983, over 2 million tons of phosphorus were used in US detergents. Since one pound of phosphorus can grow 700 pounds of algae, this excess phosphorus had significant effects on the health of the waterways.

Lakes went from crystalline to algal green. When algae die, they settle to the bottom of the water body and decompose. This strips oxygen from the bottom of the lake or pond and destroys deep-water fisheries. In addition, anoxic bottom waters release hydrogen sulfide, which causes the waterways to smell like rotten eggs and makes recreation less plausible. Nationwide, detergents accounted for about half of the phosphorus in the waterways. Vermont's Lake Champlain grew underwater castles of algae in bays that had always been clear, as did lakes around the country. By the late 1960s, nearly 10,000 lakes were blighted by detergents.

Lake Erie is the shallowest Great Lake, and the smallest by volume. Through the 1960s, about 20,000 pounds of phosphorus entered Lake Erie every day, about half from cities and industries and half from fertilizer runoff. Soon algal mats covered the shoreline, and the populations of sport fish had dwindled or disappeared.

∘ ∘ ∘

As air and water quality declined, more people were enjoying outdoor recreation. In the 1950s, automobile ownership increased and low-density suburbs sprouted across the landscape. The interstate highway system knit the country together, but consumer society led to increased solid wastes, litter, and mounting concerns over smog and corporate pollution. Billboards and pollution created urban blight, seen as both ugly and unhealthy. People could see that nature was under siege.

The Cuyahoga River burned again in 1969, and it was a turning point for environmental consciousness. This was a relatively tame fire, all considered, that damaged two railroad bridges and was extinguished in half an hour by the fire tugs. It was gone before anyone had a photograph of it. But five weeks after the fire, *Time* magazine ran a piece in the Friday, August 1, 1969, issue under the headline "America's Sewage System and the Price of Optimism."

> Some river! Chocolate-brown, oily, bubbling with subsurface gases, it oozes rather than flows. "Anyone who falls into the Cuyahoga does not drown," Cleveland's citizens joke grimly. "He decays." The Federal Water Pollution Control Administration dryly notes: "The lower Cuyahoga has no visible life, not even low forms such as leeches and sludge worms that usually thrive on wastes."

Time used a photograph from the 1952 fire to illustrate the article, and people were shocked. A burning river is almost biblical. It is epically wrong.

People were becoming aware that the nation was facing an environmental crisis. Nature was literally dying. There were mounds of detergent foam ten to twelve feet high at the base of Niagara Falls, and around the country streams and creeks were foaming. Something had to be done. Citizens were going to have to save nature before it was too late.

11

Protecting Nature

On January 28, 1969, an oil well failed in the Santa Barbara Channel, six miles off the California coast. "Uneventful Day," read the *Los Angeles Times* headline, "Then Well No. 5 Blew Out." The oil flowed freely for eleven days, and lesser leaks plagued the channel for the rest of the year. The Santa Barbara spill created the third-largest oil slick in US history, after the 2010 British Petroleum Deepwater Horizon blowout in the Gulf of Mexico and the 1989 *Exxon Valdez* crash off Alaska.

Santa Barbara is a cupcake of a university town nestled between the Pacific Ocean and the Santa Ynez Mountains. In

1969, it was home to an engaged citizenry of about 70,000 students, surfers, artists, and upper-middle-class liberals. At the time, no place was off-limits to resource extraction. The Santa Barbara Channel saw its first drilling rigs in 1958. A decade later, when the Lyndon B. Johnson administration was trying to finance the Vietnam War without raising taxes, more oil leases in the Santa Barbara Channel seemed like a good idea. Oil companies bid for leases on more than 450,000 acres under the Santa Barbara Channel, and the government received $624 million for seventy leases.

Disaster struck in less than a year.

An oil slick of about 800 square miles formed in the channel, and a storm finally pushed the oil ashore eight days after the accident. Oil containment booms were laid to keep the spill away from the harbors and beaches, but they failed. Sticky, black crude oil–covered birds, seals, sea lions, dolphins, kelp beds, and mile after mile of beaches. In the end, roughly 4 million gallons of oil were released and over thirty miles of California's coastline were besmirched. On some beaches, the oil was six inches deep.

"A week after the blowout," recalled one resident, "you'd go to the beach and you couldn't hear the waves. . . . Just . . . slop, slop, slop, slop. And people just stood there and cried."

Another person recalled that there were "miles of beach— as far as the eye could see—covered in black oil. Beaches that you walked on, swam off of, just gazed at countless times. And the smell of oil was just everywhere."

Meanwhile, no one knew how to manage an oil slick. Straw was thrown down to soak up oil in the harbors and on beaches, and pitchforked into waste barrels that were dumped in a canyon; subsequent rainstorms swept the blackened hay back to the shoreline. Eventually more than 5,200 dump trucks of oily wastes were landfilled. Six months after the blowout, oil continued to wash ashore and some beaches were still closed.

The oil slick in the channel took more than a year to dissipate.

Many of the townspeople had objected to the government auction of oil-drilling rights off Santa Barbara, and they were furious. These Santa Barbara residents held protests, signed petitions, and demanded a ban on offshore drilling. They staged plays, sang protest songs, and wrote hundreds of letters to the editor. The nearby Los Angeles news community featured the Santa Barbara spill on nightly television news, and lawsuits filed by the city and county of Santa Barbara sought $1 billion in damages from oil companies and the federal government. This oil spill caught the nation's attention.

Before the days of federal regulation, everyday environmental degradation was so profound that action had become imperative. The public was agitating for pollution control at the local, state, and federal levels. Local organizations sprang up in communities near polluted water bodies, particularly the Great Lakes, and citizen action groups were formed across the country. The Student Council on Pollution and the Environment, Buffalo's Housewives to End Pollution, the Society Against Violence to the Environment, the Clean Air Coordinating Committee, Chicago's Campaign Against Pollution, the Group Against Smog and Pollution, and Santa Barbara's Get Oil Out all lobbied their local city councils, state legislatures, and national representatives. By 1970, there were thirty-six Chicago groups working for a cleaner environment, and thirty organizations in northern California alone.

At the time of the Santa Barbara spill, Republican president Richard Nixon had just been inaugurated. Nixon, caught in a historic moment, was our nation's most effective environmentalist. Southeast Asia and China were more interesting to Nixon than the US environment, yet he signed a far-reaching pile of laws to prevent his Democratic rivals from claiming the issue as their own.

Nixon's tapes reveal more than you'd want to know about what he really thought. In a meeting with automakers in the Oval Office, he explained that environmentalists wanted to "go back and live like a bunch of damned animals." They weren't even sincere, according to Nixon. They're "a group of people that aren't one really damn bit interested in safety or clean air. What they're interested in is destroying the system. They're enemies of the system." Nixon clearly did not see himself as an environmentalist, but he presided over an astonishing amount of environmental legislation.

After the Santa Barbara spill, bills to protect the environment were introduced by both parties, and Nixon's January 1970 State of the Union address was a call to action: "Clean air is not free, and neither is clean water. . . . Through our years of past carelessness we incurred a debt to nature, and now that debt is being called." The *New York Times*' above-the-fold headline was "Nixon, Stressing Quality of Life, Asks in State of Union Message for Battle to Save Environment."

Nixon set up the framework for US environmental policy because he had to. "Restoring nature to its natural state is a cause beyond party and beyond factions," he said. "It has become a common cause of all of the people of this country." Laissez-faire capitalism had resulted in unbreathable air and unswimmable waterways, and the times were changing.

The new environmentalists were different from conservationists like Teddy Roosevelt, John Muir, and Gifford Pinchot. Those men wanted to protect beauty and resources from people who would kill all the animals and cut all the trees for money. Saving nature, to them, meant regulating commercial hunters and reserving forestland from loggers. New environmentalism wanted to do a lot more than that: their intent was to readjust the relationship between humans and the Earth. By the 1960s, the air and water had been compromised, and protecting these commons would take a wholesale change in the way business was done. The new activists rejected the assumption that environmental degradation was a necessary corollary of affluence. Capitalism itself would have to be curbed to save the country.

Opinion polls from the late 1960s show a dramatic upswing in public concern about environmental issues, particularly water pollution. National organizations that pushed an environmental agenda were multiplying: 1969 saw the first meetings of the League of Conservation Voters and Friends of the Earth, the Natural Resources Defense Council was formed in 1970, and Greenpeace was launched in 1971.

Civil rights, the counterculture, the music, and mass demonstrations in the streets were signs of a fundamental shift in American culture. In the Age of Aquarius, happiness was no longer contingent on simply having enough money to purchase material goods. Instead, people were starting to believe that living without nature makes us poor.

When Stewart Brand wrote the first *Whole Earth Catalog* in 1968, his preface read, "We are as gods and might as well get good at it." Until now, he noted, power has been held by "government, big business, formal education, church." But "a realm of intimate, personal power is developing—power of the individual to conduct his own education, find his own inspiration, shape his own environment and share his adventure with whoever is interested. Tools that aid this process are sought and promoted by the *Whole Earth Catalog*." Long before the Internet and the personal computer, Stewart Brand promoted self-sufficiency through networks of like-minded people. *The Last Whole Earth Catalogue* won the National Book Award in 1972, in the category "Contemporary Affairs."

"Stay Hungry," wrote Brand. "Stay Foolish."

Change the world.

People were rejecting established norms in favor of an individualistic nature-centered worldview. Communes and the back-to-the-land movement were based on a personal connection to nature, and Nixon guided Congress to embrace a new role in environmental protection. "Our current environmental situation calls for fundamentally new philosophies of land, air, and water use," said Nixon, "for stricter regulation, for expanded government action, for greater citizen involvement, and for new programs."

Nixon's environmental engagement was backdropped by the first Earth Day on April 22, 1970, when over 20 million people—about one-tenth of the country—demonstrated across the United States for action on the environment. Nixon signed an executive order creating the US Environmental Protection Agency (EPA) at the end of the year, with the mission of protecting public health and the environment. The Clean Air Act and its tough automobile emission standards followed.

The foaming rivers and algae-clogged lakes—one of the most visible signs of nature gone askew—came next. Lake Erie had been declared dead in the late 1960s, thanks to the 1.5 billion daily gallons of sewage and industrial effluent pouring into the lake from Detroit, Cleveland, and 120 other cities.

Canada's response to the Great Lakes' distress was the 1970 Canada Water Act, which reduced phosphorus in detergents. The United States took longer. In classic American fashion, the soap manufacturers bound together to form the Soap and

Detergent Association with the purpose of questioning whether phosphates really caused eutrophication, where excess nutrients in water leads to excessive growth of algae and plants. As with tobacco and lung cancer or fossil fuels and global warming, doubts over whether detergents caused lakes to be clogged with algae were funded by corporations with profits at stake.

In the face of federal inaction, cities in six different states outlawed detergents with phosphates in 1971. The result was a patchwork of laws until the federal government (and its friends, the soap manufacturers) caught up with the will of the people.

The Clean Water Act was like a miracle. When you stop dumping industrial and municipal wastes into the waterways, they become healthy. It worked every time: soon after a wastewater treatment plant was built, clean water and fish replaced the turds and algae that had clogged the local river, lake, or seashore. The trash that littered the waterways was cleared out, often by citizen groups, and over time many of the country's rivers and lakes have became vibrantly alive. Boston, for example, was the last major US city to build adequate wastewater treatment facilities. Until the 1980s, Boston Harbor was a fetid mess, and the prevailing currents deposited human feces onto Winthrop Beach. Thanks to the EPA, dolphins and seals now swim in the harbor, and Winthrop Beach smells like the seashore.

Without federal regulations, cities and industries ruined our commons because costs incurred by damaging public health and the environment aren't paid by the polluters, and it is always cheaper to dump wastes into the air and water. Pollution control is expensive, and federal environmental laws are the sole reason that our cities are no longer dark with smog, our waterways don't burn, and many lakes and rivers are now swimmable. As Nixon said, clean air and clean water aren't free.

○ ○ ○

We've been focusing on air and water pollution, but there was also an ongoing fight to save animals from extinction. We left species protection back in 1918, when overharvesting was the biggest problem, and the Migratory Bird Treaty Act was passed to increase waterfowl populations. It didn't work, and a 1934 report listed migratory waterfowl as the most significant issue in wildlife conservation. Conservationist Jay Darling testified that migratory waterfowl populations were a quarter of what they had been in 1910, and his Duck Stamp Act of 1934 funded an expansion of the national wildlife refuge system before ducks disappeared. Mammals, however, were on their own. Director of the National Park Service Arno Cammerer warned Congress that unless "fur-bearers, notably the wolf, wolverine, badger, otter, and fisher" were protected, they would be gone. The government did nothing, and citizens formed national organizations to advocate for wildlife, including the Wilderness Society in 1935, the National Wildlife Federation in 1936, and Ducks Unlimited in 1937.

The first attempt to protect the bald eagle was the 1930 House Resolution 7994. The National Audubon Society presented evidence that the bald eagle was in danger of extinction, and many conservation groups supported the bill. But it took a decade for the law to pass because ranchers saw eagles as dangerous predators (in fairness, eagles can eat a lot of chickens, are notorious for eating lamb eyes as well as lambs, and can kill small calves). In 1940, the Bald and Golden Eagle

Protection Act finally safeguarded these apex predators from humans.

Sport hunters and ranchers had a mutual distaste for predators, and guided most wildlife management decisions in the 1950s and '60s. Government agencies worked to increase the populations of certain species and eradicate others, and there was no room for wolves or grizzlies on public land.

The World Wildlife Fund (WWF) was created in 1961 as an arm of the International Union for Conservation of Nature (IUCN) to save the world's most endangered species. They believed that $4.2 million (about $35 million in 2018) was enough to save the California condor, the whooping crane, the giant tortoise, the Ceylon elephant, the African lion, and more than a dozen other species from extinction. According to the *New York Times*, WWF scientists believed that about 200 species of mammals and birds had become extinct "since the time of Jesus," and more than a third of these extinctions took place in the first half of the twentieth century. Their list of species that needed saving included several that were native to the United States.

A world list of endangered and threatened species—the IUCN's Red List of Threatened Species—was first published in 1964. The US Fish and Wildlife Service created the Committee on Rare and Endangered Species that same year, and nine biologists determined that some thirty-five to forty species had gone extinct in North America since the American Revolution, and sixty-two US species were currently threatened with extinction. They faulted habitat destruction, overhunting, and pollution.

Most of the species that caught people's imagination were charismatic megafauna. In particular, people loved whales and other cetaceans, and Dr. John C. Lilly was largely responsible for their popularity. *Man and Dolphin*, which a review in *Science* magazine described as "one of the frankest and most egotistical accounts of a research project ever placed before a sensation-loving public," was his first bestseller.

Lilly first studied dolphin intelligence by implanting electrodes in their brains. Later research projects on dolphin communication included giving dolphins LSD and interspecies sex. (Both of these research projects are less shocking than they sound, since psychoactive drugs were new, and given to many species for research—a paper on drugged spiders is a classic of the genre—and dolphins are one of the few species that enjoy year-round recreational sex.)

Lilly was a fan of anecdotal evidence, and little of his research was peer reviewed. But he was very enthusiastic. According to Lilly, dolphins were peaceful, generous, and sexually liberated. Lilly waxed poetic about dolphins' social compassion, intelligence, and complex phonations: dolphins use whistles and clicks to communicate. Other cetaceans, particularly whales, have elaborate songs constructed with individual variations on common forms, lasting from six to thirty minutes. Whales repeat their song very precisely, and their songs change slowly from year to year. As a child, my dad told me that blue whales would go extinct because there were so few left they couldn't find each other in the oceans. Then we learned about whale songs, and our understanding of the oceans changed. Whales are the voice of the ocean, and their songs can be heard for hundreds of miles.

How smart are cetaceans? Really smart. One guess is that their intelligence is equivalent to a three-year-old human, or a smart dog. Which might sound insulting except that three-year-olds are really smart, as are dogs. Plus they echolocate, using sound to "see" objects.

Bottlenose dolphins have bigger brains than humans (1,600 grams versus 1,300–1,400 grams), and when body size is taken into account they have the largest brains of all animals but humans. Considering that dolphins swim in cold water and need a layer of blubber for insulation, their ratio of brain weight to body weight is very impressive. Their neocortex, the area of the brain used for language, cognition, sensory perception, and spatial reasoning, is more convoluted than ours. Complex social relationships are linked to large brains, and research has revealed that wild dolphins, like elephants, apes, and humans, have highly complex social lives.

The new discoveries about cetaceans led people to reconsider their beliefs about marine mammals and animal intelligence. To some people, cetaceans represented an alternate evolutionary path for an intelligent mammal. Cetaceans are like better human beings with a more enlightened relationship with nature.

Flipper, the television show that ran from 1964 to 1967, featured a dolphin who befriends a Florida park ranger and his sons. *Flipper* was marketed like *Lassie*, on lunch boxes, souvenir spoons, swim trunks, and a glow-in-the-dark watch, in comics, puzzles, songbooks, coloring books, and a children's novel. *Flipper* did not have an ecological message. There was no attempt to show bottlenose dolphins as anything but a human sidekick. And no attempt to be accurate: his voice is reportedly a slowed-down version of the song of an Australian kingfisher, or kookaburra. But the television show presented these mammals as clever, worthy, and kind.

Naturalist Marlin Perkins hosted *Mutual of Omaha's Wild Kingdom*, an educational series centering on the lives of animals, which ran from 1963 to 1971. *The Undersea World of Jacques Cousteau* was a documentary television series, which ran from 1966 to 1976, hosted by conservationist Jacques-Yves Cousteau and the crew of his ship, the *Calypso*. They went to different areas of the globe to film episodes like "Sharks" and "Octopus, Octopus," teaching people about the oceans at a time when our understanding of these biomes was in its infancy. Both of these programs presented the intrinsic value of different species to people who may not have thought about nature in that way.

In 1966, the *New York Times* reported that only forty-four whooping cranes and thirty-eight condors remained, and that bald eagles and Florida's Key deer were on the brink of disappearing forever. In the past, this news would have spurred collectors to harvest and stuff the last few individuals for museums and private collections. That's how the auk went extinct. But this time, people were thinking about other species with more respect.

Congress passed the 1966 Endangered Species Preservation Act because the public was demanding that the federal government step in and save iconic American species. The act pulled together existing wildlife refuges and other federal lands to create the National Wildlife Refuge System, and hunters were barred from killing endangered species in the refuges (but not on private, state, or other federal lands).

Florida's Key deer was the first species saved by the Endangered Species Preservation Act. These strange, fairy-like creatures weigh between sixty-five and eighty-five pounds, about the size of a Labrador retriever. There may have been just twenty-five deer left when the government intervened and created Key deer refuges that grew to 9,200 acres. These little deer are common now on some of the Keys, living testimony to the fact that we can save endangered species from extinction.

The Fish and Wildlife Service's list of endangered species

now included seventy-eight species. The *New York Times* kept writing about the impending extinctions, and a September 9, 1967, editorial noted that the global list of species facing extinction included 250 species, including the "blue whale, the polar bear and the leopard, the fearsome tiger and the humble alligator." A few weeks later, the newspaper was decrying the fur trade as preying on some of the rarest and most beautiful creatures alive. Jackie Kennedy's leopard coat of 1962 had inspired a national craze that, at eight pelts per coat, was driving the big cat to extinction.

Hunters had become very efficient, as had whalers. Modern industrial whaling started soon after 1900, with large factory ships, fast catching boats, and specialized crews. The largest and fastest whales could now be caught and rendered, and soon the factory ships had rear slipways so whales could be winched directly onto the deck up a ramp.

"One modern factory ship can take more whales in one season than the entire American whaling fleet of 1846 which number over 700 vessels," said US Coast Guard lieutenant junior grade Quentin R. Walsh in 1938 after a year on the whale factory ship *Ulysses*. (During his tour, the *Ulysses* crew killed 3,665 whales.)

Close to 3 million whales were processed during the twentieth century alone. Just looking at sperm whales, about 300,000 were killed in the eighteenth and nineteenth centuries, another 300,000 were killed between 1900 and 1962, and 300,000 more were killed between 1962 and 1972. The problem with these numbers is that females do not physically mature until about the age of thirty, and males do not physically mature until they are about fifty. Populations of these slow-growing, long-lived mammals had no way to recover from ships that could process a hundred sperm whales a day.

Whales were common property and an open-access resource: no one owned them and anyone could take them. They were initially plentiful and when one species dwindled from overhunting, another species would become the favored prey. The cost of a factory ship was so high that, in practice, the world's whales were divided between a handful of ships.

Blue whales had been too fast to catch and too big to process until factory ships started being built. Between 1910 and 1966, an impressive 330,000 blue whales were killed in the Antarctic alone. According to the IUCN, a female reaches sexual maturity when she is about thirty-one years old and seventy-eight feet long. The 1937 International Agreement for the Regulation of Whaling allowed whalers to take blue whales at seventy feet, so whalers harvested the adolescents as well as the adults. The average length of the blue whales caught in 1965 was seventy-three feet. They were catching the teenagers, and there was no hope for the next generation.

Old harpoons stuck in the blubber of recently harvested bowhead whales show that they can live to be over 200 years old. We don't know how old sperm whales and blue whales can be, but a species that doesn't reach sexual maturity for fifty years could be very long-lived indeed.

Whaling has been regulated since 1931, when twenty-two nations signed the Geneva Convention for the Regulation of Whaling and agreed to stop bowhead whaling; right and gray whales were protected in 1935. The International Convention for the Regulation of Whaling was signed in Washington, DC, in December 1946, and the International Whaling Commission (IWC) was set up "to provide for the proper conservation of whale stocks and thus make possible the orderly development of the whaling industry."

In spite of the regulated harvest, species after species of

whales were harvested to near extinction. In its first thirty years, the IWC authorized the harvest of 1.5 million whales, about half of the total killed in the twentieth century. Some populations were slaughtered completely, and others were reduced to a small fraction of their original abundance. The IWC banned humpback whaling in the North Atlantic in 1955, the hunting of blue whales in 1966, and fin whale hunting in the southern hemisphere and the northern Pacific in 1976.

And yet hunting continued. In *The Blue Whale*, which won the 1972 National Book Award, George Small described case after case of illegal whaling. The most gruesome account was of Aristotle Onassis's factory ship *Olympic Challenger*, a notorious pirate whaler. In 1954, Onassis was charged in court with slaughtering 4,648 sperm whales, 285 blue whales, 169 fin whales, 105 humpbacks, and 21 sei whales during a year in which he had a modest declared catch of 2,348 sperm whales. After many protests, Onassis paid a fine of $3 million, and upholstered the barstools on his private yacht with leather made from sperm whale penises (which, according to the Amsterdam Zoo, is the only skin on a whale that can be tanned and used as leather). I can only hope that Jackie Kennedy Onassis never wore her leopard-skin coat while perched on a barstool on the *Christina*, lest the gates of hell yawn open.

Onassis liked his factory ship, and kept using it even when regulations limited his allowed catch. So did the Soviet Union, which owned seven factory ships, each with a fleet of catcher boats that numbered from three to over a dozen. In a single day, the largest factory ships could process up to 200 small sperm whales or 100 humpback whales, and they weren't inclined to stop. Even with multiple international observers living on factory ships, whalers figured out how to cheat the rules. The USSR whaling fleet is estimated to have illegally killed about 180,000 whales worldwide after hunting was banned, and was responsible for a number of population crashes. By the time blue whale hunting stopped, there may have been as few as 200 left.

The most disturbing part of this story is that there was no need to harvest whales. In the twentieth century, whale oil, baleen, and ivory were products with viable substitutes. European margarine and soap makers started replacing whale oil with tastier seed and nut oils in the 1950s. The Soviets used whale oil for lubricants, and whale meat as food on fur farms; the Japanese and Norwegians eat whale meat. I ate whale meat in Norway in 1970, where it was sold in the market as *hvalbiff* (whale steak). My mother bought it thinking of halibut, but hvalbiff is nearly purple, like liver, because whales have more myoglobin in their muscles than cows (or humans). Myoglobin stores oxygen, allowing whales to stay underwater for up to ninety minutes at a time. The meat tasted like rich, lean beef.

A series of recordings of humpback songs was released in 1970 as the album *Songs of the Humpback Whale*. This became the bestselling environmental record in history, achieving multiplatinum status. In 1979, *National Geographic* magazine inserted a flexible sound page of *Songs of the Humpback Whale* inside the back cover of all of its editions, with 10 million copies sent around the world in a single month, perhaps the greatest single pressing of any album ever. Humpback whale songs are psychedelic and a little trippy, perfect for the era. The songs were recorded by whale biologist Roger Payne and his sidekick, Scott McVay, a former lab researcher for dolphin aficionado John C. Lilly. Their article in *Science* magazine introduced humpback songs to the world: "The humpback whale," they wrote, "emits a surprisingly beautiful series of sounds."

Whale music helped inspire the worldwide movement to

save the whales. The songs ranged from heartfelt moans and deep growls to high wails and riffles of clicks, encompassing the full range of emotions. As an engineering student, I did years of problem sets with *Songs of the Humpback Whale* playing in the background. What better way to set up graphs than by listening to animals who can see sound?

At first, the United States tried to save the whales by itself. The US secretary of the interior put all the great whales on the endangered species list, whether or not they needed to be there. No US company had harvested whales since World War II, but hunting or selling whales became illegal in 1971 when the US secretary of the interior banned commercial whaling. Whaling fleets were owned by many other countries, though, and saving the whales was an international problem. Congress passed a resolution calling on the secretary of state to negotiate a ten-year moratorium on commercial whaling with other nations.

The harsh truth about whaling is that factory fleets are too efficient. A single whaling factory fleet is capable of deconstructing 35,000 humpbacks a year, if they can find them. That means that a factory ship's annual quota of 3,000 whales leaves the vessel woefully underused. There are plenty of minke whales—over half a million—but they're much smaller than humpbacks and a single factory ship might be capable of processing 100,000 to 150,000 a year. Should only one country be allowed to harvest minke whales? Shall we allow three or four factory fleets to harvest them all? When a single ship is capable of eradicating an entire species in a single decade, it's good to remember that when profits are balanced against regulations, profits often win.

Nixon signed the Marine Mammal Protection Act in 1972, which protected every marine mammal from harassment or harvest. The United States would no longer attempt to harvest any of these animals because the factory ships were so enormous and the remaining populations of marine mammals so remote that, in practice, the harvest could not be regulated.

In 1972, Nixon ran against George McGovern. The protests against the Vietnam War were escalating, and the Republican Party's adoption of environmental protection made Nixon a more attractive candidate. The Republican Party platform of 1972 included a promise of "vigorous environmental protection . . . [to] restore the water quality of the Great Lakes in cooperation with Canada . . . [and] protect and conserve marine mammals and other marine species."

"We commit ourselves to comprehensive pollution control laws," claimed the Republicans, and "vigorous implementation of those laws and rigorous research into the technological problems of pollution control." They even liked public land: "We have proposed 36 new wilderness areas, adding another 3.6 million acres to the National Wilderness Preservation System." And they liked whales most of all.

The Nixon White House tapped into the growing energy of the anti-whaling movement as part of a larger political strategy to maintain American environmental leadership internationally. The 1972 UN Conference on the Human Environment in Stockholm was the first global meeting on the environment, and the United States pushed hard for a ten-year moratorium on commercial whaling everywhere in the world. The ten-year moratorium on commercial whaling was adopted by nearly all nations, and the International Whaling Commission voted in favor of sustaining the moratorium in 1982. It is still in effect today. This was the first time all of the world's nations worked together to solve an environmental problem.

The USSR was a rogue operator in the 1970s, and nearly

pushed some species of cetaceans to extinction. But they stopped whaling in the 1980s, and the whales have in fact been saved. The blue whale population is now somewhere between 10,000 and 25,000 from a low of perhaps 200. They survived.

∘ ∘ ∘

Published in 1972 by Dennis Meadows, Donella Meadows, Jørgen Randers, and William W. Behrens III, *Limits to Growth* became an international phenomenon, selling over 30 million copies in more than thirty languages. The thesis was that if current rates of economic growth, resource use, and pollution continued, then modern civilization would face environmental and economic collapse in the mid-twenty-first century. This tied in nicely with ecologist Garrett Hardin's well-named 1968 *Science* article "The Tragedy of the Commons," where he explains that rational individuals will exploit common property like forests and fields without considering the effects on other people because the individual reaps all of the benefits, and the costs to the community are evenly distributed: I win a lot, and everyone else loses a little. Individuals, acting independently and rationally, will behave against the community's long-term interests by overusing the commons. The same year, biologist Paul Ehrlich wrote the bestselling book *The Population Bomb*, predicting that overpopulation would lead to mass starvation unless there was an international effort to slow population growth.

While the 1973 Endangered Species Act (ESA) was debated, the whole nation was thinking that there were too many people, too much pollution, and not enough room for wild animals. Eagle and condor populations had still not recovered, and a 1972 study showed that between 1968 and 1970, furriers in the United States imported 18,456 leopard skins, 31,105 jaguar skins, and 249,680 ocelot skins. The current laws weren't working. Aldo Leopold's line from *A Sand County Almanac*, "To keep every cog and wheel is the first precaution of intelligent tinkering," was passed around like a mantra, along with the tautology "extinction is forever."

The ESA passed unanimously in the Senate, and the House vote was 355–4. When Nixon signed it, his camera-ready quote was, "Nothing is more priceless and more worthy of preservation than the rich array of animal life with which our country has been blessed."

The ESA protected habitats as well as individual animals. This led to the practice of shoot, shovel, and shut up, where ranchers would kill and bury endangered species they found on their property, fearful that the government would tell them how to manage their land. But at the time, when our native species were fading away in front of our eyes, Republicans and Democrats both wholeheartedly supported the ESA.

Within the United States, a new kind of environmental consciousness was taking root. Before major projects were built, input from a variety of stakeholders was taken into account. Impacts and alternatives were considered, and decisions were made after public hearings and comments. New oil leases and drilling-rig proposals had to be evaluated for their environmental impacts, and could be prohibited on those grounds. Untreated sewage and industrial wastes could no longer be discharged into the waterways, cars could no longer belch smoke, and freeways could no longer be built through the middle of a neighborhood. People finally had a voice, which was often clamoring to decrease pollution, and before long environmental considerations even played a part in factory design and plant location. Protecting the environment became part of the way we do business.

We have cleaned up our air and water. The EPA, Clean

Water Act, and Clean Air Act were largely successful, but in the 1970s a number of invisible international threats emerged. Ozone depletion came first, and then acid rain.

It is astonishing how quickly the world came together to solve the ozone problem. In 1974, Sherry Rowland and Mario Molina wrote a paper published in *Nature* that explained how human-made chlorofluorocarbons (CFCs), used as refrigerants, in air conditioners, and as an aerosol propellant in cans, could damage the Earth's protective ozone layer. They postulated that loss of ozone would allow more ultraviolet light to reach the Earth's surface, and skin cancer and cataracts would become much more common. Although ozone loss had not been observed in the stratosphere—this was just a theory—these researchers recommended that CFCs be banned.

CFCs were an $8 billion business and DuPont, who made a quarter of the world's CFCs, claimed there was no proof that CFCs were harming the ozone layer. DuPont's chairman, quoted in *Chemical Week*, commented that the ozone depletion theory was "a science fiction tale . . . a load of rubbish . . . utter nonsense." In the same July 16, 1975, issue, Sherwin-Williams Company announced that it was removing CFCs from its spray cans and adding a cheerful endorsement to their labels: "Use with confidence, contains no Freon® or other fluorocarbons claimed to harm the ozone layer."

Before there was scientific consensus on ozone depletion and before anyone saw any ozone depletion in the atmosphere, the United States, Canada, Norway, Sweden, and Denmark all banned the use of CFCs in aerosol cans. The terms *ozone shield* and *hole in the ozone* were easily understood, and Americans voluntarily stopped buying aerosol sprays even before CFCs were banned in spray cans in 1978. The US ban on CFCs as a propellant in aerosol cans made a big dent in global production of CFCs, but they were still used as a refrigerant and to clean circuit boards.

In the spring of 1981, the Japanese and British research stations in Antarctica both observed a 20 percent reduction in ozone. None of the scientists involved made their findings public because each research team assumed that their low measurements were due to faulty instruments. The following spring, the ozone depletion was noted again. In 1984, researchers from the Japanese station authored a paper on the ozone findings, and scientists at the British station published their findings in *Nature*. The ozone hole had first appeared in 1981 and had been observed every year since then, just like Rowland and Molina's 1974 paper had predicted.

Under Ronald Reagan, the United States pushed for the international regulation of CFCs. A year after the ozone paper in *Nature*, the 1985 Vienna Convention for the Protection of the Ozone Layer was signed by twenty nations, including most of the CFC producers. A 1986 front-page article in the *New York Times* warned that "Americans could suffer 40 million cases of skin cancer and 800,000 cancer deaths in the next 88 years because of depletion of atmospheric ozone." DuPont, possibly thinking of potential lawsuits from 40 million excess cancer sufferers, suddenly supported CFC limits, and the Montreal Protocol on Substances That Deplete the Ozone Layer, with forty-three signatory nations, followed in 1987. Decades later, the hole in the ozone layer over the Antarctic has finally started to mend.

Acid rain was also curbed by the federal government's quick action. Until recently, the smoke from burning wood and coal went up the chimney in a cloud of alkaline soot and fly ash particles along with the acids produced during combustion, so the acids were neutralized by the soot. After World

War II, tall smokestacks caused regional acid rain problems because the heavier ash and soot would fall to the ground while the lighter precursor chemicals for acid rain would stay high, un-neutralized by the soot. Acid rain is a complex mess, chemically, but direct measurements of rainwater have sometimes shown it to be as acidic as lemon juice or vinegar.

When huge coal plants with high smokestacks were built in the Midwest, the eastern states of the United States started to be affected by acid compounds carried on the jet stream. Mountain forests and ponds in the Northeast started dying of acid deposition in the 1960s. One problem with acid rain is that the low pH allows heavy metals, particularly aluminum, to become bioavailable. Fish and birds were killed by overdoses of aluminum in high-altitude ponds throughout New England, and soon ponds in the White Mountains of New Hampshire, the Green Mountains of Vermont, and the Adirondacks of New York were completely devoid of life and ringed with small, pale skeletons. These dead ponds near the top of forested, seemingly wild mountains were surreal, and the soil was also affected: acid rain binds the calcium in soil, robbing plants of critical nutrients.

As fate would have it, a long-term forest monitoring project in central New Hampshire, the Hubbard Brook Experimental Forest, was the first place where the effects of acid rain were quantified. They found that throughout high-altitude New England, the acid rains stripped the buffers from the soil and released heavy metals, while the long-term biogeochemical measurements from Hubbard Brook show a decades-long decline in calcium levels in soil and plants. Thanks to *New York Times* reports on acid rain research, the Acid Precipitation Act was passed in 1980 to study the problem.

The northeastern mountains were acidified by a handful

of power plants, and the problem was solved using a clever, low-cost model. The 1990 Clean Air Act Amendments demanded that overall sulfur emissions from these plants be cut in half to reduce acid rain, but it did not specify which type of air pollution–control equipment should be used, or limit the pollutants emitted by each plant. Instead a cap-and-trade approach was written into the legislation.

Cap-and-trade is based on two principles: there is an overall cap or limit on pollutant emissions within a certain boundary, and there are tradable allowances that permit allowance holders to release a specific quantity of the pollutant. This allows environmental goals to be met, and provides flexibility for individual polluters to figure out how to reduce emissions. Since pollution allowances can be bought and sold, cap-and-trade programs are often classified as market-based. Power companies could use the plants with the least emissions, retire plants that polluted the most, conserve their way to fewer emissions, substitute fuels to reduce emissions, clean their fuel before combustion, or actually sell or buy emission rights, so plants that reduced their emissions cheaply can sell their reductions to plants that pollute more.

Acid rain faded away. According to the Environmental Defense Fund, sulfur emissions went down more quickly than expected at a quarter of the anticipated cost. The US experience with cap-and-trade was a big success, and the rain in the northeastern mountains is much sweeter.

Since the 1960s, a number of global environmental issues have been solved by nations working together. The United States helped save the whales, heal the ozone hole, and halt acid rain, and was well positioned to lead the world in curbing climate change.

12

Embracing Nature—Thinking Globally, Acting Locally

The primeval forests—what was left of them—exposed a toxic fault line running through the American body politic. Nearly everyone agreed that we should save the whales, but whales were part of the global commons and no one owned them. The whaling fleets were all owned by foreigners or foreign governments, so Americans had nothing to lose from a whaling ban.

In contrast, old-growth forests were rooted on land owned by lumber companies and managed as a crop, and on government forestland where trees are managed by the Department of Agriculture as a crop. Depending on your point of view, old-growth forests were either Nature's cathedral or a whole lot of standing timber. There was no agreement whatsoever about whether these forests should be preserved.

A conservative backlash against environmental regulation started with the Sagebrush Rebellion in 1976, when the Federal Land Policy and Management Act joined the Wilderness Act and the Endangered Species Act to shrink the amount of public land available for grazing, mining, and timbering. Ranchers, miners, and other property owners balked at the new environmental restrictions, and fought for greater local control of federally owned land. Ronald Reagan rode these issues into office, slashed funding for regulators, and removed the solar panels Jimmy Carter had mounted on the White House roof.

James Watt, Reagan's head of the Department of the Interior, said his job was to "follow the Scriptures, which call upon us to occupy the land until Jesus returns," and called the environmental movement a left-wing cult. Watt rescinded regulations, leased huge tracts of land to coal-mining companies, opened sweeping areas of the continental shelf to offshore drilling, and agreed to allow more local control over the management of federal lands. He loved cutting old-growth forests. There was suddenly far less for ranchers and miners to object to, and the rebellion fizzled.

In the go-go 1980s, a time of leveraged buyouts and Gordon Gekko's ethos of "Greed Is Good," both the lumber companies and the US Forest Service were keen to liquidate their big trees. The corporate and federal view of old-growth forests was neatly encapsulated by Ronald Reagan: "You know, a tree is a tree. How many more do you need to look at?"

The Reagan administration was eager to increase the volume of wood harvested from the national forests, and an easy way to do that was to cut the old trees in the virgin stands and replace them with fast-growing young trees. Reagan's forest manager, timber attorney John Crowell, believed we could double or even triple the production of board feet from the nation's forests by clearing out the overmature timber.

Soon large clear-cuts were replacing formerly pristine landscapes, and activists started demanding that the country's remaining old-growth forests—both public and private—be preserved. From one point of view, you'd have to be out of your mind to cut down the nation's last acres of primeval forest. From another, you must be mad to think of taking away the private property rights this nation was built on, or telling the government how to manage its forest resources. More than a generation later, the clear-cutters and the tree huggers still struggle to understand each other.

California's giant redwoods had been harvested since the 1850s, and by the 1980s over 90 percent of the coastal redwoods were gone. East of the Mississippi, almost all of the old forests had already been cut. The forests of the Rockies were nearly all second- and third-growth. The only substantial patches of primeval forest left in the country were in California, Oregon, and Washington. Too bad for the big trees, though, because the US Forest Service had no intention of preserving any additional acreage of old-growth forest. The Reagan plan was to create younger, more productive forests to be harvested every 70 to 120 years.

The largest private owner of redwood trees on the West

Coast was the Pacific Lumber Company (PALCO), which had been selectively cutting its 200,000 acres of forestland since the 1930s (200,000 acres is 312.5 square miles, a patch of land just thirty miles long by ten miles wide, and this was the largest privately owned redwood forest in existence). PALCO was cited as a model of wise forest management because they did a selective cut of 70 percent of the redwoods on a given plot every 50 years. This harvest schedule does not allow for old trees, but a properly done selective cut is nearly invisible. The big trees disappear, but you don't really see it happening. The forest just gets younger, year by year.

In the 1980s, PALCO was debt free with an overfunded pension fund and about $1.8 billion of standing timber. Charles Hurwitz, a corporate raider, and Michael Milken, the king of junk bonds, teamed up to do a hostile takeover of PALCO (which was not for sale). In the fall of 1985, Hurwitz bought PALCO with $800 million in junk bonds. In 1986, he started clear-cutting the redwood forest to cash out. PALCO's land was in Humboldt County, the unofficial hippie mecca and pot capital of California. There is no way this story was going to end well.

Clear-cutting commenced on PALCO's old-growth forest in California, and was already under way on public land in Oregon and Washington. Old-growth clear-cuts in the Willamette National Forest in Oregon had inspired direct action by members of the radical environmental organization Earth First!

Earth First! coalesced in 1979 as a leaderless group that used litigation and creative civil disobedience to protect wilderness. It was a group with philosophical underpinnings: they particularly liked Norwegian philosopher Arne Næss and deep ecology. Grounded in the teachings of Baruch Spinoza, Gandhi, and Buddha, Næss claimed that every living being, be it plant, fungus, animal, or insect, has an equal right to live and flourish. This doesn't mean that you can't kill a mosquito, just that the mosquito has as much right to a happy life as you do. According to Næss, the natural order—wildness—has intrinsic value that transcends human values. He takes it a step further, too: humans can only attain "realization of the Self" as part of the ecosphere because human beings, as individuals, are a tiny part of the web of life on Earth. Which is to say, whatever harm we do to the balance of life, we do to ourselves. That's the easy part. The difficult part of deep ecology is that the monocultures of industrial life destroy the Earth's cultural and biological diversity for convenience and profit—*human* convenience and profit, that is. And unless we reduce the human footprint on the world, we will destroy its diversity and beauty. Deep ecology claims that the point of protecting ecosystems is not just for humans, but for the Earth itself, and that the human population needs to be much, much lower. The Earth First! slogan is "No Compromise in the Defense of Mother Earth!" and they mean it.

Earth First! members had tried roadblocks to stop the harvest in the Willamette, and soon found that tree-sitting was an effective deterrent. Tree-sits in PALCO's Humboldt County forest started nearly as soon as clear-cutting commenced.

In 1985, Dave Foreman, one of the earliest members of Earth First!, wrote *Ecodefense: A Field Guide to Monkeywrenching*. This how-to book for environmental resistance, or ecoterrorism, includes information on how to disable equipment and destroy roads, how to make a smoke bomb, and how to spike a tree by hammering a metal rod into its trunk, which causes no lasting damage to the tree but deters loggers, who risk injury and damaged saws. *Ecodefense* is a cultural artifact from a time when sabotage—ecotage—seemed like the only way left to preserve the wilderness.

The hedge-fund manager Hurwitz, who ordered the clear-cutting of the last big chunk of privately owned old-growth forest in the United States, made a speech in which he told his loggers that "he who has the gold makes the rules." The eco-terrorists explained to the media that the sequoias are the elder spirits of the Earth plane. These people were speaking different languages, and the fight to save this particular patch of forestland lasted fifteen years.

Before it was resolved, a car bomb nearly killed Earth First! organizers Judi Bari and Darryl Cherney in 1990, 1,000 people were arrested at the then-largest forest protest of 6,000 demonstrators in 1996, Humboldt County deputies swabbed protesters' eyes with pepper spray at a protest of 9,000 in 1997, an activist was killed by a falling tree cut by a furious logger in 1998, and Julia "Butterfly" Hill completed an internationally famous tree-sit of 738 days in 1999 and finally descended when PALCO agreed to save the tree, affectionately dubbed "Luna," along with a 200-foot buffer zone. The state and federal government bought 10,000 acres of the forest. The rest is gone.

Earth First! members' rhetoric and actions seemed over the top until I spent a few days camping in an ancient forest in Idaho. When you start looking for old-growth forests, you begin to understand how rare they are. The National Commission for Science on Sustainable Forestry published an assessment of the nation's old-growth forest in 2008 that shows that less than 1 percent of the Northeast forest is old growth, and some states have just a few dozen acres. The forests of the Adirondacks have been protected for a century, but nearly all of the trees are second-growth, and the forest will take another few centuries to fully mature. Less than half a percent of the southeast forests is old growth, and around the Great Lakes old forests are even scarcer. The Southwest has a few pockets of old-growth ponderosas, and there are some very old individual trees in folds of land so steep that they couldn't be extracted, but nearly all of the Rockies were cut long ago. Trees were free money in a time when cash was hard to come by, and humans have enormous ingenuity. If a tree could be transported to the lumber mill, it was.

∘ ∘ ∘

Bob and I heard of an old-growth forest that was about ten miles long and three miles wide off a tributary to the Selway River in Idaho. The timber was still standing because it was nearly inaccessible, with a ten-mile hike down a slope so steep that a road (and equipment access) was impossible. It was a hike into a forgotten garden of ancient trees.

We all know what a forest looks like. But this Idaho forest of never-harvested cedars was unlike any place I've ever been. There were a few different species of trees along the river, but there was only one type of tree in the forest and no shrubbery. Cedars ruled as if they had held a council and decided that every other kind of tree would be excluded.

Instead of being evenly spaced, many of the trees grew in groups of two, three, and even four or five trees together. They seemed like old friends who had lived together peaceably, helping each other, for many centuries. And the forest was ageless, or timeless. One of the very largest trees in the forest had clearly grown on an ancient nurse log that had been equally large. A thousand-year tree growing on top of a thousand-year tree creates a vignette that begins at the time of the Roman Empire, and the tree still stands.

Forest Service employees had built a hiking trail that

passes through the valley, and many of the animal trails were equally clearly defined. The difference between a Forest Service trail and an animal trail, I learned, is that you can find axe-cut trees beside the human trail. Of course, animals use the human trail as well, and at one muddy stream crossing we saw the footprints of a wolf, a bear, elk, moose, and deer. The wolf print was so big it was unmistakable and I know bear tracks from Colorado, but I could not have distinguished between the elk and the moose without professional assistance. We were hiking with a retired Forest Service botanist, a friend who carried a can of pepper spray on his belt. There are lots of bears in southwest Colorado, and Bob and I know how to make ourselves big—take a wide stance and spread your arms like an X—so the bear runs away. It works in Colorado. But in a remote Idaho valley that's home to a pack of wolves, pepper spray is de rigueur because the bolder grizzlies might have displaced the shy black bears. (Fun fact: Forest Service employees don't shoot charging bears because if you wound the bear you've escalated the conflict and your life is now in danger; instead, you release a cloud of pepper spray so the bear runs into it and veers off.)

The old-growth forest and its wide array of animals seemed like a single organism, and we were part of it, walking inside an isolated snow globe of an ancient world. Everything in the forest worked together seamlessly, from the mushrooms on the forest floor to the lichens in the canopy. The air of an old-growth forest holds the magic of the Earth. It is a landscape that inspires wonder.

"Wonder is like grace," wrote novelist David James Duncan, "in that it's not a condition we grasp; it grasps us. Wonder is not an obligatory element in the search for truth. We can seek truth without wonder's assistance. But seek is all we'll do; there will be no finding. Unless wonder descends, unlocks us . . . truth is unable to enter. Wonder may be the aura of truth, the halo of it. Or something even closer. Wonder may be the caress of truth, touching our very skin."

The wildness embodied by an ancient forest is inclusive, inviting you to be part of it as well. It is wondrous. And yet the forests of the Pacific Northwest would have disappeared without the Endangered Species Act and the spotted owl. The spotted owl—a species that depends on northwestern old-growth forests—was recognized as an impediment to Forest Service clear-cutting by 1982, when the Reagan plan for rejuvenating the nation's forests included preserving enough old timber to support at least 375 pairs of spotted owls. (Biologists estimate that 2,000 pairs survive today.)

Spotted owls are a species with a low population density and a large home range. They are a classic umbrella species, where a single protected species can shield many other species in the entire assemblage. It is simpler to get legal protection for one species than for many, and the Endangered Species Act was designed to preserve habitat. Protecting the spotted owl was a way to save the remaining old-growth forests, and everything in them. In early 1987, the environmental organization Greenworld petitioned the US Fish and Wildlife Service to list the owl as an endangered species; they were joined by another twenty-nine environmental organizations that summer.

o o o

The concept of sustainable development entered the public consciousness in 1987 with the help of Norway's prime minister Gro Harlem Brundtland, who chaired a committee that published a visionary report, *Our Common Future*. The

Brundtland report showed linkages between environmental degradation and poverty, and presented a version of sustainability that included the environment, the economy, and social equity. "Humanity has the ability to make development sustainable to ensure that it meets the needs of the present without compromising the ability of future generations to meet their own needs," wrote Brundtland.

Sustainability was a concept that made intuitive sense. Ecologically, sustainability is "the property of biological systems to remain diverse and productive indefinitely." Instead of overpopulation, overconsumption, pollution, and the resulting societal collapse predicted by *Limits to Growth*, we could live within limits that allowed wildness to exist. We could live, and let live.

Razing the last old-growth forests did not meet anyone's definition of sustainable. The argument had been that these forests were not important, and it didn't matter if they were cut. Framing this as a problem of sustainability brings up the awkward fact that these forests were not being replaced. There's a charming old tale from Oxford's New College, in which administrators had set aside a forest to be harvested a thousand years hence when the timbers of the college's great hall, built of thousand-year oak, would need replacing, but that is not the American way. The spotted owl was threatened with extinction because nearly all of the old-growth forests were already gone, and they weren't being regrown.

Conservatives had learned from the fierce public backlash to Reagan's environmental deregulation that it was more effective to question the seriousness of environmental problems and discredit environmentalists as radicals who distort evidence and exaggerate problems than to openly support pollution and clear-cutting. The spotted owl and the Endangered

Species Act became a political meme. The issue was framed as jobs vs. owls, or money vs. the environment, but the reality was more complex. The sad truth is that sawmills and towns had been built to harvest old-growth forests, and by 2015 all of the forests would have been cut and the sawmills would have become obsolete. The loggers' jobs were scheduled to disappear, and the forests would have been gone as well.

The rhetoric around logging old-growth forests and preserving a way of life in lumber towns was like wool carders centuries ago and coal miners today: people should be able to do the same work as their fathers. But it wasn't just that people valued these forests differently; it was a full-fledged clash of American cultures. Free market ideology bumped up against the Endangered Species Act, private property rights clashed with the public's desire to preserve the last acres of old-growth forest, and representative democracy was not receptive to public participation in federal policy. And that is putting it politely.

The Bureau of Land Management and the US Forest Service both agreed that cutting should continue, and offered a grab bag of reasons. Sawmills built for large trees would become obsolete, they argued, and up to 28,000 jobs would be lost, leading to "increased rates of domestic disputes, divorce, acts of violence, delinquency, vandalism, suicide, alcoholism, and other problems." Consumer prices for wood would rise. The BLM pointed out that fine furniture and musical instruments have to be made with old-growth wood, and as a society we have no choice but to cut these trees. Our public servants were making feeble arguments to cut the last old forests in the contiguous United States, but it was really about money—one estimate put the loss of state revenues from old-growth forests in Oregon and Washington at $1.96 billion.

Citizens organized sit-ins at company offices, tree-sits, blockades of logging trucks, lawsuits, and demonstrations attended by tens of thousands of protesters. Folk singer U. Utah Phillips summed up the problem: "The earth is not dying, it is being killed, and the people who are killing it have names and addresses." After a fractious period of public disagreement and legal intervention, the US Fish and Wildlife Service finally listed the spotted owl as a threatened species in 1990.

In the end, some of the old forests in California, Oregon, and Washington were preserved: a 2009 study found that 6 percent of the forestland in these three states is old-growth. That's a lot, compared to the rest of the country. The spotted owl and the Endangered Species Act were accused of ruining people's lives, but the region has changed since then. Instead of an economy based on natural resources—fishing, agriculture, and lumber—Oregon, for example, now relies on a mix of manufacturing, services, high-technology, and agriculture. Many tourists visit for the scenery and craft beers. The big trees are worth more standing than they would have been cut, and their total value is much less than the annual value of Oregon computer and electronic products today. Saving those trees was a net gain for the northwest (and of course the sawmills were retooled to manage smaller trees). There was no economic disaster, but in some forest towns there aren't any jobs cutting trees anymore, and new businesses have not taken root. Economic transitions are never painless.

A study by Massachusetts Institute of Technology professor Stephen Meyer showed how the Endangered Species Act affected the economies of all fifty states from 1975 through 1990: It didn't. He found no adverse economic impact of ESA species' listings in the states with the most listed species, and many of these states actually had higher economic growth.

Protecting endangered species enhances the economy. A healthier ecosystem has wide-ranging benefits, and some of them are financial.

With the protection of the old-growth forests came the realization that within the United States, some types of ecosystems have nearly been eradicated. The grasslands have been relentlessly plowed, and less than 4 percent of the tallgrass prairie remains. In some states the only remnants of these grasslands were found in country graveyards and railroad right-of-ways. In the 1970s, it was found that this ecosystem (then at 1 percent of its original range) is easily restored by returning to old patterns of fire and grazing, and tens of thousands of acres of tallgrass prairie reserves, complete with buffalo, have been created since then.

New research shows that you can mimic the biotic complexity of an old-growth forest by knocking down trees in a young forest and leaving them to decompose on the forest floor. This simple step increases the variety of habitat in a forest, and could help speed forest restoration. About half of the country's wetlands, land that cleans flowing water and allows it to percolate down to the groundwater, have disappeared since the 1700s. Wetlands were relentlessly filled or drained until 1989, when President George H. W. Bush adopted the policy of "no net loss of wetlands," a compromise that requires new wetlands acreage to be created or restored whenever wetlands are filled. Many types of habitat are being protected and improved.

Animals depend on specific habitat, and to save wildlife you have to preserve the ecosystems they depend on. But until quite recently, wildlife managers saw their job as preserving songbirds and game and saving a few species from extinction.

In 1933, Aldo Leopold described game management as the "art of making land produce sustained annual crops of wild game for recreational use." To protect songbirds, hawks and owls were shot on sight. To protect game, larger predators, including wolves, bears, and mountain lions, had been reduced to remnant populations by the early 1900s. The public wanted their national parks to be like outdoor zoos, and the Park Service tried to accommodate them. Tourists wanted to see deer and elk, so these animals were guarded and sometimes fed, while predators were killed to save the innocent grazers.

By the twentieth century, smaller predators like coyotes and bobcats still preyed on sheep herds, and prairie dogs still ate grass. Woolgrowers were the best-organized livestock group in the West, and they controlled the stock growers' associations, so they controlled many state capitals and delegations to Washington. The federal government made a quiet project of creating a varmint-free range to aid the sheep that grazed on public land.

The US Fish and Wildlife Service protected wildlife with one hand, and poisoned coyotes and prairie dogs (and everything else) with the other. Before World War II, the federal government paid to have coyotes poisoned with strychnine-laced carcasses; after World War II, the new poison sodium fluoroacetate (named Compound 1080 after its wartime test number) was found to be extremely toxic to rodents and canids (a lethal coyote dose is 1.6 grams per hundred pounds of horsemeat). Prairie dogs were also aggressively poisoned, using thallium-covered grain that killed millions of game birds and songbirds as well. In the 1950s, the US Fish and Wildlife Service annually distributed many tons of 1080-baited meat, sometime sowing whole areas with poisoned bait dropped from airplanes. About half the land in the West was in reach of a poisoning station, including 91 percent of the rangeland in Idaho.

"Coyote getters" are stand-alone devices that kill coyotes. A mixture of sodium cyanide is packed into a .38 special cartridge case, and a primer ejects the poison into the coyote's mouth when it takes the bait; they were pegged into the ground by the tens of thousands. In the 1960s, government trappers used over 6 million strychnine pellets coated with a paste of sugar and lard. Some of the sheepmen with grazing allotments in national forests would prep their piece of public land with sacks of strychnine pellets, some in peanut butter, some in honey, and kill everything in the area before they brought their sheep in.

Predator control decreased the need for herders, fences, lambing sheds, and even dogs. In the early 1960s, a rancher marveled that he had raised "7,000 lambs that spring without a single known loss to predators! And this was accomplished on lambing in the open range, no herders, no fences!" (He was so shocked by the lack of predation that he couldn't stop using exclamation marks.)

By the 1950s and '60s, public land in the West had been effectively sterilized by poison. Charles Orlosky, a retired government trapper in a remote area of the Rocky Mountains, spoke to a writer for *Sports Illustrated* in 1971.

Around here the poisoners have wiped out weasel, marten, mink, fox, badger, and they've got the coyote hanging on the ropes. . . . There aren't enough fur-bearing animals left in these mountains to support a trapper, and I don't care how hard he works at it. Mostly, I blame the 1080 poison. They say it's only dangerous to canine species, but that's just not true. I've found all kinds of birds feeding on 1080 stations—eagles, magpies, Canada jays, Clarke's nutcrackers, woodpeckers—and those that don't get killed pack away the poisoned meat in places where the martens and the weasels can find it and get poisoned themselves. Last winter was the first time in years that we didn't have a pair of eagles feeding up here. They just disappeared. And where there used to be magpies all over the place, we didn't see one all winter. These are major changes, crucial changes. My God, if they can wipe out whole species way back here in this part of the Rockies, they can wipe them out anywhere.

There was no incentive for the US Fish and Wildlife Service to accurately count how many non-target animals were killed by strychnine and Compound 1080. Strychnine baits were recently used in Alberta, Canada, to kill wolves in an attempt to increase woodland caribou herds. Their kill lists were incomplete, but they counted 154 poisoned wolves, 36 coyotes, 91 ravens, 31 foxes, 2 fish, 2 weasels, 4 martens, and 3 lynx. Another Alberta study using strychnine to protect livestock counted 183 wolves, 42 coyotes, 99 ravens, 45 magpies, 3 eagles, and 7 foxes.

Poisons emptied the West, and if you ever hear anyone say that we have more wildlife now than in the 1950s, gently explain that's because we had almost killed absolutely everything by then, first with guns and traps, and then with poison.

When predators are eradicated, irruptions—big increases in prey populations—follow, along with the inevitable population crash when the food runs out. Deer irruptions became common after the 1920s, when most of the predators were gone (except in the southeast, where screw worms and hound dogs trimmed the herds). A famous deer irruption occurred in the Kaibab Plateau, adjacent to the Grand Canyon. The predators were eradicated to boost the deer herd, starting in 1906, and the scheme worked all too well. Aldo Leopold wrote that it was "as if someone had given God a new pruning shears and for-bidden him all other exercise." Every twig and leaf below the height of a deer standing on its hind legs was gone. The deer herd had multiplied, all right, and eaten themselves out of a food supply. The range was damaged, and some of the weak-ened survivors died of disease. Without predators, the deer herd became weak, sickly, and sparse, and the environment was degraded.

"Harmony with land is like harmony with a friend," wrote Aldo Leopold. "You cannot cherish his right hand and chop off his left. That is to say, you cannot love game and hate pred-ators; you cannot conserve the waters and waste the ranges; you cannot build the forest and mine the farm. The land is one organism." It is fairly recent news that predators, instead of be-ing evil, are a necessary part of the web of life.

In the process of conquering the wilderness, we extermi-nated prairie dog towns, shot wolves, poisoned coyotes, and clubbed the pups. But starting in the 1960s, bears, wolves, coy-otes, foxes, owls, and hawks were suddenly valued instead of vilified. Ronald Ingelhart developed a theory in *The Silent Rev-olution* that industrial societies, including the United States, shifted in the 1960s and '70s from an emphasis on materialist values—jobs, security, religion, and traditional sex roles—to post-materialist values centered on quality of life issues. Sud-denly, some people expected the government to protect the environment, humanities, and arts. Some people wanted to engage in direct democracy, and to address issues of race, gen-der, and diversity. Included in this post-materialist mind-set is an increase in the political skills of the citizens, allowing people to play a greater role in political decisions.

∘ ∘ ∘

President Nixon's February 18, 1972, State of the Union address set the goal of eliminating predator poisons. He announced an end to the use of Compound 1080, strychnine, and cyanide on public land, and his intent to prevent their use on private land. There would be no more general reduction of predator populations; instead, the offending animal would be removed. A month later, the EPA banned all interstate shipments of thallium, cyanide, strychnine, and 1080 for predator control.

Starting in the 1970s, people wanted their national parks to be fully functional ecosystems instead of outdoor zoos. They wanted to see a landscape with the full complement of wild mammals, birds, reptiles, amphibians, fish, mollusks, and insects, and with all their behaviors intact. In the New Age, people wanted to save everything.

Australian moral philosopher Peter Singer wrote *Animal Liberation* in 1975. He believes that we should seek to maximize pleasure and minimize pain, and that all pleasure or suffering counts equally. "If a being suffers, there can be no moral justification for refusing to take that suffering into consideration . . . [and] I don't think we should discount the suffering of a being because of its species."

By the 1980s, the United States was getting pretty good at saving bird species. The populations of trumpeter swans and nene (the Hawaiian goose), whooping cranes, herons, egrets, and ducks were all recovering. There were fewer than seventy wild trumpeters in 1933, and over 46,000 birds by 2010. There were about thirty nene in 1952, and in 2004 there were an estimated 1,800 birds, with 800 in the wild. The whooping crane numbered twenty-three in 1941 (including two captives); by 2015, there were about 600, including 161 captive birds.

The condor was more problematic, though, because its

impending extinction was not from hunting or habitat loss. The condors had been common enough in the Gold Rush days in California that their quills were used to store gold dust, at about 10 cubic centimeters per quill. Hunting had thinned the ranks of these giant birds, but it was poisons and lead bullets aimed at other species that destroyed them. In 1987, the last twenty-two wild California condors were captured for a captive breeding program; condors were reintroduced to the wild starting in 1991. At the end of 2016, there were about 450 California condors, more wild birds than captives, soaring off the cliffs of California, Utah, Arizona, and Mexico.

Bears and wolves were the hardest sell for the new ethic of keeping all species in the ecosystem, because plenty of ranchers hate large predators, and ranchers ran the range for many years. In Colorado, the spring hunting of black bears (along with bear dogs and bear baiting) was outlawed in 1992. The bear population has grown substantially since then, which many people enjoy. Many ranchers, however, do not. Sheep herds used to be sent into the national forest to their grazing allotment with almost no protection, but now that predators have returned the herds have to be protected with dogs or llamas. Meanwhile, sheep dogs that protect flocks in high mountain pastures are different creatures than homebound Fidos. Some of these dogs are bred to rip out the throats of wolves or coyotes. Dogs that live with the herd can be so intensely protective of their sheep that they're dangerous to hikers who don't know to steer clear of a flock.

As predators become more plentiful, people who don't use guardian animals to protect their sheep are more likely to lose them. It doesn't help that predators can wreak havoc in a herd, killing animals in gruesome, careless ways. A local sheep farmer elected to state representative was outraged when a hungry spring bear killed fifty of his sheep by tearing off all of their udders as an especially tasty treat. A bear killed my fifty sheep, he said; we need to restore the spring bear hunt. His constituents replied, your fifty sheep killed my bear, and you need a bigger guard dog. Spring hunts were not reinstated.

Yellowstone National Park, nearly 3,500 square miles, was the first national park where wildlife biologists tried to restore the original biota by bringing back wolves and allowing the population of grizzly bears to increase. It was the only place grizzlies had survived in the lower forty-eight states—there were 136 in 1975—and the 1982 recovery plan included five additional zones for grizzlies in the contiguous forty-eight states. Today, there are an estimated 1,200 to 1,400 grizzly bears, and they are still feared, but they are welcomed. Wolves had also been fearsome, back when the wilderness was feared, but when wilderness became wonderful, so did the wolf. There are now more than 5,500 wolves in the contiguous United States.

In 1999, the first of more than 200 lynx were released in southwestern Colorado, and the population has become self-sustaining. The unexpected part of this reintroduction is that these lynx aren't afraid of people, and they are often seen and photographed during the winter (when they are easier to see). They live in a world without traps or guns, and the people they meet would leave them mounds of cat food if they could. And it's not just the newly reintroduced lynx that people embrace. Our neighborhood bobcat leaves footprints in the mud when it rains and was recently sitting on our porch. When I see him, I feel lucky.

There has been a change in the western zeitgeist, an embrace of nature that has resulted in wildlife being welcomed virtually everywhere. Jackrabbits overran Fargo, North Dakota, in 2015, and no one unholstered his or her gun. Humpback whales have returned to New York Harbor after 150 years, dolphins play in Boston Harbor, and sea lions have taken over Pier 39 in San Francisco Bay. Sea turtle populations are recovering after more than fifty years of protections. When young loggerhead and green turtles were swept ashore by Hurricane Irma, more than 1,500 baby turtles were brought in to Florida's Brevard Zoo. People really want to help.

No matter how warmly people feel towards wildlife, there is a big logistical difference between saving bird species or marine mammals and saving terrestrial mammals. Bird species fly to their various feeding and mating grounds and marine mammals swim, while terrestrial mammals need to walk from place to place.

Some of the predators that have been reintroduced since the 1970s have gigantic ranges. The lynx needs a modest twenty square miles, cougars use tens to hundreds of square miles, black bears from five square miles to a thousand square miles; wolf packs need from tens to thousands of square miles, and a grizzly bear needs up to 1,500 square miles. Like the whales, it's a wonder these animals can even find each other.

To successfully reintroduce large predators into the landscape, they have to be able to meet other family groups that might live far away. The problem of finding an unrelated mate led people to think about the importance of landscape connectivity in wildlife habitats. What else do habitats need to provide for these predators to survive?

It is currently believed that a functional ecosystem depends on flows of organisms, materials, energy, and information across the landscape. An ecosystem depends on connectivity. Without any one of these flows, biodiversity will not be maintained and you end up with an unsustainable system: an outdoor zoo. This means that without functional linkages between blocks of wildlife habitat, the number of species in any block of habitat will dwindle. Unless refuges are connected, gene flow, migration, recolonization of areas without populations, and adaptation to climate change will be impossible.

Meanwhile, there are four broad categories of ecosystem services that wild land provides for humans: production of food, fiber, and water (provisioning); control of climate, floods, and disease (regulating); nutrient cycling, oxygen production, soil formation, water cycling, and crop pollination (supporting); and spiritual, aesthetic, and recreational benefits (cultural). In general, ecosystem services depend on the ecological flows across the landscape, so connectivity is an essential part of the system. If we want ecosystems to be sustainable, or if we want them to provide the services that we need, then our wildlife refuges and pieces of public land will need to be connected into an integrated whole.

Improving the connectivity of land-based refuges goes hand in hand with the recognition that waterways have also lost their connectivity. Dams fragment the watershed and change free-flowing, cold, highly oxygenated rivers into series of warm, still lakes. A free-flowing river carries sediment and nutrients downstream, and plants and animals move freely along it. Dams are being removed from waterways across the United States, often with spectacular results. When fish are able to return to their ancestral spawning grounds, the waterways are cleaner, the wildlife is better fed, and the soil has more nutrients in it.

∘ ∘ ∘

We understand more about how to support nature, but the US political system has become polarized around environmental issues. When the Soviet Union fell, conservatives replaced "the

Red scare" with "the Green scare" that tree huggers cripple the country's economy with environmental regulations. Bill Clinton was flanked by Al Gore, a vice president who wrote *Earth in the Balance*, a bestselling book about global warming. It was easy to make a clear distinction between environmentalists and Republicans.

The 1992 Rio Earth Summit was the first international attempt to address global warming. Under Reagan, the United States had successfully tackled ozone depletion with international cooperation, and used market-based pollution credits to sweeten acid rain. Instead of continuing to provide the world with bipartisan environmental leadership, the Republicans chose a different direction. According to sociologist Aaron Mc-Cright, the rise of global environmentalism generated a heightened level of antienvironmental activity by both congressional Republicans and the conservative movement as a whole.

Newt Gingrich became Speaker of the House in 1994, and positioned the GOP as the official party of the fossil-fuel industry. Oil, gas, and coal companies had traditionally donated to both parties, but in the 1990s, they started to funnel their money to Republicans and front groups and think tanks that were devoted to undermining climate science. Unlike the simple-minded denial used by cigarette manufacturers, climate change deniers used a multifaceted approach that came to be known as environmental skepticism.

Environmental skepticism was the strategy used in the uproar over the spotted owl. The first step is to establish that the problem is not important and the science is wrong. After rejecting environmental science, the next step is to prioritize economic, social, and environmental problems, with the environment pulling up last. The low priority assigned to the environment dovetails with the anti-regulatory ethos and the urge to reduce corporate liability for environmental degradation. The final theme of environmental skepticism is defending modernity from environmentalists, who are "waging a war against progress."

In the decades since Newt Gingrich's Contract with America, the GOP has become reliant on campaign cash from the fossil-fuel industry, particularly the Koch brothers, whose donations of hundreds of millions of dollars to Republican politicians and think tanks are predicated on the recipients actively opposing climate change legislation. Think tanks that promote climate change denial have published over a hundred books based on environmental skepticism since the early 1990s, weakening the United States' commitment to environmental protection. Climate change denial has become part of the Republican identity.

Proposed solutions to climate change include government intervention in the form of pollution taxes or emissions restrictions. Add in environmental skepticism, and you arrive at the rubric of "climate change is a hoax, and all proposed solutions are plots to grow the government and raise taxes." Republicans who embrace the seriousness of climate change can face a well-funded primary challenger, or see their donations evaporate. As with gun control, it is currently politically safer for Republicans to embrace skepticism than to align with Democrats. And with the GOP takeover of Congress, the committees that oversee climate policies are now led by avid deniers. Unless people start to vote on this issue, the Republicans may continue to be the world's only political party that embraces climate change denial.

Humans and nature are facing unprecedented challenges in the coming decades, and changes in rainfall patterns will surely trigger mass migration. If ever there was a time to work with other nations to reduce our output of carbon dioxide and methane, to prepare for rising seas, increased migration, and shifting agricultural regions, it's now. And yet our politics are frozen, with half of the population convinced that we can't deal with these problems.

∘ ∘ ∘

But we know how to fix things. We have done terrible things to the environment in the past, and corrected a lot of our depredations. Nature has proved to be remarkably resilient. Our progress in transitioning from fossil fuel to sustainable energy sources has depended on which political party is in power, but as people learn more about nature's benefits, more people want to protect the environment. As environmentalist activist and author Edward Abbey wrote, "It's not enough to understand the natural world, the point is to defend and preserve it." Individual actions, like tree-sitting and planting native species in our gardens and towns, are changing the landscape. Collective actions involving hundreds and sometimes thousands of people in decades-long projects like wolf restoration and dam removal are also changing the landscape.

The United States has about 74,000 dams, most of which are relatively small. We think of dams as permanent structures, but they're not. Over time, dams fill with silt and their capacity decreases, ultimately to zero. As dams age, they may become unstable, and many dams have a design life of fifty years. According to the National Registry of Dams, more than half of them are over fifty years old.

Federal Energy Regulatory Commission (FERC) licenses are required for non-federal dams that are used to generate hydropower, and they need to be renewed every thirty to fifty years. Since the last time most dams were licensed, American attitudes towards nature have undergone a sea change. In 1986, the Electric Consumers Protection Act required FERC to give "equal consideration to the purposes of energy conservation, the protection, mitigation of, damage to, and enhancement of fish and wildlife, the protection of recreational opportunities, and the preservation of other aspects of environmental quality." To get their licenses renewed, dams now have to be environmentally friendly. And sometimes that's just not possible.

Today, dams are being taken down. From the East Coast to the West, hundreds of small- and medium-size dams have been removed, allowing rivers to oxygenate and clean themselves up. In the South, everyone from local town councils to the US Army Corps of Engineers are starting to see dam removal as a way to flush out dirty rivers. "No other action can bring ecological integrity back to rivers as effectively as dam removals," wrote John Waldman, a biology professor at Queens College in New York, in 2015. It is the most economical way to restore a watershed.

In total, about 1,300 dams have been removed, and around 1,000 of these have been taken down since 1996. According to a meta-analysis done by the US Geological Survey, a river changes fast after a dam is removed—much more quickly than anyone had anticipated. Fish often swim upriver to recolonize empty habitat within days or weeks. Fish, amphibians, and mussels lay thousands of eggs (which comes in handy for recolonizing habitat) and their populations are reviving in years rather than decades. The sediment trapped behind a dam is washed downstream into a new, stable location, often within months.

This is especially true of large dams. Of the 1,300 dams

that have been removed, there were eighty-three dams over ten meters tall. The sixty-four-meter Glines Canyon Dam and the thirty-two-meter Elwha Dam in northwestern Washington State, removed in 2014, were among the largest, releasing over 10 million cubic meters of stored sediment. Removing these dams restored access to high-quality fish habitat, and the salmon are moving right back in.

Large dam removal projects in the Pacific Northwest get the most public attention, and are often the result of failing to meet FERC relicensing requirements: when dams are not in compliance with the Clean Water Act or the Endangered Species Act, it is often cheaper to take them down than to fix them. But most dams are structures too small to need FERC licenses, and are removed by local grassroots groups working to revive their river. As a rule, these people are trying to improve river vitality and bring back the fish. Many of these dams are so low that spring waters rush over them, but they are still high enough to block most spawning fish.

In Maine, entire watersheds have been rewilded in the last decade. Maine has three great rivers: the Kennebec, the Penobscot, and the St. Croix. Before the construction of the 7.3-meter-high and 280-meter-long Edwards Dam in 1837, the Kennebec River was a spawning ground for Atlantic salmon, striped bass, river herring (alewife and blueback herring), and sturgeon comparable to the Chesapeake Bay. When the dam's license expired in 1997, FERC refused to issue a license unless a significant fish ladder was installed.

Before the dams were removed, the official count of the spring spawning run was down to just 3,500 in the Kennebec. The Edwards Dam was taken out in 1999 and the upstream Fort Halifax Dam in 2008, releasing more than a thousand miles of river habitat. The Kennebec is now home to one of the largest river herring runs in North America. Nearly 3.8 million fish were counted at its fish passages in 2016, including shad, salmon, eels, and alewives. There are a thousand times more fish in the Kennebec now that the dams are gone.

On the Penobscot River, two dams were removed between 2010 and 2013 and a fish lift was installed at a third dam, reconnecting almost a thousand miles of freshwater habitat. The Penobscot now sees nearly 2 million fish a year, including thousands of endangered sturgeon—up from one lonely fish when it was dammed. The return of sturgeon was big news to the Penobscot Indian Nation. "Our members are very excited to see our relatives coming back to this reservation," said John Banks, the tribe's director of natural resources.

The opening of fish passages on the St. Croix in 2013 restored access to another thousand-plus square miles of habitat across the Maine interior, some of which was seeded with thousands of fry by the Department of Marine Resources; the St. Croix's 2016 run was 158,000 fish, the largest in twenty years, and these rivers are just getting started.

There are about 6 million new fish in Maine rivers since 1999, and it's likely that millions more will be swimming upstream in the coming decade. These fish transform algae and insects into fish flesh, cleaning lakes and ponds while improving water quality. They are a key forage species for larger animals, packed with the fat craved by halibut and cod, otters and mink, kingfishers, ospreys, and eagles. In 1970, there were fewer than thirty breeding pairs of bald eagles in Maine, and today there are more than 2,500 pairs feasting on millions of river herrings. Ted Ames, a fisheries researcher and MacArthur Foundation genius fellow, predicts that Maine's new fish runs will allow the cod populations to rebound.

Farther south, watersheds are being rewilded and changing

the species balance in other ways. An old dam torn down on the Neuse River in North Carolina opened more than 900 miles of spawning grounds, bringing back shad, striped bass, and sturgeon. The giant mud cats—flathead catfish and blue catfish—are gorging and growing enormous, and photos from recent Carolina catfish tournaments show men straining to hold up fifty- and sixty-pound cats by their wide, whiskery mouths.

Dam removal cleans a river by allowing the water to flow more quickly, and by removing toxic materials that may be leaching from the silt trapped behind an old dam. Columbus, Ohio, removed two dams and restored nine miles of river for public use. Even the Cuyahoga is being restored to a wild river. After spending about $2 billion to clean it, some sections still do not meet EPA clean water standards. The Gorge Dam, about thirty-five miles upstream, is scheduled for removal in 2019, fifty years after the fire that gave birth to the EPA. It's possible that the Cuyahoga River will soon be swimmable.

The connectivity of cities is also changing. Cities are re-connecting with nature by developing riverfront and shoreline parks and recreation, and promoting swimming, rowing, pad-dling, and sailing in their newly clean waterways. Many mu-nicipalities are starting to integrate cars, bicycles, buses, and rail into transportation networks that allow people to move around more efficiently, reducing our collective carbon foot-print. Millions of individuals are recycling, millions of build-ings are more energy efficient, millions of solar panels have been installed. Town by town, millions of people are address-ing climate change, and when the people lead, the leaders will eventually follow.

Local foods are enjoying a renaissance, along with community-supported agriculture. Every city, town, and village has a farmer's market now, where people sell produce they picked the day before. The fruits and vegetables are fresher, and likely to be heirloom varieties bred for taste rather than the hardiness demanded by industrial agriculture. But the best part of the farmer's market is that you get to know who's growing your food. I get pig parts from Margaret, eggs from Rick, and dried beans from Jim. It's personal. The beans are really tender, and I get to report back: "Gee, they're great." I sold seedlings at the market on a Saturday in May, and covered my greenhouse costs for the year. Connecting people with the food they eat, and connecting small producers to a larger market, is part of the process of reconnecting the countryside to the cities they feed.

There is growing agreement across western nations that we are all connected to the Earth, and that the natural world must be respected and preserved for the future. Climate change poses enormous challenges, and we stand on the brink of disaster. Our landscape is wracked by floods and fires, the Earth's biota is disappearing, and the way forward is unclear. At a time of great uncertainty, many Americans have embraced aboriginal attitudes toward wildness.

Like the Hopi, we must sign up to be nature's guardians.
Like the Abenaki, we seek balance.
Like the Chinook, we give thanks.

Epilogue

It was a cold and rainy spring this year, and the moisture gave the old junipers a spring halo of new growth "so vivid, so pure and trembling in the air, as to fairly cry out that they were as they were, limitlessly." So wrote American philosopher Henry Bugbee, who found enlightenment through nature. "And it was there in attending to this wilderness, with unremitting alertness and attentiveness, yes, even as I slept, that I knew myself to have been instructed for life, though I was at a loss to say what instruction I had received."

Appendix

Environmental Laws

1964

The **Wilderness Act**, signed into law by President Lyndon B. Johnson, redesignated existing wild areas, canoe areas, and wilderness areas as wilderness.

1966

The **Endangered Species Preservation Act** created the National Wildlife Refuge System, and barred killing endangered species in the refuges. The secretary of the interior was required to list the country's endangered domestic fish and wildlife species, and the Fish and Wildlife Service was authorized to spend up to $15 million per year to acquire critical land. Federal land agencies are directed to preserve endangered species on their lands "insofar as is practicable and consistent with their primary purpose."

1970

The passage of the **National Environmental Policy Act (NEPA)** was the first time the federal government took responsibility for curbing environmental destruction. It starts with a Declaration of National Environmental Policy that "requires the federal government to use all practicable means to create and maintain conditions under which man and nature can exist in productive harmony." NEPA tries to balance the needs of nature and industry. It requires federal agencies to consider the environmental effects of their projects and conduct public hearings and include comments before a project is approved.

The **Clean Air Act** was an expansion of an existing law to include cars and much more stringent restrictions on air emissions from stationary sources like power plants, smelters, and factories.

The **Environmental Protection Agency (EPA)** consolidated many environmental responsibilities of the federal government under one agency to "protect human health and the environment by writing and enforcing regulations based on laws passed by Congress."

1972

The **Clean Water Act (CWA)** was written to restore and maintain the waterways of the United States. Pollutants dumped into rivers and lakes were regulated and permitted, and the EPA set industrial discharge standards. In addition, cities no longer flushed their toilets directly into the waterways; instead, the federal government funded the construction of wastewater treatment plants. Water-quality standards were finally established for the surface waters of the United States, with useful classifications like fishable and swimmable.

DDT was banned by the EPA a decade after the official count of brown pelican chicks hatched in Louisiana fell to zero. In her book *Silent Spring* (1962), Rachel Carson asked, "Who has decided—who has the *right* to decide—for the countless legions of people who were not consulted that the supreme value is a world without insects, even though it be also a sterile world ungraced by the curving wing of a bird in flight? The decision is that of the authoritarian temporarily entrusted with power." William Ruckelshaus, the first head of the EPA, issued a cancellation order for DDT based on adverse environmental effects and potential human health risks.

The **Marine Mammal Protection Act** set aside all marine mammals as untouchable. Whales, dolphins, seals, sea lions, sea otters, and polar bears were all banned from harassment or harvest of any kind.

1973

The **Endangered Species Act** (the revised 1966 law) now protected habitat in addition to individual animals. This far-reaching legislation allows listing of threatened and endangered species, authorizes funds, and makes it illegal to harass or harm a listed species. If an endangered species is found on private land, the landowner must stop doing anything that would bother the protected animals.

Acknowledgments

This book is the brainchild of my agent, Vicky Bijur, who dreamed it up and shaped it throughout the entire process. Alexandra Franklin's thoughtful comments were always interesting, and David Duncan gets credit for the book starting with tribes rather than immigrants. Elisabeth Dyssegaard's deft guidance over the past three years coaxed this book from an inkling to a fully fledged concept, and her editing was a work of art. Thanks to my husband, Bob Lang, for just about everything else, including fixing the irrigation pump and plowing the drive. Grateful doesn't begin to describe it.

Notes

Introduction

2 *"the world does not."* John Arthur Passmore, *Man's Responsibility for Nature: Ecological Problems and Western Tradition* (New York: Scribner, 1974).

2 *"dash about uncooked"*: Roderick Frazier Nash, *Wilderness and the American Mind*, 3rd ed. (New Haven, CT: Yale University Press, 1982).

2–3 *"creatures you may have missed."* Anna L. Peterson, *Being Animal: Beasts and Boundaries in Nature Ethics* (New York: Columbia University Press, 2013), 177–179.

6 *"we actually* are *animals."* Mary Midgley, *Beast and Man: The Roots of Human and Nature* (New York: Columbia University Press, 2013), Introduction.

7 *"uninhabited from that time to this."* Louis Samuel Warren, *The Hunter's Game: Poachers and Conservationists in Twentieth-Century America* (New Haven, CT: Yale University Press, 1997).

7 *"where wilderness is Nature's cathedral."* William Cronon, ed., *Uncommon Ground: Rethinking the Human Place in Nature* (New York: W. W. Norton, 1995), 69–90.

7 *"wild place and always will be"*: Gary Snyder, quoted in "Week in Review," *New York Times*, September 18, 1994, 6.

1. Nature and Native America

10 *"called them Indian bankers."* Stephenie Ambrose Tubbs with Clay Straus Jenkinson, *The Lewis and Clark Companion: An Encyclopedic Guide to the Voyage of Discovery* (New York: Henry Holt and Company, 2003), 92.

11 *"feathers, and even slaves."* Robert H. Ruby and John A. Brown, *The Chinook Indians: Traders of the Lower Columbia River* (Norman, OK: University of Oklahoma Press, 1976).

11 *"Europeans until the 1700s."* Mary Beth Norton, Carol Sheriff, David W. Blight, and Howard Chudacoff, *A People and a Nation: A History of the United States, vol. 1* (Independence, KY: Wadsworth Cengage Learning, 2012), 460.

11 *"runs never failed."* Ruby and Brown, *The Chinook Indians: Traders of the Lower Columbia River,* 14, 21.

12 *"received more things."* Marcel Mauss, *The Gift: The Form and Reason for Exchange in Archaic Society* (New York: Routledge, 1990; originally printed in 1950), 58–59.

13 *"rights to a gift."* Lewis Hyde, *The Gift: Imagination and the Erotic Life of Property* (New York: Vintage, 1983).

15 *"a deeply non-threatening position."* James P. Ronda, *Lewis & Clark Among the Indians* (Lincoln, NE: University of Nebraska Press, 1984), ch. 8.

15 *"cost fifty to seventy shells."* Ruby and Brown, *The Chinook Indians: Traders of the Lower Columbia River,* 10, 21, 116.

15 *"were wider ear to ear."* Willard R. Espy, *Oysterville: Roads to Grandpa's Village* (Seattle, WA: University of Washington Press, 1992).

16 *"the river in great numbers."* Robert T. Boyd, Kenneth M. Ames, and Tony A. Johnson, *Chinookan Peoples of the Lower Columbia.* (Seattle and London: University of Washington Press, 2013).

18 *"Promifcuoufly fcattered about the beach."* George Vancouver, *A Voyage of Discovery to the North Pacific Ocean, and Round the World* (London: G. G. and J. Robinson, 1798), 254.

18 *"had lost an eye."* Menzies' *Journal of Vancouver's Voyage April to October, 1792,* ed. by C. F. Newcombe (Victoria, B.C.: Printed by William H. Cullin, 1923), 29.

20 *"provided for us."* David Monongye, Hopi Hearings, July 15–30, 1955, United States Department of the Interior, Bureau of Indian Affairs, Phoenix Area Office, Hopi Agency, Keams Canyon, AZ, 45.

20 *"adheres to the Hopi way."* *The Hopi Dictionary Project* (Phoenix, AZ: Bureau of Applied Research in Anthropology, University of Arizona, 1998), 99–100.

20 *"depends upon her thrift."* "A Hopi petition signed by all the chiefs and the headmen of the tribe asking the federal government to give them title to their lands collectively instead of individually allotting each

tribal member," Department of the Interior, Office of Indian Affairs, ARC Identifier 300340, 1894, National Archives.

21–22 *"symbols laden with meaning."* "Dolls: More Than Toys," Peabody Museum, Harvard University, Cambridge, MA, 2014.

23 *"and the dancer become one."* Barton Wright, "Chapter 4. Hopi Kachinas: A Life Force," *Hopi Nation: Essays on Indigenous Art, Culture, History, and Law,* Edna Glenn, John R. Wunder, Willard Hughes Rollings, and C. L. Martin, eds. (Lincoln, NE: UNL Digital Commons, 2008). Copyright © 2008 the Estate of Edna Glenn, Willard Hughes Rollings, Abbott Sekaquaptewa, Barton Wright, Michael Kabotie, Terrance Talaswaima, Alice Schlegel, Robert H. Ames, Peter Iverson, and John R. Wunder.

23 *"rebuilt in 1972."* The age of the kiva was determined by dendrochronology, where tree rings in the timbers can provide an exact date of construction.

25 *"altered state of consciousness."* Mircea Eliade, *Shamanism: Archaic Techniques of Ecstasy* (Princeton, NJ: Princeton University Press, 1951).

25 *"seven animal forms."* Fanny H. Eckstorm, *Old John Neptune and Other Maine Indian Shamans* (Portland, ME: Southworth-Anthoensen Press, 2012).

25 *"a positive necessity."* James Hastings, John Alexander Selbie, and Louis Herbert Gray, *Encyclopaedia of Religion and Ethics,* vol. 1 (New York: T. & T. Clark, 1908), 321.

26 *"do they perform miracles?"* in Bonnie Horrigan, "Shamanic Healing: We Are Not Alone: An Interview of Michael Harner," *Shamanism* 10, no. 1 (Spring/Summer 1997).

26 *"on personal charisma."* Email interview with Dr. Philip S. LeSourd, January through April, 2018. Dr. LeSourd, a linguist and anthropology professor at Indiana University, is one of the world's foremost experts on the Algonquian language family, which includes Abenaki.

26 *"most inclined to Christianity,"* from John Romeyn Brodhead, *Documents Relative to the Colonial History of the State of New York: Procured in Holland, England and France* (Albany, NY: Weed, Parsons, and Company, 1855), 441.

26 *"admirably sober and Christian."* Colin G. Calloway, *The Western Abenakis of Vermont, 1600–1800: War, Migration, and the Survival of an Indian People* (Norman, OK: University of Oklahoma Press, 1990).

27 *"human and animal needs."* Dean R. Snow, "Wabanaki 'Family Hunting Territories,'" *American Anthropologist* 70 (1968).

27 *"near disappearance of the tribe."* Elise A. Guyette, "Gathering and Interactions of Peoples, Cultures, and Ideas, Native Americans in Vermont: The Abenaki," Flow of History c/o Southeast Vermont

Community Learning Collaborative, accessed June 8, 2018, www
.flowofhistory.org.

28 *"the Pilgrims in 1620."* Billee Hoornbeek, "An Investigation into the
Cause or Causes of the Epidemic Which Decimated the Indian Popu-
lation of New England, 1616–1619," *New Hampshire Archeologist* 19
(1976–1977); Gorges Ferdinando, *A Briefe Narration of the Originall
Undertakings of the Advancement of Plantations into the Parts of America*
(London: E. Brudenell, 1658).

28 *"traditional culture fractured."* Roger L. Nichols, *The American Indian: Past and Present* (Norman, OK: University of Oklahoma Press,
2008), 40.

28 *"98 percent of their people."* Gordon M. Day, "Western Abenaki," in
Handbook of North American Indians, vol. 15, Bruce G. Trigger, ed.
(Washington, DC: Smithsonian Institution, 1978), 148–159.

2. Nature as Sublime

31 *"waste howling wilderness."* Deuteronomy 32:1.

31 *"wild beasts and wild men."* Samuel Eliot Morison, *Of Plymouth Plantation, 1620–1647 by William Bradford* (New York: Alfred A. Knopf,
1952), 62.

31 *"solitary, poore, nasty, brutish, and short."* Thomas Hobbes, *Leviathan or
the Matter, Fore and Power of a Common-Wealth Ecclesiastical and Civill*
(Andrew Crooke, Green Dragon in St. Paul's Churchyard, 1651).

31 *"winner-take-all society."* Patrick Nolan and Gerhard Lenski. "The
Agricultural Economy," in *Human Societies: An Introduction to Macrosociology*, 12th ed. (New York: Oxford University Press, 2014),
156–201.

32 *"commoners took a nosedive."* Trevor George William Bark, "Custom
Becomes Crime, Crime Becomes Custom" (Thesis, Middlesex University, London, UK, 2006), 118–119; G. Slater, "Historical Outline of
Land Ownership in England," in *The Land: The Report of the Land Enquiry Committee* (London: Hodder and Stoughton, 1913).

33 *"their food with money."* F. L. Pryor, "The Adoption of Agriculture: Some
Theoretical and Empirical Evidence," *American Anthropologist* 88
(2006): 879–897.

34 "handsome tea services in Staffordshire ware." William Radcliffe, *Origin of the New System of Manufacture, Commonly Called "Power-Loom
Weaving" and the Purposes for Which This System Was Invented and
Brought into Use, Fully Explained in a Narrative* (Stockport: James Lo-
max, 1828), p. 67.

35 *"assisted by his two sons."* Andrew Ure, *Cotton Manufacture of Great
Britain Systematically Investigated*, vol. 1 (London: Knight, 1836), 191.

36 *"through the mob"*: Charles Dickens, ed., *All the Year Round*, vol. 3 (London: Chapman and Hall, 1860), 63.

36 *"continued for thirty years."* P. Mantoux, "The Beginnings of Machinery in the Textile Industry," in *The Industrial Revolution in the Eighteenth Century: An Outline of the Beginnings of the Modern Factory System in England* (New York: Routledge, 2015; originally published in 1961), 207–208.

36 *"later sixteen or more."* Sven Beckert, *Empire of Cotton: A Global History* (New York: Vintage Books, 2014), 65.

37 *"six feet in the same time"*: British Parliamentary Proceeding, 1837–1838 (VIII).

38 *"England and Scotland were children."* Douglas A. Galbi, "Child Labour and the Division of Labour in the Early English Cotton Mills," Centre for History and Economics, King's College, Cambridge.

39 *"the contents of a dye vat."* W. O. Henderson and Hans Caspar Escher, *Industrial Britain Under the Regency; The Diaries of Escher, Bodmer, May, and de Gallois, 1814–1815* (New York: A. M. Kelley, 1968), 136.

40 *"Robert Wood, Thos. Blackburn."* J. F. C. Harrison, *Society and Politics in England, 1780–1960* (New York: Harper & Row, 1965), 71–72.

40 *"by the restrictions of government."* T. K. Gaspard, *A Political Economy of Lebanon, 1948–2002: The Limits of Laissez-Faire* (Leiden: Brill, 2004), 2.

41 *"aligned with their own interests."* Sidney Fine, *Laissez Faire and the General-Welfare State* (Ann Arbor: University of Michigan Press, 1964).

41 *"collective bargaining by riot."* E. J. Hobsbawm, "The Machine Breakers," *Past & Present* 1, no. 1, (1 February 1952), 57–70.

42 *"proclamations were signed 'Ned Ludd.'"* Kirkpatrick Sale, "The Achievements of 'General Ludd': A Brief History of the Luddites," *The Ecologist* 29, no. 5 (August/September 1999).

42 *"Now the Hero of Nottinghamshire,"* Adrian Randall, *Riotous Assemblies: Popular Protest in Hanoverian England* (Oxford: Oxford University Press, 2006), 273.

43 *"the subject of surprise."* Thomas Moore, *The Life, Letters and Journals of Lord Byron* (London: John Murray, 1860), 156.

44 *"raised chests and spinal flexures."* P. Gaskell, *The Manufacturing Population of England* (London: Baldwin and Cradock, 1833), 161–162.

44 *" rocks, twigs and clouds."* Mary D. Garrard, *Brunelleschi's Egg: Nature, Art and Gender in Renaissance Italy* (Berkeley, CA: University of California Press, 2011).

45 *"Anne-Caroline was born."* Laura Boyle, "William Wordsworth: Poet of the Lake District," *Jane Austen Centre Online Magazine*, July 15, 2011.

45 *"bushwhacked through the fields."* Anne Fadiman, "Coleridge the Runaway," in *At Large and At Small* (New York: Penguin, 2007).

48 *"Nature and the Soul.";* *"the world exists for you."* and *"Nature is everything."* are from Ralph Waldo Emerson, *Nature* (Boston: James Munroe and Company, 1836).

49 *"School of landscape painting."* Thomas Cole Papers, 1821–1863, New York State Library, SC10635.

50 *"American symbol of nature."* Environmental historian William Cronon is the person who tied Niagara Falls to the American concept of nature.

50 *"dangers and delights of love."* Barbara Penner, *Newlyweds on Tour: Honeymooning in Nineteenth-Century America* (Durham, NH: University of New Hampshire Press, 2007), 55.

50 *"was very great indeed."* Frances Milton Trollope, *Domestic Manners of the Americans* (London: Whittaker Treacher and Company, 1832), 303.

3. Nature and Health

51 *"healthier by reducing stress."* Terry Hartig, Richard Mitchell, Sjerp de Vries, and Howard Frumkin, "Nature and Health," *Annual Review of Public Health* 35, no. 1 (2014): 207–228.

52 *"become a shorter adult."* T. Paul Schultz, "Wage Gains Associated with Height as a Form of Health Human Capital," *American Economic Review* 92, no. 2 (2002): 349–353.

52 *"routinely measured their members."* Howard Bodenhorn, Timothy W. Guinnane, and Thomas A. Mroz, "Problems of Sample-Selection Bias in the Historical Heights Literature: A Theoretical and Econometric Analysis," Yale Economics Department Working Paper No. 114 and Yale University Economic Growth Center Discussion Paper No. 1023, May 5, 2013.

53 *"until the age of thirty."* Ariell Zimran, "Does Sample-Selection Bias Explain the Industrialization Puzzle? Evidence from Military Enlistment in the Nineteenth-Century United States," *Journal of Economic History* 77, no. (2015): 171–207.

53 *"taller than northerners."* T. C. G. Nicholas Mascie-Taylor, Akira Yasukouchi, and Stanley Ulijaszek, *Human Variation: From the Laboratory to the Field* (Boca Raton, FL: CRC Press, 2010), ch. 12.

53 *"5,000 calories a day."* Paul Clayton and Judith Rowbotham, "How the Mid-Victorians Worked, Ate and Died," *International Journal of Environmental Research and Public Health* 6, no. 3 (2009): 1235–1253.

54 *"children ate bread and water."* Andrea Broomfield, *Food and Cooking in Victorian England: A History* (Santa Barbara, CA: Praeger, 2007), 89.

54 *"worker's biological standard of living."* John Komlos, "A Three-Decade 'Kuhnian' History of the Antebellum Puzzle: Explaining the Shrink-

ing of the US Population at the Onset of Modern Economic Growth," SSRN (2012): 212.

54 *"boys from industrial schools."* Roderick Floud, Jane Humphries, and Paul Johnson, eds., *The Cambridge Economic History of Modern Britain*, vol. 1 (Cambridge: Cambridge University Press, 2014), 141.

54 *"shortchanged in height, weight, and years."* J. M. Prince, "Intersection of Economics, History, and Human Biology: Secular Trends in Stature in Nineteenth-Century Sioux Indians," *Human Biology* 67, no. 3 (1995): 387–406.

55 *"tallest measured people in the world."* C. G. Nicholas Mascie-Taylor, Akira Yasukouchi, and Stanley Ulijaszek. *Human Variation: From the Laboratory to the Field* (Boca Raton, FL: CRC Press, 2010), 192–193.

55 *"expand into global pandemics."* US Census Bureau, *Report on Transportation Business in the United States at the Eleventh Census*, 1890, 4.

55 *"400,000 Europeans a year."* Stefan Riedel, "Edward Jenner and the History of Smallpox and Vaccination." *Baylor University Medical Center Proceedings* 18, no. 1 (2005): 21–25.

55 *"100,000 to 150,000 graves."* K. D. Patterson, "Yellow Fever Epidemics and Mortality in the United States, 1693–1905," *Social Science and Medicine* 34 (1992): 855–865.

56 *"in quick succession."* James Copland, *A Dictionary of Practical Medicine* (New York: Harper and Brothers, 1845), 610.

56 *"lavender and yarrow."* John Duffy, *From Humors to Medical Science: A History of American Medicine* (Chicago: University of Illinois Press, 1993), 14.

57 *"all smell is disease."* Chadwick's evidence, Parliamentary Papers, London, UK, 1846, vol. 10, p. 651.

57 *"proving the point."* W. H. McNeill, *Plagues and People* (New York: Anchor Press, 1976).

58 *"detailed in Chadwick's report."* Liverpool death statistics are from Edwin Chadwick, *Report on the Sanitary Condition of the Labouring Population and on the Means of Its Improvement* (London: May 1842).

59 *"broth, beer, or wine."* Emily E. Stevens, "A History of Infant Feeding," *Journal of Perinatal Education* 18, no. 2 (2009).

59 *"allow me to urge you never to stuff a babe"*: Pye Henry Chavasse, *Advice to a Mother on the Management of Her Children and on the Treatment on the Moment of Some of Their More Pressing Illnesses and Accidents* (London: Churchill, 1878).

60 *"princesses went cold and hungry."* Robert Massie, *Nicholas and Alexandra* (New York: Atheneum, 1967).

61 *"plain pudding at dinner":* Quoted in Ruth Goodman, *How to Be a Victorian* (London: Penguin, 2013), 241.

61 *"signs of rickets."* M. T. Weick, "A History of Rickets in the United States," *American Journal of Clinical Nutrition* 20, no. 11 (November 1967); John W. Ward and Christian Warren, *Silent Victories: The History and Practice of Public Health in Twentieth-Century America* (New York: Oxford University Press, 2007).

61 *"left people biologically vulnerable."* John Fielden, *The Curse of the Factory System* (London: A. Cobbett, 1836), 34–35.

63 *"more widely available."* Walter Hilliard Bidwell, ed., *The Eclectic Magazine: Foreign Literature*, vol. 58 (New York: John A. Gray, 1863): 520.

64 *"vendors and street stalls."* Matthew Brennan, "The Civil War Diet" (Master's thesis, Virginia Polytechnic Institute and State University, Blacksburg, VA, 2005), 28.

65 *"for the uninoculated."* Anne Eriksen, "Cure or Protection? The Meaning of Smallpox Inoculation, ca 1750–1775," *Medical History* 57, no. 4 (2013): 516–536.

66 *"feces saturating the soil."* Steven J. Burian, Stephan J. Nix, Robert E. Pitt, and S. Rocky Durrans, "Urban Wastewater Management in the United States: Past, Present and Future," *Journal of Urban Technology* 7, no. 3 (December 2000): 33–62.

66 *"for 28 years past."* Marilyn Thornton Williams, *Washing the Great Unwashed: Public Baths in Urban America, 1840–1920* (Columbus, OH: Ohio State University Press, 1991), 12.

68 *"by dilution with air."* Quoted in Judith Flanders, *Inside the Victorian Home: A Portrait of Domestic Life in Victorian England* (New York: W. W. Norton, 2004), 355.

69 *"died of the disease."* C. J. Finnegan, S. M. Brookes, N. Johnson, J. Smith, K. L. Mansfield, V. L. Keene, and A. R. Fooks, "Rabies in North America and Europe," *Journal of the Royal Society of Medicine* 95, no. 1 (2002): 9–13.

70 *"in the line of duty."* Harriet Ritvo, *The Animal Estate: The English and Other Creatures in the Victorian Age* (Cambridge, MA: Harvard University Press, 1987), 194.

70 *"the Institute Pasteur."* King-Thom Chung and Dean Hammond Ferris, *The True Master of Microbiology* (New York: McGraw-Hill, 2010).

71 *"long and healthy life."* John Brown, *Health: Five Lay Sermons to Working-People* (New York: Robert Carter & Brothers, 1862), 88.

71 *"level of life itself."* Hailey Charlie, "From Sleeping Porch to Sleeping Machine: Inverting Traditions of Fresh Air in North America," *Traditional Dwellings and Settlements Review* 20, no. 2 (2009), 32.

4. Collecting Nature

73 *"woven into everyday life."* Philip Blom, *To Have and to Hold* (New York: Overlook Press, 2004), 20–25.

74 *"birds of paradise had feet."* Sabrina Richards, "The World in a Cabinet, 1600s: A 17th Century Danish Doctor Arranges a Museum of Natural History Oddities in His Own Home," *The Scientist*, April 1, 2012.

75 *"wheat and a dirty shirt."* Quoted in Jean Le Conte, *Les oeuvres de Jean-Baptiste Van Helmont*, trans. Alex Levine (Lyon, 1671), pt. 1, ch. 16, 103–109.

75 *"divided animals into"*: Joseph Strutt, *The Sports and Pastimes of the People of England from the Earliest Period to the Present Time* (London: Chatto and Windus, 1876).

76 *"is not to be fathomed."* Carl von Linné, *Systema naturae, Edition 12*, vol. 1, part 1 (Stockholm, 1766).

76 *"was easily understood."* Judith Flanders, *Inside the Victorian Home: A Portrait of Domestic Life in Victorian England* (New York: W. W. Norton, 2004), 117.

79 *"further botanizing excursions."* P. D. A. Boyd, "Ferns and Pteridomania in Victorian Scotland," *Scottish Garden* (Winter 2005).

79 *"other animals and birds."* Harriet Ritvo, *The Animal Estate: The English and Other Creatures in the Victorian Age* (Cambridge, MA: Harvard University Press, 1987), 208.

79 *"and several hyenas."* Richard Phillips, *Modern London* (London: Richard Phillips, 1804).

80 *"Regent Park Zoo alone."* Richard Daniel Altick, *The Shows of London* (Cambridge, MA: Belknap Press, 1978), 318.

80 *"half million specimens."* *Museo di Storia Naturale*, translated by the author (pamphlet, Universita degli Studi Firenze, 2016).

81 *"collections around the world."* Fernando Marte, Amandine Pe Quignot, and David W. Von Endt, "Arsenic in Taxidermy Collections: History, Detection, and Management," *Collection Forum* 21 (2006): 143–150.

82 *"the plant-collecting public."* Toby Musgrave, "The Remarkable Case of Dr. Ward: A Victorian Fern Enthusiast Changed Gardening Forever," *The Telegraph*, January 19, 2002.

84 *"even some villages."* Oscar Edward Norman, *The Romance of the Gas Industry* (Chicago: A. C. McClurg & Company, 1922).

86 *"gallery of paintings."* Thomas Allston Brown Dodd, *A History of the New York Stage from the First Performance in 1732 to 1901*, vol. 1 (New York: Mead, 1903), 71.

87 *"railway and boundary surveys."* Antony Adler, "From the Pacific to the

Patent Office: The US Exploring Expedition and the Origins of America's First National Museum," *Journal of the History of Collections* 23, no. 1 (May 2011): 49–74.

89   *"both Carabi & Panagæus!"* Charles Darwin, letter to Leonard Jenyns, October 17, 1846.

92   *"partially closed bureau drawers."* Theodore Roosevelt, *The Autobiography of Theodore Roosevelt* (New York: Charles Scribner's Sons, 1913).

5. Selling Nature

96   *"less expensive than beeswax."* Emily Irwin, "The Spermaceti Candle and the American Whaling Industry," *Historia* 21 (Spring 2012): 45–53.

96   *"little over $15 per month."* "Whales and Hunting: How the Profits Were Divided," New Bedford Whaling Museum, New Bedford, MA, accessed June 7, 2018, https://www.whalingmuseum.org/learn/research -topics/overview-of-north-american-whaling/whales-hunting.

96   "$8.1 billion in 2018." State Street Trust Company, *Whale Fishery of New England: An Account* (Boston: Walton Advertising and Printing Company, 1915), 44.

97   *"peculiar to most animal oils."* John Murray, "Voyages de Decouverte, Tome II," *Quarterly Review* (April and June 1817): 238.

98   *"walrus-skin rope."* Joel Asaph Allen, *History of North American Pinnipeds: A Monograph of the Walruses, Sea-Lions, Sea-Bears and Seals of North America*, vol. 12 (Washington, DC: US Government Printing Office, 1880), 133.

99   *"after the whales were gone."* Alexandre N. Zerbini, Janice M. Waite, Jeffrey L. Laake, and Paul R. Wade, "Abundance, Trends and Distribution of Baleen Whales Off Western Alaska and the Central Aleutian Islands," *Deep-Sea Research Part 1* 53, no. 11 (November 2006): 1772–1790.

100 *"items that had international markets."* Charles Robinson Toothaker, S. F. Aaron, and B. H. A. Groth, *Commercial Raw Materials: Their Origin, Preparation and Uses* (Boston: Ginn, 1905).

100 *"made from porpoise jaws."* Walter Sheldon Tower, *A History of the American Whale Fishery*, vol. 20 (Philadelphia: University of Pennsylvania, 1907).

101 *"Laysan Island near Hawaii."* Carrol L. Henderson, *Oology and Ralph's Talking Eggs: Bird Conservation Comes Out of Its Shell* (Austin, TX: University of Texas Press, 2009), 10.

102 *"employment to many hundreds."* Clyde MacKenzie, "History of Oystering in the United States and Canada, Featuring the Eight Greatest Oyster Estuaries," *Marine Fisheries Review* 58, no. 4 (1996): 4–21.

103 *"serve 'the luscious bivalves.'"* Frederick J. Parks, *The Celebrated Oyster House Cookbook* (Allentown, PA: F. J. Parks, 1985).

105 *"everything around in destruction."* Alexander Wilson, *American Ornithology; or, The Natural History of the Birds of the United States* (New York: Collins & Co., 1839), 399–400.

107 *"chomp down on the skull."* Joel Greenberg, *A Feathered River Across the Sky: The Passenger Pigeon's Flight to Extinction* (New York: Bloomsbury, 2014), 142.

108 *"hundred and fifty thousand dozen."* "The Pigeon Trade," *Plattsburgh Republican,* August 2, 1851.

108 *"$1.30 and $1.60 per dozen."* Daniel McKinley, "A History of the Passenger Pigeon in Missouri," in *The Auk: Ornithological Advances* 77, no. 4 (Oct., 1960): 407.

108 *"144 dozen passenger pigeons":* A. W. Schorger, *The Passenger Pigeon: Its Natural History and Extinction* (Madison, WI: University of Wisconsin Press, 1955).

109 *"and many other cities."* Bill Loomis, *Detroit's Delectable Past: Two Centuries of Frog Legs, Pigeon Pie and Drugstore Whiskey* (Charleston, SC: History Press, 2012), 91–103.

110 *"complexity of the forest landscape."* J. W. Ellsworth and B. C. McComb, "Potential Effects of Passenger Pigeon Flocks on the Structure and Composition of Presettlement Forests of Eastern North America," *Conservation Biology* 17, no. 6 (2003): 1548–1558.

111 *"back under the wing."* G. A. McFetridge, *Poultry: A Concise Treatise on All Branches. How to Hatch, Feed, Brood and Prepare for Market* (Syracuse, NY: Clarence de Puy, 1897).

111 *"insects, and snails."* Richard C. Banks, "The Decline and Fall of the Eskimo Curlew, or Why Did the Curlew Go Extaille?" *American Birds* 31, no. 2 (1977): 127–134.

112 *"hatch of nestlings and insects."* Wells W. Cooke, *Our Shorebirds and Their Future* (Washington, DC: Government Printing Office, 1915).

113 *"more than a century."* Farley Mowat, *Sea of Slaughter* (Berkeley, CA: Douglas and McIntyre Publishers, 2012; originally published in 1984), 62–74; Richard Vaughan, *In Search of Arctic Birds* (London: T. & A. D. Poyser, 1992), 12; Randy Hoffman, "A Birdwatcher at Peggy's Cove, Nova Scotia, Reports Seeing a Bird Presumed to Be Extinct: An Eskimo Curlew," *Bird Watching* 1 (October 2007).

113 *"the area of California."* The *Guinness Book of World Records* claims 12.5 trillion insects in the swarm compared to Jeff Lockwood's 3.5 trillion insects; I used the more conservative estimate. Jeffrey A. Lockwood, *Locust: The Devastating Rise and Mysterious Disappearance of the Insect That Shaped the American Frontier* (New York: Basic Books, 2004).

114 *"down the Mississippi."* Ian D. Whyte, *A Dictionary of Environmental History* (New York: I. B. Tauris, 2013), 64.

116 *"will be wholly exhausted."* George Brown Goode et al., *The Fisheries and Fishery Industries of the United States: Natural History of Useful Aquatic Animals* (Washington, DC: US Government Printing Office, 1884).

116 *"sent to distant friends."* *Luggage and Leather Goods*, vol. 18–19 (Business Journals Incorporated, 1906), 92.

116 *"said to be abundant."* Karl P. Schmidt, *The American Alligator* (Chicago: Field Museum of Natural History, 1922), 10–11.

6. Erasing Nature

123 *"enslaved people for resident labor."* The Thomas Jefferson Encyclopedia, Monticello, accessed May 27, 2018, https://www.monticello.org/site/research-and-collections/the.

124 *"under the age of twenty-five."* Christopher Tomlins, "Reconsidering Indentured Servitude: European Migration and the Early American Labor Force, 1600–1775," *Labor History* 42, no. 1 (2001): 5–43; footnotes 31, 42, 66.

125 *"about 5,800 today."* Randolph B. Marcy, *The Prairie Traveler: A Handbook for Overland Expeditions* (Washington, DC: War Department, 1859).

125 *"half years to five years."* Ewing Matheson, *Aid Book to Engineering Enterprise Abroad* (New York: E. and F. N. Spon, 1878), 252; W. J. Gordon, "The Omnibus Horse," in *The Horse World of London* (London: Religious Tract Society, 1893).

126 *"Native Americans until 1860."* William Klingaman and Nicholas P. Klingaman, *The Year Without a Summer: 1816 and the Volcano That Darkened the World and Changed History* (New York: St. Martin's Press, 2013), 23.

126 *"person cost about $1,000."* Memorial of the Permanent Committee of the New York Convention of the Friends of Domestic Industry, 2nd Cong., 2nd sess., 1833, doc. 78, p. 15. See also, Avery Craven, *Soil Exhaustion as a Factor in the Agricultural History: Virginia and Maryland, 1806 to 1860* (Columbia, SC: University of South Carolina, 2006).

126 *"plantation was seven years."* Calvin Schermerhorn, *The Business of Slavery and the Rise of American Capitalism, 1815–1860* (New Haven, CT: Yale University Press, 2015).

126 *"on his capital investment."* Alfred H. Conrad and John R. Meyer, "The Economics of Slavery in the Ante Bellum South," *Journal of Political Economy* 66, no. 2 (April 1958): 109.

127 *"best man on the farm."* Ira Berlin, *Many Thousands Gone: The First Two Centuries of Slavery in North America* (Cambridge, MA: Harvard University Press, 1998), 126–127.

129 *"pulse is incalculable."* William Klingaman and Nicholas P. Klingaman, *The Year Without a Summer: 1816 and the Volcano That Darkened the World and Changed History* (New York: St. Martin's Press, 2013), 114.

130 *"on herbage and grains."* Ibid., p. 112.

131 *"who has not seen them."* Garcilaso de la Vega, *Royal Commentaries of the Incas* (Austin, TX: University of Texas Press, 1966; originally published in 1609), 1:246–247.

131 *"on the Chincha Islands."* Cecilia Méndez, *Los trabajadores guaneros del Perú, 1840–1879* (Lima: Universidad Nacional Mayor de San Marcos, 1987).

132 *"Age of Manure."* A. J. Duffield, *Peru in the Guano Age; Being a Short Account of a Recent Visit to the Guano Deposits, with Some Reflections on the Money They Have Produced and the Uses to Which It Has Been Applied* (London: R. Bentley and Son, 1877).

133 *"common in the 1800s."* Gregory Clark, *A Farewell to Alms: A Brief Economic History of the World* (Princeton, NJ: Princeton University Press, 2007), 286.

134 *"clean out the present crop."* *The Papers of Thomas Jefferson*, vol. 26, *11 May–31 August 1793*, ed. John Catanzariti (Princeton, NJ: Princeton University Press, 1995), 61–63.

138 *"miles of North America."* A. Alyokhin, "Colorado Potato Beetle Management on Potatoes: Current Challenges and Future Prospects," in P. Tennant and N. Benkeblia, eds., *Potato II: Fruit, Vegetable and Cereal Science and Biotechnology* 3, no. 1 (2009): 10–19.

139 *"were nearly as expensive."* Derek Thompson, "How the Tractor (Yes, the Tractor) Explains the Middle Class Crisis," *The Atlantic*, March 13, 2012.

7. Conserving Nature

142 *"over 100,000 visitors a year."* P. M. Eckel, "The Village of Niagara Falls," *Res Botanica*, July 22, 2003; S. D. Scott and P. K. Scott, *The Niagara Reservation Archaeological and Historical Resource Survey* (New York: New York Office of Parks, Recreation, and Historic Preservation, Historic Sites Bureau, March 1983).

142 *"aspect of a colossal carnival."* William Dean Howells, *Niagara, First and Last* (New York: Niagara Book, 1901).

142 *"a secondary wonder."* R. L. Way, *Ontario's Niagara Parks, A History* (Niagara Falls, ON: Niagara Parks Commission, 1946).

142 *"sloped banks of the Park."* P. M. Eckel, "The Village of Niagara Falls" *Res Botanica*, Missouri Botanical Garden, July 22, 2003, quoted from S. D. Scott and P. K. Scott, *The Niagara Reservation Archaeological and Historical Resource Survey* (New York: New York Office of Parks, Recreation, and Historic Preservation, Historic Sites Bureau, March 1983).

142 *"Twain's jumping frog)."* Richard J. Hartesveldt, "The 'Discoveries' of the Giant Sequoias," *Journal of Forest History* 19, no. 1 (1975): 20.

143 *"the London* Athenaeum.*"* Eric Rutkow, *American Canopy: Trees, Forests, and the Making of a Nation* (New York: Simon and Schuster, 2013), 72–73.

143 *"majestic of nature's marvels."* Horace Greeley, *An Overland Journey from New York to San Francisco in the Summer of 1859* (New York: C. M. Saxton, Barker & Co., 1860), 105.

144 *"Himmal'yeh in its precipices."* Fitz High Ludlow, "Seven Weeks in the Great Yo-Semite," *Atlantic Monthly,* June 1864.

144 *"inalienable for all time."* Josiah D. Whitney for the Geological Survey of California, *The Yosemite Guide-book: a Description of the Yosemite Valley And the Adjacent Region of the Sierra Nevada, And of the Big Trees of California* (Cambridge, MA: University Press, Welch, Bigelow, 1869), 2.

145 *"thousands of years to prepare."* Marlene Deahl Merrill, *Yellowstone and the Great West: Journals, Letters, and Images from the 1871 Hayden Expedition* (Lincoln, NE: University of Nebraska Press, 2003), 210–211.

146 *"there with their guns"* and *"the game in that park":* Congressional *Globe*, 42nd Cong., 2nd Sess., part 1, p. 697.

146 *"Native Americans alike."* Emily A. Vernizzi, "The Establishment of the United States National Parks and the Eviction of Indigenous People" (Thesis, Social Sciences Department, California Polytechnic State University, San Luis Obispo, CA, 2011).

147 *"country in considerable numbers":* J. T. Headley, "The Adirondack; or Life in the Woods, New and Enlarged Edition," *New York Times*, August 15, 1854.

147 *"health-giving qualities."* W. H. H. Murray, 1840–1904. (1869). *Adventures in the Wilderness, Or, Camp-Life in the Adirondacks.* Tourist's ed. (Boston: Fields, Osgood, & Co., 1869), 15.

147 *"accommodations for 1,200":* Evelyn Barrett Britten, "Writer Gathers Old Data on Grand Union Hotel," *Chronicles of Saratoga*, September 26, 1952.

148 *"voice, and dancing."* Gladys Montgomery, *An Elegant Wilderness* (New York: Acanthus Press, 2011), 26, 32.

148   *"Park for the world."* "Adirondack," *New York Times,* August 9, 1864, 4.

148   *"kept as wild forest lands."* In 1894, a New York State Constitutional Convention approved a new Article VII (now XIV), bringing New York's Forest Preserve lands under the state's highest level of protection. This proposal became effective on January 1, 1895.

149   *"pleasure glow not explainable."* John Muir, *The Writings of John Muir,* vol. 2 (Boston and New York: Houghton Mifflin, 1911), 131.

150   *"novel species of jewellery":* Peter Lund Simmonds, *Science and Commerce: Their Influence on Our Manufactures: A Series of Statistical Essays and Lectures, Etc* (London: Robert Hardwick, 1872); Robin W. Doughty, *Feather Fashions and Bird Preservation: A Study in Nature Protection* (Berkeley, CA: University of California Press, 1975).

152   *"shilling for each wing."* R. J. Moore-Colyer, "Feathered Women and Persecuted Birds: The Struggle Against the Plumage Trade, c. 1860– 1922," *Rural History* 11, no. 1 (April 2000): 57–73.

152   *"cost a mere $20.67."* Merle Patchett, "Fashioning Feathers: Dead Birds, Millinery Crafts and the Plumage Trade," at the FAB Gallery, University of Alberta, Edmonton, 2011.

153   *"quick to respond."* George Bird Grinnell, "The Audubon Society" *Forest and Stream,* February 11, 1886.

153   *"antelope for hides."* George Bird Grinnell, *Blackfeet Indian Stories* (Helena, MO: Riverbend Publishing, 2005).

154   *"true from the false."* Kim Heacox, *John Muir and the Ice That Started a Fire: How a Visionary and the Glaciers of Alaska Changed America* (New York: Rowman & Littlefield, 2014).

155   *"from near-certain extinction."* Alexandra Mogan, "Theodore Roosevelt and the Boone and Crockett Club: The Saving of America's Buffalo," *Global Tides* 6 (May 2012).

157   *"consideration comes as secondary":* Richard Levine, "Indians, Conservation, and George Bird Grinnell," *American Studies* 28 (1987): 41–55.

157   *"else in the Universe."* John Muir, *My First Summer in the Sierra* (Boston: Houghton Mifflin, 1911), 110.

158   *"wear feathers would not join."* William Souder, "How Two Women Ended the Deadly Feather Trade," *Smithsonian Magazine,* March 2013.

158   *"protection of our native birds."* Minna B. Hall, "Letter 5, 'A New Audubon Society,'" *Forest and Stream,* April 18, 1896.

158   *"but not for sale."* "The Feather Trade and the American Conservation Movement," National Museum of American History, Smithsonian Institution, February and August 1999.

8. Nature in the City

162 *"scavengers, these pigs."* Charles Dickens, *American Notes for General Circulation* (New York: Harper, 1842), chapter 6.

163 *"in fetid slop."* Joel A. Tarr, "Urban Pollution: Many Long Years Ago the Old Gray Mare Was Not the Ecological Marvel, in American Cities, That Horse Lovers Like to Believe," *American Heritage Magazine*, October 1971.

164 *" in a quiet sleep."* Jay Ruby, *Secure the Shadow: Death and Photography in America* (Cambridge, MA: MIT Press, 1995), 53.

164 *"all types of adornments."* Briony D. Zlomke, "Death Became Them: The Defeminization of the American Death Culture, 1609–1899" (Thesis, University of Nebraska-Lincoln, April 19, 2013).

165 *"bereavement without asking."* Fernando Quintero, "A Culture Speaks Through Its Ritual of Death: The Victorians' Elaborate Mourning Customs Are Important to an Understanding of Their Society," *Berkeleyan*, March 27, 1996.

165 *"embraced by nature."* David Charles Sloane, *The Last Great Necessity: Cemeteries in American History* (Baltimore, MD: Johns Hopkins University Press, 1991)

166 *"a bit of nature."* Joseph Story, "Consecration Address," in *The Picturesque Pocket Companion Through Mount Auburn* (Boston: Otis Broaders and Co., 1839), 79; Tate Williams, "In the Garden Cemetery: The Revival of America's First Urban Parks," *American Forests* (Spring/Summer 2014).

168 *"reinvigoration of the whole system."* Witold Rybczynski, *A Clearing in the Distance: Frederick Law Olmsted and America in the Nineteenth Century* (New York: Scribner, 1999).

169 *"city from our landscapes."* Frederick Law Olmsted, *Public Parks: Being Two Papers Read Before the American Social Science Association in 1870 and 1880, Entitled, Respectively, Public Parks and the Enlargement of Towns and A Consideration of the Justifying Value of a Public Park* (Brookline, MA, 1902), 48.

169 *"ecological health of the area."* http://www.olmsted.org/the-olmsted -legacy/olmsted-theory-and-design-principles/design-principles, accessed June 11, 2018.

170 *"growth are to be preserved"*: Frederick Law Olmsted, letter to William Seward Webb, March 17, 1887, Olmsted Papers, reel Al:68, in Alan Emmet, "A Park and Garden in Vermont: Olmsted and the Webbs at Shelburne Farms," *Arnoldia* (Fall 1996).

171 *"brings these details to life."* "American Scenery: Different Views in Hudson River School Painting," Blanton Museum, Austin, TX, February to May 2012.

171 *"careless utterance of nature"*: Frederick Law Olmsted, letter to Ignaz Anton Pilat, September 26, 1863, Panama, in *The Papers of Frederick Law Olmsted: The California Frontier, 1863–1865*, vol. 5, Victoria Post Ranney, Gerard J. Rauluk, and Carolyn E. Hoffman, eds. (Baltimore, MD: Johns Hopkins University Press, 1990).

171 *"humans to create."* Charles Beveridge interview, *Olmsted and America's Urban Parks,* directed by Rebecca Messner, George deGolian, and Michael White (PBS, 2010).

175 *"more than 34,000 miles."* Joel A. Tarr and Josef W. Konvitz, "Patterns in the Development of Urban Infrastructure," in *American Urbanism*, eds. Howard Gillette Jr. and Zane L. Miller (Westport, CT: Greenwood Press, 1987), 204.

175 *"provided by private businesses."* Sam Bass Warner, *Streetcar Suburbs: The Process of Growth in Boston, 1870–1900* (Cambridge, MA: Harvard University Press, 1962), 28, 31.

176 *"the Devil's playthings."* Pamela Horn, *The Victorian Town Child* (New York: New York University Press, 1997), 100.

176 *"paralyse its domestic existence."* Theodore Martin, *The Life of His Royal Highness the Prince Consort*, vol. 4 (Cambridge, UK: Cambridge University Press, 1879), 62.

177 *"poverty and hard work."* John Clarke, *Children and Childhood* (New York: Blackwell Publishing, 2002), 8; Thomas E. Jordan, *Victorian Child Savers and Their Culture: A Thematic Evaluation* (Lewiston, NY: Edwin Mellen Press, 1998).

178 *"decline before mortality did."* Michael R. Haines, "The Population of the United States, 1790–1920," National Bureau of Economic Research Historical Working Paper No. 56, New York, June 1994, 31, 64.

178 *"was readily available."* James C. Mohr, *Abortion in America: The Origins and Evolution of National Policy* (New York: Oxford University Press, 1978), 76–82.

179 *"spermicide in one."* Fahd Khan, Saheel Mukhtar, Ian K Dickinson, and Seshadri Sriprasad, "The Story of the Condom," *Indian Journal of Urology* 29, no. 1 (2013): 12–15.

179 *"problem of child abandonment."* Richard A. Shweder and Thomas R. Bidell, *The Child: An Encyclopedic Companion* (Chicago: University of Chicago Press, 2009).

181 *"study nature, not books."* Sally Gregory Kohlstedt, "Nature, Not Books: Scientists and the Origins of the Nature-Study Movement in the 1890s." *Isis* 96, no. 3 (September 2005): 325.

181 *"outdoors from textbooks."* Kevin C. Armitage, *The Nature Study Movement: The Forgotten Popularizer of America's Conservation Ethic* (Lawrence, KS: University of Kansas Press, 2009), 3–4, 15.

182 *"every state in the Union."* Kevin C. Armitage, *The Nature Study Movement: The Forgotten Popularizer of America's Conservation Ethic* (Lawrence, KS: University of Kansas Press, 2009), 4.

9. Rearranging Nature

186 *"and finally, settling dams."* E. B. Wilson, *Hydraulic and Placer Mining* (New York: J. Wiley & Sons, 1904), 2.

186 *"290 miles, to do the work."* *Minutes of Proceedings of the Institution of Civil Engineers*, vol. 144 (Great Britain: Institution of Civil Engineers, 1901), 184.

186 *"40,000 gallons a day."* B. A. Etcheverry, *Irrigation Practice and Engineering*, vol. 3 (New York: McGraw-Hill, 1915).

192 *"ready to be swept away."* Richard C. Hanes and Sharon M. Hanes, eds., "Dust Bowl 1931–1939," *Historic Events for Students: The Great Depression* (Farmington Hills, MI: Gale, 2002), 168–185.

193 *"that cannot be used up."* US Bureau of Soils, "Bulletin 55," 1909, 66.

194 *"for himself alone."* Arthur Meier Schlesinger, *The Coming of the New Deal, 1933–1935* (New York: Houghton Mifflin Harcourt, 2003), 72.

194 *"soil conservation activities."* Robert A. McLeman et al., "What We Learned from the Dust Bowl: Lessons in Science, Policy, and Adaptation," *Population and Environment* 35, no. 4 (2014): 417–440.

195 *"by the Ogallala Aquifer."* *Ogallala Aquifer Initiative 2011 Report* (Washington, DC: Natural Resources Conservation Service, US Department of Agriculture, 2011).

196 *"use in the United States."* David H. Getches, *Water Law in a Nutshell* (Saint Paul, MN: West Publishing Co., 1997).

197 *"over $27 billion."* *NIGC Tribal Gaming Revenues* (PDF). National Indian Gaming Commission (NIGC), 2018.

197 *"for storage and distribution."* Tim Talley, "Tribes, Oklahoma Reach Deal on Water Rights Dispute," Associated Press, August 11, 2016.

198 *"half a billion dollars."* Jedediah S. Rogers, "Animas-La Plata Project," Historic Reclamation Projects, Bureau of Reclamation, 2009.

200 *"biodiversity on Earth."* R. A. Abell, D. M. Olsen, E. Dinerstein, P. T. Hurley, J. T. Diggs, W. Eichbaum, S. Walters, W. Wettengel, T. Allnutt, C. J. Loucks, and P. Hedao, *Freshwater Ecoregions of North America: A Conservation Assessment* (Washington, DC: Island Press, 2000).

201 *"that of land animals."* Anthony Ricciari and Joseph B. Rasmussen, "Extinction Rates of North American Freshwater Fauna," *Conservation Biology* 13, no. 5 (October 1999): 1220.

201 *"nation's mussel species."* Charles Lydeard and Richard L. Mayden, "A Diverse and Endangered Aquatic Ecosystem of the Southeast United States," *Conservation Biology* 9, no. 4 (August 1995).

201 *"freshwater biota since 1988."* Allen Press, "Why Are Freshwater Mussels in Decline?" *ScienceDaily*, September 21, 2007.

10. Poisoning Nature

204 *"of the Monongahela River."* W. E. Edmunds, *Coal in Pennsylvania: Pennsylvania Geological Survey, 4th series*, 2nd ed. (Harrisburg, PA: Commonwealth of Pennsylvania Department of Conservation and Natural Resources, 2002), 2.

205 *"smoke—everywhere smoke."* James Parton, "Pittsburg." *Atlantic Monthly*, January 1868.

205 *"that is hostile to life."* Joel Tarr, "The Changing Face of Pittsburgh: A Historical Perspective," In *Institute of Medicine (US) Roundtable on Environmental Health Sciences, Research, and Medicine*, eds. B. D. Goldstein et al. (Washington, DC: National Academies Press, 2003).

205 *"healthy coal smoke"* is from "Pittsburgh and Its Business," *Pittsburgh Post-Gazette*, June 27, 1835.

205 *"without a trace of irony."* Cliff I. Davidson, "Air Pollution in Pittsburgh: A Historical Perspective," *Journal of the Air Pollution Control Association* 29, no. 10 (1979): 1037.

205 *"justification for coal smoke disappeared."* P. Thorsheim, *Inventing Pollution: Coal, Smoke, and Culture in Britain Since 1800* (Athens, OH: Ohio University Press, 2006), 2.

205 *"physical and mental defects."* Dale M. Bauer, *Edith Wharton's Brave New Politics* (Madison, WI: University of Wisconsin Press, 1994), 16; Lee Jackson, *Dirty Old London: The Victorian Fight Against Filth* (New Haven: Yale University Press, 2014), 234.

205–06 *"instead of bituminous coal":* Cliff I. Davidson, "Air Pollution in Pittsburgh: A Historical Perspective," *Journal of the Air Pollution Control Association* 29, no. 10, (1979): 1039.

206 *"the pride, the spirit of the city."* David L. Lawrence's inaugural address as mayor of Pittsburgh in 1946 can be found in Michael P. Weber, *Don't Call Me Boss: David L. Lawrence, Pittsburgh's Renaissance Mayor* (Pittsburgh: University of Pittsburgh Press, 1988).

206 *"of the plant was dead."* American Steel and Wire Company, Donora Works Records, 1919–1920, HCLA 1874, Penn State University Library, Special Collections.

206 *"sulphuric acid, cadmium, and lead."* Lynne Page Snyder, "Revisiting Donora, Pennsylvania's 1948 Air Pollution Disaster," in *Devastation and Renewal: An Environmental History of Pittsburgh and Its Region*, ed. Joel A. Tarr (Pittsburgh, PA: University of Pittsburgh Press, 2003).

207–8 *"air quality sampling.";* *"an overflow morgue."* Lynne Page Snyder, "'The Death-Dealing Smog over Donora, Pennsylvania': Industrial Air Pollution, Public Health Policy, and the Politics of Expertise, 1948–1949," *Environmental History Review* 18, no. 1 (1994): 119–132.

209 *"an "atmospheric freak."* Benjamin Ross and Steven Amter, "A Long History of Chemical Pollution," *Utne Reader,* August 2012.

209 *"responsibility for the disaster."* Benjamin Ross and Steven Amter, *The Polluters: The Making of Our Chemically Altered Environment* (New York: Oxford University Press, 2010); Sean D. Hamill, "Unveiling a Museum, a Pennsylvania Town Remembers the Smog That Killed 20," *New York Times,* November 1, 2008.

210 *"Bureau of Air Pollution Control."* Allegheny County Health Department, Bureau of Air Pollution Control Records, AIS.1980.07, University of Pittsburgh Library System, Allegheny County, PA.

210 *"measurements of sulfur dioxide."* Michelle L. Bell, Devra L. Davis, and Tony Fletcher, "A Retrospective Assessment of Mortality from the London Smog Episode of 1952: The Role of Influenza and Pollution," *Environmental Health Perspectives* 112, no. 1 (2004).

210 *"from November 15 to 24."* Leonard Greenburg et al., "Report of an Air Pollution Incident in New York City, November 1953," *Public Health Reports* 77, no. 1 (1962): 9, 14.

210 *"or any combination thereof."* "What Makes Smog? Cities Do Not Agree; Los Angeles and St. Louis Say It Is Controllable by Law—Pittsburgh Blames Nature," *New York Times,* November 22, 1953.

210 *"to air pollution control".* Air Pollution Control Act of 1955 (Pub.L. 84–159, ch. 360, 69 Stat. 322), Sec. 2.

213 *"dumped with impunity."* N. William Hines, "Nor Any Drop to Drink: Public Regulation of Water Quality; Part III: The Federal Effort," *Iowa Law Review* 52, no. 799 (1967): 803–804. In the 1960s, the Rivers and Harbors Act would eventually be applied to the disposal of some liquid wastes, such as oil, gasoline, and other flammable materials. See *United States v. Standard Oil Co.,* 384 U.S. 224 (1966).

213 *"effort to get rid of it".* Ron Chernow, *Titan: The Life of John D. Rockefeller* (New York: Vintage, 1998), 78, 101.

213 *"carried a $10 fine."* "Oils in River Menace Lives and Property," *Cleveland Press,* May 1, 1912.

214 *"water erupted in flames."* Ron Chernow, *Titan: The Life of John D. Rockefeller* (New York: Vintage, 1998), 101, supra note 38.

214 *"thickness of several inches."* D. Stradling and R. Stradling, "Perceptions of the Burning River: Deindustrialization and Cleveland's Cuyahoga River," *Environmental History* 13, no. 3 (2008): 523–524.

215 *"growing source of alarm."* D. Stradling and R. Stradling, "Perceptions of the Burning River: Deindustrialization and Cleveland's
Cuyahoga River," *Environmental History* 13, no. 3 (2008): 525.

215 *"flared again in 1930."* "Fight Oil Fire on Cuyahoga," *Cleveland Press*,
April 2, 1930.

215 *"solution: fire tugs!"* David D. Van Tassel, ed., *The Encyclopedia of
Cleveland History* (Bloomington, IN: Indiana University Press, 1996);
Robert H. Clifford, "City's Lake and River Fronts in Constant Peril of
Conflagration Without the Protection of Fire Tugs," *Cleveland Press*,
April 25, 1936.

215 *"a lack of fire tugs."* Dan Williams, "Rivermen Cite Fire Peril, Ask
City for Protection," *Cleveland Press*, March 11, 1941.

215 *"slicks and other potential hazards."* Julian Griffin, "Fire Hazards
Peril Cuyahoga Shipping," *Cleveland Press*, August 11, 1948.

215 *"fire hazard in Cleveland."* "Sohio Blamed for Oil Slick Fire Hazard,"
Cleveland Press, May 1, 1952.

215 *"river in some places."* Maxwell Riddle, "River Trip Bares Oil Waste
Peril," *Cleveland Press*, May 6, 1952.

215 *"$500,000 and $1.5 million."* "Three Tugs," *Cleveland Plain Dealer*,
November 2, 1952.

216 *"forty miles from Akron."* "Cuyahoga River Seen in Good Condition,"
Cleveland Plain Dealer, March 28, 1957.

216 *"on bridges to watch them."* John H. Hartig, *Burning Rivers: Revival of
Four Urban-Industrial Rivers That Caught on Fire* (Burlington, VT:
Aquatic Ecosystem Health and Management Society, 2010).

217 *"Beware the lactating mammal."* Steven Simon, André Bouville, and
Charles Land, "Fallout from Nuclear Weapons Tests and Cancer Risks:
Exposures 50 Years Ago Still Have Health Implications Today That
Will Continue into the Future," *American Scientist*, January–February
2006.

218 *"do not break down."* Peter Montague, "The History of Chlorinated
Diphenyl (PCB's)," Rachel's Environment and Health blog, March 4,
1993.

218 *"Monsanto."* Robert Risebrough and Virginia Brodine, "More Letters
in the Wind," in *Our World in Peril: An Environment Review*, Sheldon
Novick and Dorothy Cottrell, eds. (Greenwich, CT: Fawcett, 1971).

218 *"moves up the food chain."* National Research Council, *A Risk-
Management Strategy for PCB-Contaminated Sediments* (Washington, DC: National Academies Press, 2001), 40.

219 *"lactation (for mammals)."* A. A. Jensen, "Transfer of Chemical Contaminants into Human Milk," in *Chemical Contaminants in Human
Milk*, A. A. Jensen and S. A. Sorach, eds. (Boca Raton, FL: CRC Press,
1991), 9–19.

219 *"changes we know about)."* US Public Health Service, the Agency for Toxic Substances and Disease Registry, US Department of Health and Human Services, and the US Environmental Protection Agency, *Public Health Implications of Exposure to Polychlorinated Biphenyls (PCBs)* (2015).

219 *"daily intake for an adult."* Kristin Bryan Thomas and Theo Colborn, "Organochlorine Endocrine Disruptors in Human Tissue," in *Chemically-Induced Alterations in Sexual and Functional Development: The Wildlife/Human Connection*, Theo Colborn and Coralie Clement, eds. (Princeton, NJ: Princeton Scientific Publishing Co., 1992), 365–394.

220 *"fifteen to thirty years."* Qiang Ju, Christos C. Zouboulis, and Longqing Xia, "Environmental Pollution and Acne: Chloracne," *Dermatoendocrinology* 1, no. 3 (2009).

220 *"possibility of systematic effects."* Cecil K. Drinker et al., "The Problem of Possible Systemic Effects from Certain Chlorinated Hydrocarbons," *Journal of Industrial Hygiene and Toxicology* 19 (September 1937).

220 *"regulations, taxes and fines."* Scott Beauchamp, "A Short Way to Hell: In Sauget, Illinois, Poisons Mean Profit," *Beltmag Publishing*, September 23, 2015.

221 *"a Japanese town."* R. W. Risebrough, P. Rieche, D. B. Peakall, S. G. Herman, and M. N. Kirven, "Polychlorinated Biphenyls in the Global Ecosystem," *Nature* 220 (December 1968).

221 *"and nervous systems."* Nancy Beiles, "What Monsanto Knew: In a Small Brick House Strung Year-Round with Christmas Lights, Behind Curtains Made of Flowered Sheets, Jeremiah Smith Is Listening to His Favorite Preacher on the Radio," *The Nation*, May 11, 2000.

221 *"New Jersey scavenger,"* and *"from a single plant."* J. S. Nelson, "PCB: An Industry Problem?" General Electric Corporate Engineering, October 30, 1969, 4.

221 *"and ocean sediments."* Shinsuke Tanabe, "PCB Problems in the Future: Foresight from Current Knowledge," *Environmental Pollution* 50 (1988): 5–28.

221 *"surface-water species."* A. J. Jamieson et al., "Bioaccumulation of Persistent Organic Pollutants in the Deepest Ocean Fauna," *Nature, Ecology and Evolution* 1, no. 51 (2017).

222 *"sea mammals could disappear."* J. E. Cummins, "PCBs: Can the World's Sea Mammals Survive Them?" *The Ecologist* 28, no. 5 (September–October 1998).

223 *"every year since."* Davis Dyer, Frederick Dalzell, and Rowena Olegario, *Rising Tide: Lessons from 165 Years of Brand Building at Procter & Gamble* (Boston: Harvard Business School Press, 2004), 80—81.

224 *"health of the waterways."* Chris Knud-Hansen, "Historical Perspec-

tive of the Phosphate Detergent Conflict," Conflict Research Consortium Working Paper 94-54, Natural Resources and Environmental Policy Seminar, University of Colorado, February 1994.

224 *"dwindled or disappeared."* Congressional Report HR 91-1004, April 14, 1970.

11. Protecting Nature

227 *"stood there and cried."* and *"oil was just everywhere."* Kate Wheeling and Max Ufberg, "'The Ocean Is Boiling': The Complete Oral History of the 1969 Santa Barbara Oil Spill," *Pacific Standard*, April 18, 2017.

228 *"caught the nation's attention."* Shelby Grad, "The Environmental Disaster That Changed California—And Started the Movement Against Offshore Oil Drilling," *Los Angeles Times*, April 28, 2017.

228 *"northern California alone."* Congressional Report HR 92-918, March 15, 1972; Morris Goran, *The Conquest of Pollution* (Newtonville, MA: Environmental Design and Research Center, 1981), 212.

229 *"bunch of damned animals."* Richard Nixon, Meeting in the Oval Office: 11:08 a.m. to 11:43 a.m, April 27, 1971, Washington, DC, tape.

229 *"people of this country."* Richard Nixon's 1970 State of the Union address was given on January 22, 1970, to both houses of the 91st United States Congress.

230 *"humans and the Earth."* John McCormick, *Reclaiming Paradise: The Global Environmental Movement* (Bloomington: Indiana University Press, 1991), 48.

230 *"particularly water pollution."* Terence Kehoe, *Cleaning Up the Great Lakes: From Cooperation to Confrontation* (Dekalb, IL: Northern Illinois University Press, 1997).

230 "Whole Earth Catalog." Stewart Brand, *Whole Earth Catalog*. (Menlo Park, CA: Portola Institute, 1968).

231 *"Stay Foolish."* Stewart Brand, *The Last Whole Earth Catalogue: Access to Tools*. (Menlo Park, CA: Portola Institute; distributed by Random House, New York, 1971), back cover.

231 *"and for new programs."* Jack Doyle, "Santa Barbara Oil Spill: California, 1969," PopHistoryDig.com, February 22, 2016.

232 *"will of the people."* Chris Knud-Hansen, "Historical Perspective of the Phosphate Detergent Conflict," Conflict Research Consortium Working Paper 94-54, Natural Resources and Environmental Policy Seminar, University of Colorado, February 1994.

234 *"other species from extinction."* M. K. Tolba, ed., *Our Fragile World: Challenges and Opportunities for Sustainable Development*, vol. 1 and 3 (Encyclopedia of Life Support Systems Publications, 2001), 348–349.

234 *"first half of the twentieth century."* "New Fund Seeks to Save Near Extinct Species," *New York Times*, November 8, 1961.

234 *"destruction, overhunting, and pollution."* Dale D. Goble, J. Michael Scott, and Frank W. Davis, eds., "By the Numbers," *The Endangered Species Act at Thirty*, vol. 1 (Washington, DC: Island Press, 2006), 16–35.

235 *"a sensation-loving public."* *Science* 134 (September 29, 1961): 938.

235 *"whistles and clicks to communicate."* Francis Jeffrey and John C. Lilly, *John Lilly, So Far* (New York: Penguin, 1991), 102.

237 *"brink of disappearing forever."* "Wildlife Species Face Extinction," *New York Times*, January 9, 1966.

238 *"most beautiful creatures alive."* "78 Species Listed Near Extinction," *New York Times*, March 12, 1967; "Civilization's Prey," *New York Times*, September 9, 1967; "Traffic in Savagery," *New York Times*, September 19, 1968; Shannon Petersen, "Bison to Blue Whales: Protecting Endangered Species Before the Endangered Species Act of 1973," *Environmental Law and Policy Journal* 29, no. 71 (1999): 104.

238 *"number over 700 vessels"*: William H. Thiesen, "The Long Blue Line: Quentin Walsh's Long, Colorful Career," Coast Guard Compass blog, July 7, 2016.

238 *"killed between 1962 and 1972."* Robert C. Rocha Jr., Phillip J. Clapham, and Yulia V. Ivashchenko, "Emptying the Oceans: A Summary of Industrial Whaling Catches in the 20th Century," *Marine Fisheries Review* 76, no. 4 (March 2015).

240 *"killed in the 20th century."* C. Bright, "A Fish Story About Whales," *Wildlife Conservation* 94, no. 4 (July–August 1991): 62–69.

241 *"a number of population crashes."* Yulia V. Ivashchenko, Phillip J. Clapham, and Robert L. Brownell Jr., "Soviet Illegal Whaling: The Devil and the Details," *Marine Fisheries Review* 73 (2011): 1–19.

241 *"beautiful series of sounds."* Roger S. Payne and Scott McVay, "Songs of Humpback Whales," *Science* 173, no. 3997 (August 1971): 585–597.

243 *"a more attractive candidate."* Arne Kalland, *Unveiling the Whale: Discourses on Whales and Whaling* (Brooklyn, NY: Berghahn Books, 2009).

243 *"and other marine species."* The Republican Party Platform of 1972 (August 21, 1972), can be found online at the American Presidency Project, http://www.presidency.ucsb.edu/.

243 *"problems of pollution control."* Ibid.

244 The blue whale population numbers are from the IUCN's current population count; the American Cetacean Society claims 8,000–14,000. The minimum population number is from *The Blue Whale*. A population estimate from the IWC in 1997 was for 2,300 plus or minus 1,150 individuals, or 1,150 to 4,500, so numbers were indeed very low.

245 *"country has been blessed."* Richard M. Nixon, Statement made on signing the Endangered Species Act, San Clemente, California, 28 December 1973.

246 *"Earth's protective ozone layer."* M. J. Molina and F. S. Rowland, "Stratospheric Sink for Chlorofluoromethanes: Chlorine Atom-Catalyzed Destruction of Ozone," *Nature* 249, no. 5460 (6 June 1974): 810–812.

246 *"CFCs be banned."* Sharon L. Roan, *Ozone Crisis: The 15-Year Evolution of a Sudden Global Emergency* (New York: John Wiley & Sons, 1989).

246 *"rubbish . . . utter nonsense."* Chemical Week, July 16, 1975.

246 *"to harm the ozone layer."* Sherwin-Williams advertisement in *Chemical Week*, July 16, 1975.

247 *"their findings in* Nature." S. A. Abbasi and Tasneem Abbasi, *Ozone Hole: Past, Present, Future* (New York: Springer, 2017), 27.

247 *"depletion of atmospheric ozone."* Philip Shabecoff, "U.S. Report Predicts Rise in Skin Cancer with Loss of Ozone," *New York Times*, November 5, 1986.

248 *"lemon juice or vinegar."* Connecticut Agricultural Experiment Station, "Acid Rain: Sources and Effects in Connecticut Report of the Acid Rain Task Force," Bulletin 809, New Haven, CT, January 1983, 1–2.

12. Embracing Nature

251 *"land until Jesus returns":* Bill Prochnau, "The Watt Controversy," *Washington Post*, June 30, 1981.

252 *"you need to look at":* Ronald Reagan, speech at the Western Wood Products Association meeting, San Francisco, CA, March 12, 1966.

252 *"every 70 to 120 years."* Ivan J. Lieben, "Political Influences on USFW Listing Decision Under the ESA: Time to Rethink Priorities," *Environmental Law*, December 22, 1997.

254 *"happy life as you do."* Arne Næss, *Ecology, Community and Lifestyle* (Cambridge, UK: Cambridge University Press, 1989), 164–165.

254 *"realization of the Self":* Timothy Luke, "Deep Ecology: Living as if Nature Mattered," *Organization and Environment* 15, no. 2 (June 2002): 178–186.

254 *"of life on Earth."* Ibid.

254 *"destroy its diversity and beauty."* Alan Drengson, "Some Thought on the Deep Ecology Movement," Foundation for Deep Ecology, 2012.

254 *"much, much lower."* Walter Schwarz, "Ethical and Green Living: Arne Næss," *Guardian*, January 14, 2009.

254 *"Defense of Mother Earth."* Roderick Frazier Nash, *The Rights of Nature: A History of Environmental Ethics* (Madison, WI: University of Wisconsin Press, 1989), 190.

255 *"makes the rules":* Martin Porter, "Bad Capitalism: The Pacific Lumber Story," LinkedIn, October 12, 2014.

255 *"200-foot buffer zone."* The number of protesters, which often depends on who is doing the counting, is from Ami Chen Mills, "Headwaters: What's the deal?" *Mother Jones*, May 26, 1998.

256 *"lumber mill, it was."* National Commission on Science for Sustainable Forestry, *Beyond Old Growth: Older Forests in a Changing World* (Washington, DC: National Council for Science and the Environment, 2008).

257 *"the magic of the Earth."* Jessica Goldstein, "Descriptions of 'Old-Growth Forest' Are Somewhat Elusive," *Washington Post*, October 21, 2011.

258 *"touching our very skin":* David James Duncan, *My Story as Told By Water* (Berkeley, CA: University of California Press, 2002).

258 *"everything in them."* Erica Fleishman, Dennis D. Murphy, and Robert B. Blair, "Selecting Effective Umbrella Species," *Conservation Magazine*, July 29, 2001.

258 *"environmental organizations that summer."* Mark Bonnett and Kurt Zimmerman, "Politics and Preservation: The Endangered Species Act and the Northern Spotted Owl," *Ecology* 18, no. 105 (1991): 111–113; Ivan J. Lieben, "Political Influences on USFW Listing Decision Under the ESA: Time to Rethink Priorities," *Environmental Law*, December 22, 1997.

259 *"to meet their own needs."* United Nations General Assembly, "Report of the World Commission on Environment and Development: Our Common future" (Oslo, Norway: United Nations General Assembly, Development and International Co-operation: Environment, 1987).

259 *"wrote Brundtland."* Chris Moore, "Sustainable Land Development," *Today*, February 2009.

260 *"alcoholism, and other problems."* From a joint study by US Forest Service, US Department of the Interior and the Bureau of Land Management, 1990, quoted in T. Gup, "Owl vs Man," *Time* (June 25, 1990): 56–63.

260 *"at $1.96 billion."* Lieben, "Political Influences on USFW Listing Decision Under the ESA," *Environmental Law*, vol. 27, no. 4 (Winter 1997): 1323, 1371.

261 *"higher economic growth."* David Brittan, "Defending an Endangered Act," *Technology Review*, August–September 1995.

262 *"no net loss of wetlands."* In 1989, President George H. W. Bush established the national policy of "no-net loss of wetlands": each acre of wetland that is filled in is replaced with a new acre of wetland elsewhere.

263 *"for recreational use."* Aldo Leopold, *Game Management* (Madison, WI: University of Wisconsin Press, 1986), 3.

263 *"grazed on public land."* Jack Olsen, "The Poisoning of the West," *Sports Illustrated*, March 8, 1971.

264 *"brought their sheep in."* Jack Olsen, "A Little Bit Goes a Long Way," *Sports Illustrated*, March 15, 1971.

264 *"no herders, no fences!"* Thomas R. Dunlap, *Saving America's Wildlife* (Princeton, NJ: Princeton University Press, 1988).

265 *"4 martens and 3 lynx."* Dave Hervieux, Mark Hebblewhite, Dave Stepnisky, Michelle Bacon, and Stan Boutin, "Managing Wolves (*Canis lupus*) to Recover Threatened Woodland Caribou (*Rangifer tarandus caribou*) in Alberta," *Canadian Journal of Zoology* 92 (2015): 1029–1037.

266 *"him all other exercise."* Aldo Leopold, "Thinking Like a Mountain," *A Sand County Almanac* (New York: Oxford University Press, 1949).

266 *"The land is one organism."* Aldo Leopold, "Round River," *A Sand County Almanac* (New York: Oxford University Press, 1949).

267 *"because of its species."* Peter Singer, *Animal Liberation* (New York, Random House, 1975), 18.

267 *"800 in the wild."* Richard Ellis, *No Turning Back: The Life and Death of Animal Species* (New York: HarperPerennial, 2004), 280–281.

268 *"centimeters per quill."* Loye Miller, "Feather Studies on the California Condor," *The Condor* 39, no. 4 (1937): 160–162.

270 *"People really want to help."* Joanna Klein, "Sea Turtles Appear to Be Bouncing Back Around the World," *New York Times*, September 20, 2017; Jim Waymer, "Irma Batters Beaches, Residents and Baby Sea Turtles," *Florida Today*, September 12, 2017.

271 *"essential part of the system."* Camilo A. Correa Ayram, Manuel E. Mendoza, Andrés Etter, and Diego R. Pérez Salicrup, "Habitat Connectivity in Biodiversity Conservation," *Progress in Physical Geography* 40, no. 1 (August 2015): 7–37.

272 *"movement as a whole."* Aaron M. McCright, Chenyang Xiao, and Riley E. Dunlap, "Political Polarization on Support for Government Spending on Environmental Protection in the USA, 1974–2012," *Social Science Research* 48 (November 2014).

273 *"commitment to environmental protection."* Peter J. Jacques, Riley E. Dunlap, and Mark Freeman, "The Organisation of Denial: Conservative Think Tanks and Environmental Scepticism," *Environmental Politics* 17, no. 3 (June 2008): 349–385.

274 *"over fifty years old."* Daniel A. Farber and Jim Chen, *Disasters and the Law: Katrina and Beyond* (Aspen Publishers Online, 2006), 282.

275 *"aspects of environmental quality."* Section 4(e) of the Federal Power Act.

275 *"effectively as dam removals."* John Waldman and Karin Limburg, "Undamming Rivers Can Offer a New Source for Clean Energy." *Guardian*, August 7, 2015.

276 *"meters of stored sediment."* J. E. O'Connor, J. J. Duda, and G. E. Grant, "Ecology: 1000 Dams Down and Counting," *Science*, May 1, 2015, 496–497.

276 *"moving right back in."* M. M. Foley et al., "Dam Removal: Listening In," *Water Resources Research* 53 (2017): 5229–5246.

276 *"block most spawning fish."* Patrik Jonsson, "The Unsung Tale of a River's Restoration: A Movement to Remove Obsolete Dams Gathers Force in the East—and Fishermen Are First to Take Notice," *Christian Science Monitor*, January 30, 2001.

277 *"back to this reservation"*: Shawna Newcomb, "Sturgeon Return to Milford After Nearly 200 Years," WLBZ, August 4, 2016.

278 *"river for public use."* Anna Lieb, "The Undamming of America," NOVA, August 12, 2015.

278 *"birth to the EPA."* Daniel J. McGraw, "America's Great Dam Teardown Means Cleaner Water, More Parkland: So Why Aren't More Cities Removing These Barriers to Health and Public Space?" *Next City*, March 27, 2017.

Epilogue

280 Henry Bugbee, *The Inward Morning* (Athens, GA: University of Georgia Press, 1999), 140.

Bibliography

Abbasi, S. A., and Tasneem Abbasi. *Ozone Hole: Past, Present, Future*. New York: Springer, 2017.

Abell, R. A., D. M. Olsen, E. Dinerstein, P. T. Hurley, J. T. Diggs, W. Eichbaum, S. Walters, W. Wettengel, T. Allnutt, C. J. Loucks, P. Hedao, and C. Taylor. *Freshwater Ecoregions of North America: A Conservation Assessment*. Washington, DC: Island Press, 2000.

Adler, Antony. "From the Pacific to the Patent Office: The US Exploring Expedition and the Origins of America's First National Museum." *Journal of the History of Collections* 23, no. 1 (May 2011): 49–74.

Allegheny County Health Department, Bureau of Air Pollution Control Records, AIS.1980.07. University of Pittsburgh Library System, Allegheny County, PA.

Allen, Joel Asaph. *History of North American Pinnipeds: A Monograph of the Walruses, Sea-Lions, Sea-Bears and Seals of North America*, vol. 12. Washington, DC: US Government Printing Office, 1880.

Altick, Richard Daniel. *The Shows of London*. Cambridge, MA: Belknap Press, 1978.

Alyokhin, A. "Colorado Potato Beetle Management on Potatoes: Current Challenges and Future Prospects." In P. Tennant and N. Benkeblia, eds., *Potato II: Fruit, Vegetable and Cereal Science and Biotechnology* 3, no. 1 (2009): 10–19.

American Steel and Wire Company, Donora Works, 1919–1920, HCLA 1874, Penn State University Library, Special Collections.

Armitage, Kevin C. *The Nature Study Movement: The Forgotten Popularizer of America's Conservation Ethic*. Lawrence: University of Kansas Press, 2009.

Ayram, Camilo A. Correa, Manuel E. Mendoza, Andrés Etter, and Diego R. Pérez Salicrup. "Habitat Connectivity in Biodiversity Conservation." *Progress in Physical Geography* 40, no. 1 (August 2015).

Banks, Richard C. "The Decline and Fall of the Eskimo Curlew, or Why Did the Curlew Go Extaille?" *American Birds* 31, no. 2 (1977): 127–134.

Bark, Trevor George William. "Custom Becomes Crime, Crime Becomes Custom." Thesis, Middlesex University, London, 2006.

Barton, Andrew John. "Fishing for Ivory Worms: A Review of Ethnographic and Historically Recorded *Dentalium* Source Locations." Master's thesis, Simon Fraser University, Burnaby, BC, October 1994.

Barton Wright, *Hopi Nation: Essays on Indigenous Art, Culture, History, and Law*, Edna Glenn, John R. Wunder, Willard Hughes Rollings, and C. L. Martin, eds. (Lincoln, NE: UNL Digital Commons, 2008). Copyright © 2008 the Estate of Edna Glenn, Willard Hughes Rollings, Abbott Sekaquaptewa, Barton Wright, Michael Kabotie, Terrance Talaswaima, Alice Schlegel, Robert H. Ames, Peter Iverson, and John R. Wunder.

Bauer, Dale M. *Edith Wharton's Brave New Politics*. Madison: University of Wisconsin Press, 1994.

Beauchamp, Scott. "A Short Way to Hell: In Sauget, Illinois, Poisons Mean Profit." *Beltmag*, September 23, 2015.

Beckert, Sven. *Empire of Cotton: A Global History*. New York: Vintage Books, 2014.

Beiles, Nancy. "What Monsanto Knew: In a Small Brick House Strung Year-Round with Christmas Lights, Behind Curtains Made of Flowered Sheets, Jeremiah Smith Is Listening to His Favorite Preacher on the Radio." *The Nation*, May 11, 2000.

Bell, Michelle L., Devra L. Davis, and Tony Fletcher. "A Retrospective Assessment of Mortality from the London Smog Episode of 1952: The Role of Influenza and Pollution." *Environmental Health Perspectives* 112, no. 1 (2004).

Berlin, Ira. *Many Thousands Gone: The First Two Centuries of Slavery in North America*. Cambridge, MA: Harvard University Press, 1998.

Bidwell, Walter Hilliard, ed. *The Eclectic Magazine: Foreign Literature*, vol. 58. New York: John A. Gray, 1863.

Blanton Museum. "American Scenery: Different Views in Hudson River School Painting," Austin, TX, February–May 2012.

Blom, Philip. *To Have and to Hold*. New York: Overlook Press, 2003.

Bodenhorn, Howard, Timothy W. Guinnane, and Thomas A. Mroz. "Problems of Sample-Selection Bias in the Historical Heights Literature: A Theoretical and Econometric Analysis." Yale Economics Department Working Paper No. 114 and Yale University Economic Growth Center Discussion Paper No. 1023, May 5, 2013.

Bonnett, Mark, and Kurt Zimmerman. "Politics and Preservation: The Endangered Species Act and the Northern Spotted Owl." *Ecology* 18, no. 105 (1991): 111–113.

Boyd, P. D. A. "Ferns and Pteridomania in Victorian Scotland." *Scottish Garden* (Winter 2005).

Boyd, Robert T., Kenneth M. Ames, and Tony A. Johnson. *Chinookan Peoples of the Lower Columbia.* Seattle and London: University of Washington Press, 2013.

Boyle, Laura. "William Wordsworth: Poet of the Lake District." *Jane Austen Centre Online Magazine,* July 15, 2011.

Brittan, David. "Defending an Endangered Act." *Technology Review,* August–September 1995.

Brennan, Matthew. "The Civil War Diet." Master's thesis, Virginia Polytechnic Institute and State University, Blacksburg, VA, 2005.

Bright, C. "A Fish Story About Whales." *Wildlife Conservation* 94, no. 4 (July–August 1991).

British Parliamentary Proceeding, 1837–1838 (VIII).

Britten, Evelyn Barrett. "Writer Gathers Old Data on Grand Union Hotel." *Chronicles of Saratoga,* September 26, 1952.

Brodhead, John Romeyn. *Documents Relative to the Colonial History of the State of New York: Procured in Holland, England and France.* Albany, NY: Weed, Parsons, 1855.

Broomfield, Andrea. *Food and Cooking in Victorian England: A History.* Santa Barbara, CA: Praeger, 2007.

Brown, John. *Health: Five Lay Sermons to Working-People.* New York: Robert Carter & Brothers, 1862.

Bugbee, Henry. *The Inward Morning.* Athens: University of Georgia Press, 1999.

Bureau of Applied Research in Anthropology. The Hopi Dictionary Project. University of Arizona (1998).

Burian, Steven J., Stephan J. Nix, Robert E. Pitt, and S. Rocky Durrans. "Urban Wastewater Management in the United States: Past, Present and Future." *Journal of Urban Technology* 7, no. 3 (December 2000): 33–62.

Business Journals Incorporated. *Luggage and Leather Goods,* vols. 18–19. 1906.

Calloway, Colin G. *The Western Abenakis of Vermont, 1600–1800: War, Migration, and the Survival of an Indian People.* Norman: University of Oklahoma Press, 1990.

Carnegie Museum of Natural History. Permanent exhibit: Alcoa Foundation Hall of American Indians, American Indians and the Natural World, Hopi Peoples of the Southwest "The Katsina Season." Pittsburgh, PA, accessed June 19, 2018, https://nsew.carnegiemnh.org/.

Chadwick, Edwin. *Report on the Sanitary Condition of the Labouring Population and on the Means of Its Improvement.* London: May 1842.

Charlie, Hailey. "From Sleeping Porch to Sleeping Machine: Inverting Traditions of Fresh Air in North America." *Traditional Dwellings and Settlements Review* 20, no. 2 (2009).

Chavasse, Pye Henry. *Advice to a Mother on the Management of Her Children and on the Treatment on the Moment of Some of Their More Pressing Illnesses and Accidents.* London: Churchill, 1878.

Chernow, Ron. *Titan: The Life of John D. Rockefeller.* New York: Vintage, 1998.

Chung, King-Thom, and Dean Hammond Ferris. *The True Master of Microbiology.* New York: McGraw-Hill, 2010.

Clark, Gregory. *A Farewell to Alms: A Brief Economic History of the World.* Princeton, NJ: Princeton University Press, 2007.

Clarke, John. *Children and Childhood.* New York: Blackwell Publishing, 2002.

Clayton, Paul, and Judith Rowbotham. "How the Mid-Victorians Worked, Ate and Died." *International Journal of Environmental Research and Public Health* 6, no. 3 (2009): 1235–1253.

Cleveland Plain Dealer. "Cuyahoga River Seen in Good Condition." March 28, 1957.

———. "Three Tugs." November 2, 1952.

Cleveland Press. "Fight Oil Fire on Cuyahoga." April 2, 1930.

———. "Oils in River Menace Lives and Property." May 1, 1912.

———. "Sohio Blamed for Oil Slick Fire Hazard." May 1, 1952.

Clifford, Robert H. "City's Lake and River Fronts in Constant Peril of Conflagration Without the Protection of Fire Tugs." *Cleveland Press,* April 25, 1936.

Combe, Andrew. *Treatise on the Physiological and Moral Management of Infancy,* 5th ed. New York: Fowler & Wells, 1840.

Congressional Globe. 42nd Cong., 2nd Sess., Part 1, p. 697.

Congressional Report HR 91-1004. April 14, 1970.

Congressional Report HR 92-918, March 15, 1972.

Connecticut Agricultural Experiment Station. "Acid Rain: Sources and Effects in Connecticut Report of the Acid Rain Task Force." Bulletin 809, New Haven, CT, January 1983.

Conrad, Alfred H., and John R. Meyer. "The Economics of Slavery in the Ante Bellum South," *Journal of Political Economy* 66, no. 2 (April 1958).

Cooke, Wells W. *Our Shorebirds and Their Future*. Washington: Government Printing Office, 1915.

Copland, James. *A Dictionary of Practical Medicine*. New York: Harper and Brothers, 1845.

Craven, Avery. *Soil Exhaustion as a Factor in the Agricultural History: Virginia and Maryland, 1806 to 1860*. Columbia: University of South Carolina, 2006.

Cronon, William, ed. *Uncommon Ground: Rethinking the Human Place in Nature*. New York: W. W. Norton, 1995.

Cummins, J. E. "PCBs: Can the World's Sea Mammals Survive Them?" *Ecologist* 28, no. 5 (September–October 1998).

Darwin, Charles, letter to Leonard Jenyns, October 17, 1846.

Davidson, Cliff I. "Air Pollution in Pittsburgh: A Historical Perspective." *Journal of the Air Pollution Control Association* 29, no. 10 (1979): 1037.

Day, Gordon M. "Western Abenaki." In *Handbook of North American Indians*, vol. 15. Edited by Bruce G. Trigger. Washington, DC: Smithsonian Institution, 1978, 148–159.

De la Vega, Garcilaso. *Royal Commentaries of the Incas*. Austin: University of Texas Press, 1966; originally published in 1609, 1:246–247.

Department of the Interior, Office of Indian Affairs. ARC Identifier 300340, 1894, National Archives.

Deuteronomy 32:1.

Dickens, Charles, ed. *All the Year Round*, vol. 3. London: Chapman and Hall, 1860.

Dickens, Charles. *American Notes for General Circulation*. New York: Harper, 1842.

Dodd, Thomas Allston Brown. *A History of the New York Stage from the First Performance in 1732 to 1901*, vol. 1. New York: Mead, 1903.

Doughty, Robin W. *Feather Fashions and Bird Preservation: A Study in Nature Protection*. Berkeley: University of California Press, 1975.

Doyle, Jack. "Santa Barbara Oil Spill: California, 1969." PopHistoryDig.com, February 22, 2016.

Drengson, Alan. "Some Thought on the Deep Ecology Movement." Foundation for Deep Ecology, 2012.

Drinker, Cecil K., et al. "The Problem of Possible Systemic Effects from Certain Chlorinated Hydrocarbons." *Journal of Industrial Hygiene and Toxicology* 19 (September 1937).

Duffield, A. J. *Peru in the Guano Age; Being a Short Account of a Recent Visit to the Guano Deposits, with Some Reflections on the Money They Have Produced and the Uses to Which It Has Been Applied*. London: R. Bentley and Son, 1877.

Duffy, John. *From Humors to Medical Science: A History of American Medicine*. Chicago: University of Illinois Press, 1993.

Duncan, David James. *My Story as Told by Water.* Berkeley: University of California Press, 2002.

Dunlap, Thomas R. *Saving America's Wildlife.* Princeton, NJ: Princeton University Press, 1988.

Dyer, Davis, Frederick Dalzell, and Rowena Olegario. *Rising Tide: Lessons from 165 Years of Brand Building at Procter & Gamble.* Boston: Harvard Business School Press, 2004.

Eckel, P. M. "The Village of Niagara Falls." *Res Botanica,* July 22, 2003.

Eckstorm, Fanny H. *Old John Neptune and Other Maine Indian Shamans.* Portland, ME: Southworth-Anthoensen Press, 2012, originally published in 1945.

Edmunds, W. E. *Coal in Pennsylvania: Pennsylvania Geological Survey, 4th series,* 2nd ed. Harrisburg: Commonwealth of Pennsylvania Department of Conservation and Natural Resources, 2002.

Egan, Timothy. *The Big Burn: Theodore Roosevelt and the Fire That Saved America.* New York: Mariner Books, 2009.

Eliade, Mircea. *Shamanism: Archaic Techniques of Ecstasy.* Princeton, NJ: Princeton University Press, 1951.

Ellis, Richard. *No Turning Back: The Life and Death of Animal Species.* New York: HarperPerennial, 2004.

Ellsworth, J. W., and B. C. McComb. "Potential Effects of Passenger Pigeon Flocks on the Structure and Composition of Presettlement Forests of Eastern North America." *Conservation Biology* 17, no. 6 (2003): 1548–1558.

Emerson, Ralph Waldo. *Nature.* East Aurora, NY: Roycrofters, 1905.

Emmet, Alan. "A Park and Garden in Vermont: Olmsted and the Webbs at Shelburne Farms." *Arnoldia* (Fall 1996).

Eriksen, Anne. "Cure or Protection? The Meaning of Smallpox Inoculation, ca 1750–1775." *Medical History* 57, no. 4 (2013): 516–536.

Erlandson, Jon M., René L. Vellanoweth, Annie C. Caruso, and Melissa R. Reid. "*Dentalium* Shell Artifacts from a 6600-Year-Old Occupation of Otter Cave, San Miguel Island." *Pacific Coast Archaeological Society Quarterly* 37, no. 3 (Summer 2001).

Espy, Willard R. *Oysterville: Roads to Grandpa's Village.* Seattle: University of Washington Press, 1992.

Etcheverry, B. A. *Irrigation Practice and Engineering,* vol. 3. New York: McGraw-Hill, 1915.

Fadiman, Anne. "Coleridge the Runaway." In *At Large and At Small.* New York: Penguin, 2007.

Farber, Daniel A., and Jim Chen. *Disasters and the Law: Katrina and Beyond.* New York: Aspen, 2006.

Fenn, Elizabeth. *Pox Americana.* New York: Farrar, Straus and Giroux, 2001.

Ferdinando, Gorges. *A Briefe Narration of the Originall Undertakings of the Advancement of Plantations into the Parts of America.* London: E. Brudenell, 1658.

Fielden, John. *The Curse of the Factory System.* London: A. Cobbett, 1836.

Fine, Sidney. *Laissez Faire and the General-Welfare State.* Ann Arbor: University of Michigan Press, 1964.

Finnegan, C. J., S. M. Brookes, N. Johnson, J. Smith, K. L. Mansfield, V. L. Keene, and A. R. Fooks. "Rabies in North America and Europe." *Journal of the Royal Society of Medicine* 95, no. 1 (2002).

Fladmark, Knut R. *British Columbia Prehistory.* Ottawa, ON: National Museum of Man, 1986.

Flanders, Judith. *Inside the Victorian Home: A Portrait of Domestic Life in Victorian England.* New York: W. W. Norton, 2004.

Fleishman, Erica, Dennis D. Murphy, and Robert B. Blair. "Selecting Effective Umbrella Species." *Conservation Magazine*, July 29, 2001.

Floud, Roderick, Jane Humphries, and Paul Johnson, eds. *The Cambridge Economic History of Modern Britain*, vol. 1. Cambridge: Cambridge University Press, 2014.

Foley, M. M., et al. "Dam Removal: Listening In." *Water Resources Research* 53 (2017).

Galbi, Douglas A. "Child Labour and the Division of Labour in the Early English Cotton Mills." Centre for History and Economics, King's College, Cambridge.

Garrard, Mary D. *Brunelleschi's Egg: Nature, Art and Gender in Renaissance Italy.* Berkeley: University of California Press, 2011.

Gaskell, P. *The Manufacturing Population of England.* London: Baldwin and Cradock, 1833.

Gaspard, T. K. *A Political Economy of Lebanon, 1948–2002: The Limits of Laissez-Faire.* Leiden: Brill, 2004.

Getches, David H. *Water Law in a Nutshell.* St. Paul, MN: West Publishing, 1997.

Glenn, Edna, John R. Wunder, Willard Hughes Rollings, and C. L. Martin, eds. *Hopi Nation: Essays on Indigenous Art, Culture, History, and Law.* Lincoln, NE: UNL Digital Commons, 2008.

Goble, Dale D., J. Michael Scott, and Frank W. Davis, eds. *The Endangered Species Act at Thirty*, vol. 1. Washington, DC: Island Press, 2006.

Goldstein, Jessica. "Descriptions of 'Old-Growth Forest' Are Somewhat Elusive." *Washington Post*, October 21, 2011.

Goode, George Brown, et al. *The Fisheries and Fishery Industries of the United States: Natural History of Useful Aquatic Animals.* Washington, DC: US Government Printing Office, 1884.

Goodman, Ruth. *How to Be a Victorian.* London: Penguin, 2013.

Goran, Morris. *The Conquest of Pollution*. Newtonville, MA: Environmental Design and Research Center, 1981.

Gordon, W. J. "The Omnibus Horse." In *The Horse World of London*. London: Religious Tract Society, 1893.

Grad, Shelby. "The Environmental Disaster That Changed California—And Started the Movement Against Offshore Oil Drilling." *Los Angeles Times*, April 28, 2017.

Greeley, Horace. *An Overland Journey from New York to San Francisco in the Summer of 1859*. New York: C. M. Saxton, Barker & Co., 1860.

Greenberg, Joel. *A Feathered River Across the Sky: The Passenger Pigeon's Flight to Extinction*. New York: Bloomsbury, 2014.

Greenburg, Leonard, et al. "Report of an Air Pollution Incident in New York City, November 1953." *Public Health Reports* 77, no. 1 (1962).

Griffin, Julian. "Fire Hazards Peril Cuyahoga Shipping." *Cleveland Press*, August 11, 1948.

Grinnell, George Bird. *Blackfeet Indian Stories*. Helena, MO: Riverbend Publishing, 2005.

Guyette, Elise A. "Gathering and Interactions of Peoples, Cultures, and Ideas, Native Americans in Vermont: The Abenaki." Flow of History c/o Southeast Vermont Community Learning Collaborative, accessed June 8, 2018, www.flowofhistory.org.

Guynup, Sharon. *State of the Wild: A Global Portrait of Wildlife, Wildlands, and Oceans*. New York: Wildlife Conservation Society, 2005.

Haines, Michael R. "The Population of the United States, 1790–1920." National Bureau of Economic Research Historical Working Paper No. 56, New York, June 1994.

Hall, Minna B. "Letter 5, 'A New Audubon Society.'" *Forest and Stream*, April 18, 1896.

Hamill, Sean D. "Unveiling a Museum, a Pennsylvania Town Remembers the Smog That Killed 20." *New York Times*, November 1, 2008.

Harrison, J. F. C. *Society and Politics in England, 1780–1960*. New York: Harper & Row, 1965.

Harrison, John. "First-Salmon Ceremony." Columbia River History Project, October 31, 2008.

Hartesveldt, Richard J. "The 'Discoveries' of the Giant Sequoias." *Journal of Forest History* 19, no. 1 (1975): 20.

Hartig, John H. *Burning Rivers: Revival of Four Urban-Industrial Rivers That Caught on Fire*. Burlington, VT: Aquatic Ecosystem Health and Management Society, 2010.

Hartig, Terry, Richard Mitchell, Sjerp de Vries, and Howard Frumkin. "Nature and Health." *Annual Review of Public Health* 35, no. 1 (2014): 207–228.

Hastings, James, John Alexander Selbie, and Louis Herbert Gray. *Encyclopaedia of Religion and Ethics*, vol. 1. New York: T. & T. Clark, 1908.

Hanes, Richard C., and Sharon M. Hanes, eds. "Dust Bowl 1931–1939." *Historic Events for Students: The Great Depression*. Farmington Hills, MI: Gale, 2002.

Heacox, Kim. *John Muir and the Ice That Started a Fire: How a Visionary and the Glaciers of Alaska Changed America*. New York: Rowman & Littlefield, 2014.

Henderson, Carrol L. *Oology and Ralph's Talking Eggs: Bird Conservation Comes Out of Its Shell*. Austin: University of Texas Press, 2009.

Henderson, W. O., and Hans Caspar Escher. *Industrial Britain Under the Regency; The Diaries of Escher, Bodmer, May, and de Gallois, 1814–1815*. New York: A. M. Kelley, 1968.

Hervieux, Dave, Mark Hebblewhite, Dave Stepnisky, Michelle Bacon, and Stan Boutin. "Managing Wolves (*Canis lupus*) to Recover Threatened Woodland Caribou (*Rangifer tarandus caribou*) in Alberta." *Canadian Journal of Zoology* 92 (2015): 1029–1037.

Hines, N. William. "Nor Any Drop to Drink: Public Regulation of Water Quality; Part III: The Federal Effort." *Iowa Law Review* 52, no. 799 (1967): 803–804.

Hobbes, Thomas. *Leviathan or the Matter, Fore and Power of a Common-Wealth Ecclesiastical and Civill*. Andrew Crooke, Green Dragon in St. Paul's Churchyard, 1651.

Hobsbawm E. J. "The Machine Breakers." *Past & Present* 1, no. 1 (1 February 1952).

Hoffman, Randy. "A Birdwatcher at Peggy's Cove, Nova Scotia, Reports Seeing a Bird Presumed to Be Extinct: An Eskimo Curlew." *Bird Watching* 1 (October 2007).

Hoornbeek, Billee. "An Investigation into the Cause or Causes of the Epidemic Which Decimated the Indian Population of New England, 1616–1619." *New Hampshire Archeologist* 19 (1976–1977).

Horn, Pamela. *The Victorian Town Child*. New York: New York University Press, 1997.

Horrigan, Bonnie. "Shamanic Healing: We Are Not Alone: An Interview of Michael Harner." *Shamanism* 10, no. 1 (Spring/Summer 1997).

Howells, William Dean. *Niagara, First and Last*. New York: Niagara Book, 1901.

Hyde, Lewis. *The Gift: Imagination and the Erotic Life of Property*. New York: Vintage, 1983.

Institution of Civil Engineers. *Minutes of Proceedings of the Institution of Civil Engineers*, vol. 144. Great Britain: 1901.

Irwin, Emily. "The Spermaceti Candle and the American Whaling Industry." *Historia* 21 (Spring 2012).

Ivashchenko, Yulia V., Phillip J. Clapham, and Robert L. Brownell Jr. "Soviet Illegal Whaling: The Devil and the Details." *Marine Fisheries Review* 73 (2011).

Jackson, Lee. *Dirty Old London: The Victorian Fight Against Filth*. New Haven, CT: Yale University Press, 2014.

Jacques, Peter J., Riley E. Dunlap, and Mark Freeman. "The Organisation of Denial: Conservative Think Tanks and Environmental Scepticism." *Environmental Politics* 17, no. 3 (June 2008).

Jamieson, A. J., et al. "Bioaccumulation of Persistent Organic Pollutants in the Deepest Ocean Fauna." *Nature, Ecology and Evolution* 1, no. 51 (2017).

Jeffrey, Francis, and John C. Lilly. *John Lilly, So Far*. New York: Penguin, 1991.

Jensen, A. A. "Transfer of Chemical Contaminants into Human Milk." In *Chemical Contaminants in Human Milk*. Edited by A. A. Jensen and S. A. Sorach. Boca Raton, FL: CRC Press, 1991.

Jonsson, Patrik. "The Unsung Tale of a River's Restoration: A Movement to Remove Obsolete Dams Gathers Force in the East—and Fishermen Are First to Take Notice." *Christian Science Monitor*, January 30, 2001.

Jordan, Thomas E. *Victorian Child Savers and Their Culture: A Thematic Evaluation*. Lewiston, NY: Edwin Mellen Press, 1998.

Ju, Qiang, Christos C. Zouboulis, and Longqing Xia. "Environmental Pollution and Acne: Chloracne." *Dermato-Endocrinology* 1, no. 3 (2009).

Kalland, Arne. *Unveiling the Whale: Discourses on Whales and Whaling*. Brooklyn, NY: Berghahn Books, 2009.

Kehoe, Terence. *Cleaning Up the Great Lakes: From Cooperation to Confrontation*. Dekalb: Northern Illinois University Press, 1997.

Khan, Fahd, Saheel Mukhtar, Ian K. Dickinson, and Seshadri Sriprasad. "The Story of the Condom." *Indian Journal of Urology* 29, no. 1 (2013).

Klein, Joanna. "Sea Turtles Appear to Be Bouncing Back Around the World." *New York Times*, September 20, 2017.

Klingaman, William, and Nicholas P. Klingaman. *The Year Without a Summer: 1816 and the Volcano That Darkened the World and Changed History*. New York: St. Martin's Press, 2013.

Knud-Hansen, Chris. "Historical Perspective of the Phosphate Detergent Conflict." Conflict Research Consortium Working Paper 94-54, Natural Resources and Environmental Policy Seminar, University of Colorado, February 1994.

Komlos, John. "A Three-Decade 'Kuhnian' History of the Antebellum Puzzle: Explaining the Shrinking of the US Population at the Onset of Modern Economic Growth." SSRN (2012).

Le Conte, Jean. *Les oeuvres de Jean-Baptiste Van Helmont.* Translated by Alex Levin. Lyon, 1671, pt. 1, ch. 16.

Leopold, Aldo. *Game Management.* Madison: University of Wisconsin Press, 1986.

———."Thinking Like a Mountain." *A Sand County Almanac.* New York: Oxford University Press, 1949.

LeSourd, Dr. Philip S. Email interview with the author January through April 2018.

Levine, Richard. "Indians, Conservation, and George Bird Grinnell." *American Studies* 28 (1987).

Lieb, Anna. "The Undamming of America." NOVA, August 12, 2015.

Lieben, Ivan J. "Political Influences on USFW Listing Decision Under the ESA: Time to Rethink Priorities." *Environmental Law,* December 22, 1997.

Lockwood, Jeffrey A. *Locust: The Devastating Rise and Mysterious Disappearance of the Insect That Shaped the American Frontier.* New York: Basic Books, 2004.

Loomis, Bill. *Detroit's Delectable Past: Two Centuries of Frog Legs, Pigeon Pie and Drugstore Whiskey.* Charleston, SC: History Press, 2012.

Luke, Timothy. "Deep Ecology: Living as if Nature Mattered." *Organization and Environment* 15, no. 2 (June 2002).

Lydeard, Charles, and Richard L. Mayden. "A Diverse and Endangered Aquatic Ecosystem of the Southeast United States." *Conservation Biology* 9, no. 4 (August 1995).

MacKenzie, Clyde. "History of Oystering in the United States and Canada, Featuring the Eight Greatest Oyster Estuaries." *Marine Fisheries Review* 58, no. 4 (1996).

Mantoux, P. "The Beginnings of Machinery in the Textile Industry." In *The Industrial Revolution in the Eighteenth Century: An Outline of the Beginnings of the Modern Factory System in England.* New York: Routledge, 2015; originally published in 1961.

Marcy, Randolph B. *The Prairie Traveler: A Hand-Book for Overland Expeditions.* Washington, DC: War Department, 1859.

Marte, Fernando, Amandine Pe Quignot, and David W. Von Endt. "Arsenic in Taxidermy Collections: History, Detection, and Management." *Collection Forum* 21 (2006).

Martin, Theodore. *The Life of His Royal Highness the Prince Consort,* vol. 4. Cambridge: Cambridge University Press, 1879.

Mascie-Taylor, T. C. G. Nicholas, Akira Yasukouchi, and Stanley Ulijaszek. *Human Variation: From the Laboratory to the Field.* Boca Raton, FL: CRC Press, 2010, ch. 12.

Massie, Robert. *Nicholas and Alexandra*. New York: Atheneum, 1967.

Matheson, Ewing. *Aid Book to Engineering Enterprise Abroad*. New York: E. and F. N. Spon, 1878.

Mauss, Marcel. *The Gift: The Form and Reason for Exchange in Archaic Society*. New York: Routledge, 1990.

McCormick, John. *Reclaiming Paradise: The Global Environmental Movement*. Bloomington: Indiana University Press, 1991.

McFetridge, G. A., *Poultry: A Concise Treatise on All Branches. How to Hatch, Feed, Brood and Prepare for Market*. Syracuse, NY: Clarence de Puy, 1897.

McGraw, Daniel J. "America's Great Dam Teardown Means Cleaner Water, More Parkland: So Why Aren't More Cities Removing These Barriers to Health and Public Space?" *Next City*, March 27, 2017.

McKinley, Daniel. "A History of the Passenger Pigeon in Missouri." In *The Auk: Ornithological Advances* 77, no. 4 (October 1960).

McLeman, Robert A., et al. "What We Learned from the Dust Bowl: Lessons in Science, Policy, and Adaptation." *Population and Environment* 35, no. 4 (2014).

McNeill, W. H. *Plagues and People*. New York: Anchor Press, 1976.

McCright, Aaron M., Chenyang Xiao, and Riley E. Dunlap. "Political Polarization on Support for Government Spending on Environmental Protection in the USA, 1974–2012." *Social Science Research* 48 (November 2014).

Memorial of the Permanent Committee of the New York Convention of the Friends of Domestic Industry. 2nd Cong., 2nd sess., 1833, doc. 78, p. 15.

Méndez, Cecilia. *Los trabajadores guaneros del Perú, 1840–1879*. Lima: Universidad Nacional Mayor de San Marcos, 1987.

Menzies' Journal of Vancouver's Voyage April to October, 1792 ed. by C. F. Newcombe. Victoria, BC: Printed by William H. Cullin, 1923.

Merrill, Marlene Deahl. *Yellowstone and the Great West: Journals, Letters, and Images from the 1871 Hayden Expedition*. Lincoln: University of Nebraska Press, 2003.

Messner, Rebecca, George deGolian, and Michael White, dirs. *Olmsted and America's Urban Parks*. PBS, 2010.

Midgley, Mary. *Beast and Man: The Roots of Human and Nature*. Hertfordshire, UK: Harvester Press Limited, 1979.

Miller, Loye. "Feather Studies on the California Condor." *The Condor* 39, no. 4 (1937).

Mills, Ami Chen. "Headwaters: What's the Deal?" *Mother Jones*, May 26, 1998.

Mogan, Alexandra. "Theodore Roosevelt and the Boone and Crockett Club: The Saving of America's Buffalo." *Global Tides* 6 (May 2012).

Mohr, James C. *Abortion in America: The Origins and Evolution of National Policy*. New York: Oxford University Press, 1978.

Molina, M. J., and F. S. Rowland. "Stratospheric Sink for Chlorofluorometh-anes: Chlorine Atom-Catalyzed Destruction of Ozone." *Nature* 249, no. 810–812 (1974).

Monongye, David. Hopi Hearings. July 15–30, 1955, United States Depart-ment of the Interior, Bureau of Indian Affairs, Phoenix Area Office, Hopi Agency, Keams Canyon, Arizona.

Montague, Peter. "The History of Chlorinated Diphenyl (PCB's)." Rachel's Environment and Health blog, March 4, 1993.

Montgomery, Gladys. *An Elegant Wilderness*. New York: Acanthus Press, 2011.

Monticello. The Thomas Jefferson Encyclopedia. Accessed May 27, 2018. https://www.monticello.org/site/research-and-collections/the.

Moore, Chris. "Sustainable Land Development." *Today*, February 2009.

Moore, Thomas. *The Life, Letters and Journals of Lord Byron*. London: John Murray, 1860.

Moore-Colyer, R. J. "Feathered Women and Persecuted Birds: The Strug-gle Against the Plumage Trade, c. 1860–1922." *Rural History* 11, no. 1 (April 2000).

Morison, Samuel Eliot. *Of Plymouth Plantation, 1620–1647 by William Bradford*. New York: Alfred A. Knopf, 1952.

Mowat, Farley. *Sea of Slaughter*. Berkeley, CA: Douglas and McIntyre Pub-lishers, 2012; originally published in 1984.

Murray, John. "Voyages de Decouverte, Tome II." *Quarterly Review* (April and June 1817).

Musgrave, Toby. "The Remarkable Case of Dr. Ward: A Victorian Fern En-thusiast Changed Gardening Forever." *The Telegraph*, January 19, 2002.

Næss, Arne. *Ecology, Community and Lifestyle*. Cambridge: Cambridge University Press, 1989.

Nash, Roderick Frazier. *Wilderness and the American Mind*. New Haven, CT: Yale University Press, 1982.

National Commission on Science for Sustainable Forestry. *Beyond Old Growth: Older Forests in a Changing World*. Washington, DC: National Council for Science and the Environment, 2008.

National Museum of American History. "The Feather Trade and the Amer-ican Conservation Movement." Smithsonian Institution, February through August 1999.

National Research Council. *A Risk-Management Strategy for PCB-Contaminated Sediments*. Washington, DC: National Academies Press, 2001.

Nelson, J. S. "PCB: An Industry Problem?" General Electric Corporate En-gineering, October 30, 1969.

New Bedford Whaling Museum. "Whales and Hunting: How the Profits

Were Divided." New Bedford, MA. accessed June 7, 2018, https://www.whalingmuseum.org/learn/research-topics/overview-of-north-american-whaling/whales-hunting.

New York Times. "78 Species Listed Near Extinction." March 12, 1967.

——. "Civilization's Prey." September 9, 1967.

——. "New Fund Seeks to Save Near Extinct Species." November 8, 1961.

——. "The Adirondack; or Life in the Woods, New and Enlarged Edition." August 15, 1854.

——. "Traffic in Savagery." September 19, 1968.

——. "Week in Review." September 18, 1994, 6.

——. "What Makes Smog? Cities Do Not Agree; Los Angeles and St. Louis Say It Is Controllable by Law—Pittsburgh Blames Nature." November 22, 1953.

——. "Wildlife Species Face Extinction." January 9, 1966.

Newcomb, Shawna. "Sturgeon Return to Milford After Nearly 200 Years." WLBZ, August 4, 2016.

Nichols, Roger L. *The American Indian: Past and Present*. Norman: University of Oklahoma Press, 2008.

Nixon, Richard. Meeting in the Oval Office: 11:08 a.m. to 11:43 a.m., April 27, 1971, Washington, DC, tape.

Nolan, Patrick, and Gerhard Lenski. "The Agricultural Economy." In *Human Societies: An Introduction to Macrosociology*, 12th ed. New York: Oxford University Press, 2014.

Norman, Oscar Edward. *The Romance of the Gas Industry*. Chicago: A. C. McClurg, 1922.

Norton, Mary Beth, Carol Sheriff, David W. Blight, and Howard Chudacoff. *A People and a Nation: A History of the United States, Volume 1*. Independence, KY: Wadsworth Cengage Learning, 2012.

O'Connor, J. E., J. J. Duda, and G. E. Grant. "Ecology: 1000 Dams Down and Counting." *Science*, May 1, 2015.

Ogallala Aquifer Initiative 2011 Report. Washington, DC: Natural Resources Conservation Service, US Department of Agriculture, 2011.

Olmsted, Frederick Law. Letter to Ignaz Anton Pilat, September 26, 1863, Panama. In *The Papers of Frederick Law Olmsted: The California Frontier, 1863–1865*, vol. 5. Edited by Victoria Post Ranney, Gerard J. Rauluk, and Carolyn E. Hoffman. Balimore: Johns Hopkins University Press, 1990.

——. Letter to William Seward Webb, March 17, 1887. Olmsted Papers, reel Al:68.

Olsen, Jack. "A Little Bit Goes a Long Way." *Sports Illustrated*, March 15, 1971.

——. "The Poisoning of the West." *Sports Illustrated*, March 8, 1971.

Parks, Frederick J. *The Celebrated Oyster House Cookbook*. Allentown, PA: F. J. Parks, 1985.

Parliamentary Papers, Chadwick's evidence, London, 1846, vol. 10, p. 651.

Passmore, John Arthur. *Man's Responsibility for Nature: Ecological Problems and Western Tradition.* Duckworth, 1974.

Patchett, Merle. "Fashioning Feathers: Dead Birds, Millinery Crafts and the Plumage Trade" at the FAB Gallery, University of Alberta, Edmonton, 2011.

Patterson, K. D. "Yellow Fever Epidemics and Mortality in the United States, 1693–1905." *Social Science and Medicine* 34 (1992).

Payne, Roger S., and Scott McVay. "Songs of Humpback Whales." *Science* 173, no. 3997 (August 1971).

Peabody Museum, Harvard University. "Dolls: More Than Toys." Cambridge, MA, 2014.

Penner, Barbara. *Newlyweds on Tour: Honeymooning in Nineteenth-Century America.* Durham: University of New Hampshire Press, 2007.

Peterson, Anna L. *Being Animal: Beasts and Boundaries in Nature Ethics.* New York: Columbia University Press, 2013.

Petersen, Shannon. "Bison to Blue Whales: Protecting Endangered Species Before the Endangered Species Act of 1973." *Environmental Law and Policy Journal* 71, no. 104 (1999).

Phillips, Richard. *Modern London.* London: Richard Phillips, 1805.

Pittsburgh Post-Gazette. "Pittsburgh and Its Business." June 27, 1835.

Plattsburgh Republican. "The Pigeon Trade." August 2, 1851.

Porter, Martin. "Bad Capitalism: The Pacific Lumber Story." LinkedIn, October 12, 2014.

Press, Allen. "Why Are Freshwater Mussels in Decline?" *ScienceDaily*, September 21, 2007.

Prince, J. M. "Intersection of Economics, History, and Human Biology: Secular Trends in Stature in Nineteenth-Century Sioux Indians." *Human Biology* 67, no. 3 (1995).

Prochnau, Bill. "The Watt Controversy." *Washington Post*, June 30, 1981.

Pryor, F. L. "The Adoption of Agriculture: Some Theoretical and Empirical Evidence." *American Anthropologist* 88 (2006).

Quintero, Fernando. "A Culture Speaks Through Its Ritual of Death: The Victorians' Elaborate Mourning Customs Are Important to an Understanding of Their Society." *Berkeleyan*, March 27, 1996.

Randall, Adrian. *Riotous Assemblies: Popular Protest in Hanoverian England.* Oxford: Oxford University Press, 2006.

Reagan, Ronald. Speech at the Western Wood Products Association meeting, San Francisco, CA, March 12, 1966.

Ricciari, Anthony, and Joseph B. Rasmussen. "Extinction Rates of North American Freshwater Fauna." *Conservation Biology* 13, no. 5 (October 1999).

Richards, Sabrina. "The World in a Cabinet, 1600s: A 17th Century Danish

Doctor Arranges a Museum of Natural History Oddities in His Own Home." *The Scientist*, April 1, 2012.

Riddle, Maxwell. "River Trip Bares Oil Waste Peril." *Cleveland Press*, May 6, 1952.

Riedel, Stefan. "Edward Jenner and the History of Smallpox and Vaccination." *Proceedings (Baylor University Medical Center)* 18, no. 1 (2005).

Risebrough, R. W., P. Rieche, D. B. Peakall, S. G. Herman, and M. N. Kirven. "Polychlorinated Biphenyls in the Global Ecosystem." *Nature* 220 (December 1968).

Risebrough, Robert, and Virginia Brodine. "More Letters in the Wind." In *Our World in Peril: An Environment Review*. Edited by Sheldon Novick and Dorothy Cottrell. Greenwich, CT: Fawcett, 1971.

Ritvo, Harriet. *The Animal Estate: The English and Other Creatures in the Victorian Age*. Cambridge, MA: Harvard University Press, 1987.

Roan, Sharon L. *Ozone Crisis: The 15-Year Evolution of a Sudden Global Emergency*. New York: John Wiley & Sons, 1989.

Rocha Jr., Robert C., Phillip J. Clapham, and Yulia V. Ivashchenko. "Emptying the Oceans: A Summary of Industrial Whaling Catches in the 20th Century." *Marine Fisheries Review* 76, no. 4 (March 2015).

Rogers, Jedediah S. "Animas-La Plata Project." Historic Reclamation Projects, Bureau of Reclamation, 2009.

Roosevelt, Theodore. *The Autobiography of Theodore Roosevelt*. New York: Charles Scribner's Sons, 1913.

Ronda, James P. *Lewis & Clark Among the Indians*. Lincoln: University of Nebraska Press, 1984.

Ross, Benjamin, and Steven Amter. "A Long History of Chemical Pollution." *Utne Reader*, August 2012.

———. *The Polluters: The Making of Our Chemically Altered Environment*. New York: Oxford University Press, 2010.

Ruby, Jay. *Secure the Shadow: Death and Photography in America*. Cambridge, MA: MIT Press, 1995.

Ruby, Robert H., and John A. Brown. *The Chinook Indians, Traders of the Lower Columbia River*. Norman: University of Oklahoma Press, 1976.

Rutkow, Eric. *American Canopy: Trees, Forests, and the Making of a Nation*. New York: Simon and Schuster, 2013.

Rybczynski, Witold. *A Clearing in the Distance: Frederick Law Olmsted and America in the Nineteenth Century*. New York: Scribner, 1999.

Sale, Kirkpatrick. "The Achievements of 'General Ludd': A Brief History of the Luddites." *Ecologist* 29, no. 5 (August/September 1999).

Schermerhorn, Calvin. *The Business of Slavery and the Rise of American Capitalism, 1815–1860*. New Haven, CT: Yale University Press, 2015.

Schlesinger, Arthur Meier. *The Coming of the New Deal, 1933–1935*. New York: Houghton Mifflin Harcourt, 2003.

Schmidt, Karl P. *The American Alligator*. Chicago: Field Museum of Natural History, 1922.

Schorger, A. W., *The Passenger Pigeon: Its Natural History and Extinction*. Madison: University of Wisconsin Press, 1955.

Schultz, T. Paul. "Wage Gains Associated with Height as a Form of Health Human Capital." *American Economic Review* 92, no. 2 (2002).

Schwarz, Walter. "Ethical and Green Living: Arne Næss." *The Guardian*, January 14, 2009.

Scott, S. D., and P. K. Scott. *The Niagara Reservation Archaeological and Historical Resource Survey*. New York: New York Office of Parks, Recreation, and Historic Preservation, Historic Sites Bureau, March 1983.

Shabecoff, Philip. "U.S. Report Predicts Rise in Skin Cancer with Loss of Ozone." *New York Times*, November 5, 1986.

Shweder, Richard A., ed. *The Child: An Encyclopedic Companion*. Chicago: University of Chicago Press, 2009.

Simmonds, Peter Lund. *Science and Commerce: Their Influence on Our Manufactures: A Series of Statistical Essays and Lectures, Etc*. London: Robert Hardwick, 1872.

Simon, Steven, André Bouville, and Charles Land. "Fallout from Nuclear Weapons Tests and Cancer Risks: Exposures 50 Years Ago Still Have Health Implications Today That Will Continue into the Future." *American Scientist*, January–February 2006.

Slater, G. "Historical Outline of Land Ownership in England." In *The Land: The Report of the Land Enquiry Committee*. London: Hodder and Stoughton, 1913.

Sloane, David Charles. *The Last Great Necessity: Cemeteries in American History*. Baltimore: Johns Hopkins University Press, 1991.

Snow, Dean R. *The Archeology of New England*. New York: Academic Press, 1980.

———. "Wabanaki 'Family Hunting Territories.'" *American Anthropologist* 70 (1968).

Snow, Dean R., and Kim M. Lamphear. "European Contact and Indian Depopulation in the Northeast: The Timing of the First Epidemics." *Ethnohistory* 35 (Winter 1988).

Snyder, Lynne Page. "Revisiting Donora, Pennsylvania's 1948 Air Pollution Disaster." In *Devastation and Renewal: An Environmental History of Pittsburgh and Its Region*. Edited by Joel A. Tarr. Pittsburgh: University of Pittsburgh Press, 2003.

———. "'The Death-Dealing Smog over Donora, Pennsylvania': Industrial Air Pollution, Public Health Policy, and the Politics of Expertise, 1948–1949." *Environmental History Review* 18, no. 1 (1994).

Souder, William. "How Two Women Ended the Deadly Feather Trade." *Smithsonian Magazine*, March 2013.

State Street Trust Company, *Whale Fishery of New England: An Account*. Boston: Walton Advertising and Printing Company, 1915.

Stevens, Emily E. "A History of Infant Feeding." *Journal of Perinatal Education* 18, no. 2 (2009).

Story, Joseph. "Consecration Address." In *The Picturesque Pocket Companion Through Mount Auburn*. Boston: Otis Broaders, 1839.

Stradling, D., and R. Stradling. "Perceptions of the Burning River: Deindustrialization and Cleveland's Cuyahoga River." *Environmental History* 13, no. 3 (2008).

Strutt, Joseph. *The Sports and Pastimes of the People of England from the Earliest Period to the Present Time*. London: Chatto and Windus, 1876.

Talley, Tim. "Tribes, Oklahoma Reach Deal on Water Rights Dispute." Associated Press, August 11, 2016.

Tanabe, Shinsuke. "PCB Problems in the Future: Foresight from Current Knowledge." *Environmental Pollution* 50 (1988).

Tarr, Joel A. "The Changing Face of Pittsburgh: A Historical Perspective." In *Institute of Medicine (US) Roundtable on Environmental Health Sciences, Research, and Medicine*. Edited by B. D. Goldstein, B. Fischhoff, S. J. Marcus, et al. Washington, DC: National Academies Press, 2003.

———. "Urban Pollution: Many Long Years Ago the Old Gray Mare Was Not the Ecological Marvel, in American Cities, That Horse Lovers Like to Believe." *American Heritage Magazine*, October 1971.

Tarr, Joel A., and Josef W. Konvitz. "Patterns in the Development of Urban Infrastructure." In *American Urbanism*. Edited by Howard Gillette Jr. and Zane L. Miller. Westport, CT: Greenwood Press, 1987.

Thiesen, William H. "The Long Blue Line: Quentin Walsh's Long, Colorful Career." Coast Guard Compass blog, July 7, 2016.

Thomas Cole Papers, 1821–1863. New York State Library, SC10635.

Thomas, Kristin Bryan, and Theo Colborn. "Organochlorine Endocrine Disruptors in Human Tissue." In *Chemically-Induced Alterations in Sexual and Functional Development: The Wildlife/Human Connection*. Edited by Theo Colborn and Coralie Clement. Princeton, NJ: Princeton Scientific Publishing, 1992.

Thompson, Derek. "How the Tractor (Yes, the Tractor) Explains the Middle Class Crisis." *The Atlantic*, March 13, 2012.

Thorsheim, P. *Inventing Pollution: Coal, Smoke, and Culture in Britain Since 1800*. Athens: Ohio University Press, 2006.

Tolba, M. K., ed. *Our Fragile World: Challenges and Opportunities for Sustainable Development*, vols. 1 and 3. Encyclopedia of Life Support Systems Publications, 2001.

Tomlins, Christopher. "Reconsidering Indentured Servitude: European

Migration and the Early American Labor Force, 1600–1775." *Labor History* 42, no. 1 (2001).

Toothaker, Charles Robinson, S. F. Aaron, and B. H. A. Groth. *Commercial Raw Materials: Their Origin, Preparation and Uses*. Boston: Ginn, 1905.

Tower, Walter Sheldon. *A History of the American Whale Fishery*, vol. 20. Philadelphia: University of Pennsylvania, 1907.

Trollope, Frances Milton. *Domestic Manners of the Americans*. London: Whittaker Treacher, 1832.

Tubbs, Stephenie Ambrose with Clay Straus Jenkinson. *The Lewis and Clark Companion: An Encyclopedic Guide to the Voyage of Discovery*. New York: Henry Holt, 2003.

Universita degli Studi Firenze. *Museo di Storia Naturale*. Translated by the author. Pamphlet. 2016.

Ure, Andrew. *Cotton Manufacture of Great Britain Systematically Investigated*, vol. 1. London: Knight, 1836.

US Bureau of Soils. "Bulletin 55." 1909.

US Census Bureau. *Report on Transportation Business in the United States at the Eleventh Census*. 1890.

US Public Health Service, the Agency for Toxic Substances and Disease Registry, US Department of Health and Human Service, and the US Environmental Protection Agency. *Public Health Implications of Exposure to Polychlorinated Biphenyls (PCBs)*. 2015.

Van Tassel, David D., ed. *The Encyclopedia of Cleveland History*. Bloomington: Indiana University Press, 1996.

Vancouver, George. *A Voyage of Discovery to the North Pacific Ocean, and Round the World*. London: G. G. and J. Robinson, 1798.

Vaughan, Richard. *In Search of Arctic Birds*. London: T. & A. D. Poyser, 1992.

Vernizzi, Emily A. "The Establishment of the United States National Parks and the Eviction of Indigenous People." Thesis, Social Sciences Department, California Polytechnic State University, San Luis Obispo, CA, 2011.

von Linné, Carl. *Systema naturae, edition 12, vol. 1, part 1*. Stockholm, 1766.

Warren, Louis Samuel. *The Hunter's Game: Poachers and Conservationists in Twentieth-Century America*. New Haven, CT: Yale University Press, 1997.

Ward, John W., and Christian Warren. *Silent Victories: The History and Practice of Public Health in Twentieth-Century America*. New York: Oxford University Press, 2007.

Warner, Sam Bass. *Streetcar Suburbs: The Process of Growth in Boston, 1870–1900*. Cambridge, MA: Harvard University Press, 1962.

Way, R. L. *Ontario's Niagara Parks, A History*. Niagara Falls, ON: Niagara Parks Commission, 1946.

Waymer, Jim. "Irma Batters Beaches, Residents and Baby Sea Turtles." *Florida Today*, September 12, 2017.

Weick, M. T. "A History of Rickets in the United States." *American Journal of Clinical Nutrition* 20, no. 11 (November 1967).

Wheeling, Kate, and Max Ufberg. "'The Ocean Is Boiling': The Complete Oral History of the 1969 Santa Barbara Oil Spill." *Pacific Standard*, April 18, 2017.

Wilford, John Noble. "Site in Turkey Yields Oldest Cloth Ever Found." *New York Times*, July 13, 1993.

Williams, Dan. "Rivermen Cite Fire Peril, Ask City for Protection." *Cleveland Press*, March 11, 1941.

Williams, Marilyn Thornton. *Washing the Great Unwashed: Public Baths in Urban America, 1840–1920*. Columbus: Ohio State University Press, 1991.

Williams, Tate. "In the Garden Cemetery: The Revival of America's First Urban Parks." *American Forests* (Spring/Summer 2014).

Wilson, Alexander. *American Ornithology; or, The Natural History of the Birds of the United States*. New York: Collins, 1839.

Wilson, E. B. *Hydraulic and Placer Mining*. New York: J. Wiley & Sons, 1904.

Wright, Barton. "Chapter 4, Hopi Kachinas: A Life Force." *Hopi Nation: Essays on Indigenous Art, Culture, History, and Law*, Edna Glenn, John R. Wunder, Willard Hughes Rollings, and C. L. Martin, eds. (Lincoln, NE: UNL Digital Commons, 2008). Copyright © 2008 the Estate of Edna Glenn, Willard Hughes Rollings, Abbott Sekaquaptewa, Barton Wright, Michael Kabotie, Terrance Talaswaima, Alice Schlegel, Robert H. Ames, Peter Iverson, and John R. Wunder.

Zerbini, Alexandre N., Janice M. Waite, Jeffrey L. Laake, and Paul R. Wade. "Abundance, Trends and Distribution of Baleen Whales Off Western Alaska and the Central Aleutian Islands." *Deep-Sea Research Part 1* 53, no. 11 (November 2006): 1772–1790.

Zimran, Ariell. "Does Sample-Selection Bias Explain the Industrialization Puzzle? Evidence from Military Enlistment in the Nineteenth-Century United States." *Journal of Economic History* 77, no. (2015): 171–207.

Zlomke, Briony D. "Death Became Them: The Defeminization of the American Death Culture, 1609–1899." Thesis, University of Nebraska-Lincoln, March 19, 2013.

Index